SAVING PAPA'S TALES

Printed in the United States
by Piscataqua Press
32 Daniel Street
Portsmouth, NH 03801

ISBN: 978-1-944393-65-6

SAVING PAPA'S TALES

Richard Ebner

INTRODUCTION

If you have similar sensibilities to me when choosing to read or not read a book, then you probably won't start here, but rather, you have already skipped to the meat and potatoes; my apologies to vegetarian readers.

The fact that you are even considering reading *Papa's Tales* is gratifying for me. Since starting this story 24 years ago, I have seen many changes in the publishing world. When I began writing, eBooks were not an option. Now that electronic versions of books are in vogue, the choices of what to read seem endless. And if you are—viewing this on a screen—in the last chapter you will find hyperlinks to expand your options even more—including: the history of some scholarly icons, music, music-videos, and one full-length concert. Sometimes when you click on a hyperlink you will be accosted by an ad—this is America after all. But fear not, a countdown will begin and usually in less than four seconds you will be able to experience what I have chosen for you. After that, you can continue anywhere you wish to go.

There seems to be at least two schools of thought about how books should be produced. The tactile group likes pages to hold, a bookmark to insert when taking a break, and pages to turn while reading. Readers on electronic devices love the accessibility of reading on tablets, laptops and smart phones. Why not Coexist and produce books that satisfy everyone's needs? This is what I've tried to do. My taking so long to complete this book is due to some of my own shortcomings, as well as circumstances beyond my control. However, this delay has allowed the universe that is technology to create a new way for me to write.

In the first 33 chapters, Papa's and my story is told in a fairly traditional style, but in Chapter 34 all bets are off.

So, if you want to start at Chapter 34 and are intrigued enough to go back to the beginning—so be it—this is now your story to read any way you choose.

Even though the topic of aging can be hard at times, this is not a dark tale. Papa has a very dynamic personality and his humor is omnipresent throughout. I do warn my animal-loving readers that Chapter 16 might be too difficult for them. But you can easily skip that chapter and still get the gist of things.

For the most part our coauthored tale is, in my opinion, uplifting and optimistic. And if you make it all the way to the end, consider entering the contest. You could win 50 bucks.

CHAPTER ONE

Finding Papa

I find my father pacing in front of the nurses' station. His fists are clenched. His face is red. Mustering the brightest greeting I can, I call out, "So there you are, Papa! I've been looking for you all over." I lie.

Turning to the direction of my voice, he shouts back, "Who's that?"

"It's Richard, your son," I answer, walking to where he is standing.

"Oh, Richard, my boy! Finally, some contact from the outside world!"

"How are you doing, Pop?" I ask. Then, inexplicably to me—I reach out and throw my arms around him. Instantly I can feel the response from his body, a body so longing for touch, so thirsty for it, that as we hold each other, I can feel my father drink from my soul.

Locked in an embrace, Papa and I stand together for several seconds. Finally, Papa releases his grip and loudly declares, "I'm God damn shitty mad! I ask for answers and I get no response. What am I, a prisoner? I want to know what I am doing here."

"Come on, Papa, let's go find a spot to sit and we'll talk." I put my arm around him and we head down the corridor toward a room with some comfortable chairs and a couch.

Before we arrive, a disheveled-looking woman, barefoot, with thinning hair, and wearing a food-stained bathrobe, shuffles toward us. As she slowly moves, she repeats loudly, "Ralph, we've got to get out of here!" When closer, she starts calling, "Doctor Bones, Doctor Bones!" A nurse notices the situation and quickly whisks the woman away.

Papa looks even more disturbed now. "What am I doing here? Is this a hospital or an insane asylum? Am I sick?"

"No, Papa, you're not sick. You're in a nursing home called Littleton House."

"A nursing home?" There is an incredulous tone to his voice. "If I'm not sick, what the hell am I doing in a nursing home?"

"Donna left you here because she felt she could no longer take care of you at home."

Papa stops walking. "Take care of me," he says. There is a puzzled look on his face as he suggests, "What does she have to do, cook a few meals for me? She has to eat anyway herself, doesn't she? I make no other demands on her."

I don't answer. We start walking again toward the smaller of two living rooms that residents and guests can use for visits. It is after eight at night and the hallway is now empty in front of us. Some of the doors we pass are open. The flashing blue of a television catches my eye. I look inside the room and in the dim TV light I can barely make out a human form beneath the blankets on a bed. My gaze shifts quickly back to the corridor.

I am so new at this. I haven't installed any filters yet. Every sight, sound and smell pops up to assault me. A strong chemical odor masks the underlying scent of many sickly humans housed close to one another. I don't know if the woman we saw earlier is crazy, but she had one thing right. I've got to get Papa out of here!

As we reach the doorway to the living room, I stop for a moment to look inside. Another television, left on, feigns conversation. A sitcom provides the room with its only laughter.

Hearing what I hear, my father asks, "Is someone in there?"

"No, Papa. It's just the TV. I'll shut it off."

Across from the television a row of chairs and a couch form a straight line facing the set. A large window, the curtains drawn shut, fills the wall behind the furniture. The room is cold, drafty.

Papa follows me to the middle and we both stand there awkwardly for a few moments. "Where would you like to sit?" I ask him.

"It doesn't matter."

I pull a wing chair out to face the couch and motion for him to sit down. Seating myself on the couch, I begin by asking, "Papa, do you know where you are?"

He hesitates, looks disconcerted and then answers, "In a nursing home?"

"That's right, Littleton House. Do you know how you got here?"

"I have no idea!" Papa shakes his head.

"Donna brought you. About two weeks ago, remember?" He doesn't answer; instead he just keeps shaking his head. "You arrived early in the morning, right after breakfast, and Peter and I met you here a little later."

"Peter was here?"

"Yes, Papa."

"And how is my boy Petie?"

"He's okay, I guess."

I feel Papa drifting, losing his focus. It would be easier to just go with that, to talk about my brother Peter or my dog, Baby, and not have this conversation again and again. It would be easier to forget, like he forgets.

Instead, I place one of my hands on each of Papa's knees and start over. "Do you know why Donna left you here, why she put you in a nursing home?"

"No." Papa fiddles with the buttons on his shirt. "Does she have a new lover?"

"I don't know, Papa. I don't think so." His finger fumbling begins to annoy me. I take Papa's hands in mine. "Papa, you're in a nursing home because you forget things."

"I do? What things?"

"Donna said you left the stove on and nearly melted down a frying pan."

"She did? Well, I don't remember that. I think she exaggerates. Besides, anyone could do that. I suppose you never forget."

"Of course I do, Papa. I forget plenty of things, like people's names and phone numbers. But forgetting a phone number isn't serious—I can always look it up. Leaving the stove on could cause a fire."

"Now look!" Papa pulls his hands free and throws them out to his sides. "There was no fire, was there? I remember what I need to remember, important things. I can't fill my brain with every little detail or I would run out of room."

I back off. I'm wondering how to get through to him. When Papa's biggest impairment, his lack of memory, gets in the way of his even realizing he has a memory problem, I am at a loss on how to make him understand why he can't be free anymore.

As I'm considering another approach, I begin to question my own recollections. It occurs to me that the incident with the stove being left on actually happened more than a year and a half ago, before Donna and my father, Manny, were married. And yet,

Donna uses that as one of her reasons for putting Papa away.

I reach for a more recent complaint, "Donna said you got lost on one of your walks and she had to send the police to find you."

"Donna said, Donna said! She's a nervous woman. What can I tell you? You think I could get lost in my own neighborhood? That's ridiculous! I've lived here for 30 years, for God's sake!"

"Lived here, Papa?"

"Lived there! 24 Ruthellen Road, Chelmsford, Massachusetts. You think I don't even know my own address? Twenty-four, that's right, isn't it? I know where I live at least!" Papa waits for my confirmation.

"Absolutely! You know that address cold."

When I saw my father a few days ago, he was completely aware of his surroundings and how he came to be here. That was in the morning. I've been reading about sundown syndrome and how it affects the elderly with dementia. At times he is more agitated around sunset, but not always. And his memory loss doesn't seem to be in steady decline. Some days he is completely with it, morning or night.

We continue like this for a while, with me trying to convince Papa he has memory impairment and Papa demonstrating with the skills of a master debater that not all has been lost intellectually.

Then out of the blue he asks, "Did I marry Donna?"

"Yes, Papa, about a year ago."

"Well, then she has to take care of me, doesn't she? Didn't she agree to that? In sickness and health—till death do us part. I'm not dead, am I?"

We both laugh at the irony of his last question.

"No, you're certainly not dead. But you can't force someone to take care of you no matter what they agreed to. And even if you could, I don't think Donna would do a very good job if her heart wasn't in it."

"Well, I'll divorce her then!" he declares. Then he asks, "I still own my house, don't I?"

"Yes, you still own half your house, but Donna owns half also. Half the house became hers when you married her."

"She's not acting as my wife. How can she be entitled to my house if she doesn't act like my wife?" He considers for a moment, and then adds, "Does a wife have the right to put a man out of his home? Don't I have rights—don't I even get a day in court? I thought this was America, not some totalitarian state."

I explain to him as best as I can that he signed a power of attorney in 1991 so Donna could help him manage his financial affairs. Papa's already poor vision had gotten worse by then and he needed someone to fill out his checks before he signed them. Donna also holds his health proxy. Both documents list me as her alternate. I tell him that Peter and I plan to go to the lawyer's office tomorrow to see if things can be changed.

"Right now we're at a standoff with the lawyers. You know the phrase 'catch-22,' Papa?"

"Yes, I think so. The crazy pilot who wasn't really so crazy, isn't it?"

"That's right, exactly!" Papa sits up straight, sticks out his chin and shows off his profile. "Very nice, Papa. Now, you know your power of attorney was set up because of your eyes—so Donna could help with banking and such?" Papa nods in agreement. "And you understand it's not supposed to be fully in effect unless you've been deemed incompetent?" He nods again. "But it seems Donna is using it as her authority to put you in here. And now, because you're in a nursing home and haven't been deemed competent to leave, your lawyer doesn't want to change your power of attorney."

Papa looks dumbfounded. Although I have said essentially the same thing several times before, this seems like the first time he's grasping the full significance. Prior to this evening, Papa would say that Donna was just a little mixed-up right now, that he'd have a talk with her and she'd come to her senses.

"No, now that's crazy! Are you saying Donna had no legal right to put me here in the first place, but now because I'm here, she does, and I can't leave?"

"You've got it, Papa!"

"Well, how can this be? What if I just walked out and went home? How could she stop me?"

"She could call the police."

"So, I tell the cop it's my house and I can prove it."

"That won't work, Papa," I tell him. The next few words come hard. "Donna might not be able to convince a specialist, or the court, that you are demented, but she'd have little trouble convincing a cop."

"What do you mean 'demented'?" His expression sours and his voice hangs on the word *demented*. "Who says I'm demented? Do you think I'm demented?" Papa asks me.

"Not at all! A little eccentric perhaps, but there's nothing wrong with that," I try to reassure him.

"So what's the problem then? Why am I stuck in here?"

"It's your memory, Papa."

He takes a moment and responds with, "You know it's so strange, but I have no sense of any memory loss."

"I know, Papa. It must be difficult for you to have me keep telling you about it. It must be frustrating."

"Not really frustrating, just unbelievable. But I suppose I must believe you. You wouldn't lie to me about such a thing. Would you?"

"Of course not! And since there is nothing wrong with your

logical skills, you must realize that if not for your memory loss, Donna could not have put you in a nursing home without your consent."

"I suppose you're right. Something must not be working for me to be in such a fix," Papa concedes. Then he says, "Lay on, Macduff."

"Donna thinks you're not capable of making decisions for yourself anymore."

"She does? Well, who is she to decide such a thing? She's not a doctor! I've not been examined! How can a man be taken from his home and put in a place like this without being examined?"

"I don't know. That's one of the things we'll ask the lawyer."

"Incompetent." Papa shakes his head. "I say she's incompetent! This just isn't right."

I move from the couch, kneel at the edge of my father's chair and put an arm around him. "It'll be okay," I try to reassure him.

"I don't believe it! She put me in a nursing home. What did I do to her?"

"Nothing. You didn't do anything wrong."

"I don't want to be here. There's no one to talk to. I don't belong here!"

"I know you don't, Papa. I don't think you belong here either and I'm working on getting you sprung."

"Papa, I know we've never been close, but I do care what happens to you. You're not alone." I continue kneeling next to him for several minutes. After some time, Papa calms down. Then from the corridor come the sounds of buzzers.

"What's that?" Papa asks. There is nothing wrong with his hearing.

"Help buzzers," I tell him. Papa looks puzzled. "You know, the button next to your bed?" Papa shrugs his shoulders. "Well, if you need something—like a drink of water, or something—and let's say it's the middle of the night—you don't feel like getting up. Well, all you have to do is ring that buzzer and a nurse will come to your room."

"Fat chance," Papa tells me.

"What do you mean, Papa?"

"I hear those sounds all the time. Nobody ever comes."

"Maybe you forget. There are lots of people here. Maybe one buzzer sounds like the next," I suggest.

"No. Nobody will come," Papa insists. "At least I don't need them. Not like some of the poor souls."

After the buzzing finally stops, we remain silent for a few moments. Then I feel compelled to test Papa's memory again. "Papa, what day is this?"

"Well, do you mean the day of the week or the date?"

"Either one will do," I say, quite sure he knows neither. Asking him to answer makes me feel like shit.

"Let's see—what month are we in—it's autumn, isn't it? No, don't tell me! It must be—Saturday. That's it, it's Saturday!"

"No, Papa. It's Tuesday."

"Oh, off by four days." He does the math without missing a beat. "Big deal! I have no way of knowing what day it is in here," he defends. And he is right.

I don't know why I feel the need to keep testing him. It just seems necessary—almost as if Papa had just woken up from being knocked out and I want to find out how much damage has been done. Or perhaps, I want to see if there is anything worth trying to save.

"What did you have for lunch today, Papa?"

"For lunch? Did I have lunch today? Oh, yes, it's nighttime. I must have. Lunch? Well, that's a good question. I don't seem to remember. It couldn't have been that good."

These questions are torturous. I can feel my father's embarrassment even though he tries to hide it behind his humor. "Papa, don't worry about it. It doesn't matter."

"Yes, well, I suppose it doesn't. But I still don't understand why I can't be home in my own little house." He waits for me to answer, and then sensing I'm not going to, he adds, "I don't want to stay in this place. If I stay here much longer, I'll run my head into a wall, and Ebner will be no more, that's all." Papa often refers to himself by his surname alone.

A strange way to commit suicide. I don't think Papa will actually hurt himself, and yet I'm not really sure. But physically, he has the strength to do so.

"Papa, please don't talk about killing yourself. If you do that, we'll never get you evaluated. I don't think they test corpses for competency."

"You're probably right," he says, and then he laughs. "So, I'm going to be tested, then?"

"That's the plan."

"And when will this happen?"

"Soon, Papa. I don't have a date yet, but I'm working on it. We'll get this straightened out. You will be properly evaluated, and if need be, you'll have your day in court. Trust me."

With that said he seems satisfied for the moment. I ask him if he is tired. He tells me he is. He says he is tired from pacing the floors all day, from trying to figure out where he is and why he can't go home.

We walk back to his room. I help him get ready for bed and tuck him in, just as Papa must have done for me so many years before (although I have no clear memory of his ever doing that).

"I love you, Papa," I say. The white stubble of Papa's beard scratches my face as I kiss his cheek.

"I love you, too."

Moving to the doorway, I offer one more farewell. With a wave, I say, "See you soon, Papa. I love you."

"I love you, too. Don't forget me in here," Papa says. He is crying now.

I am 40 years old. This is the first time I have ever seen my father cry. I feel my own tears forming but hold them back. I never thought I'd feel this way for my father—that I would let myself get close enough to really care.

The nursing home has become a place of firsts for us. I called him "Papa" for the first time in my life, right here in this room. It just blurted out. Since then I've been mostly calling him "Papa." I can tell he likes hearing it. I like saying it.

Until he was put into Littleton House, I can't remember ever missing him. Moreover, if I thought about my father at all, my thoughts were usually about avoiding him. Tonight I must force myself to leave.

I head back up the corridor to go home. At first, my pace is slow, reluctant—then faster and faster I walk. Passing the nurses' station, I slow down, keeping from breaking into a run. I don't want to be noticed. I don't want anyone to ask why I'm leaving my father in a nursing home when there are extra beds at my house.

At the end of the hallway, three other corridors intersect to form a quadrangle. In the corner stands an easel with a placard. I stop for a moment to read it: "TODAY IS: TUESDAY, SEPTEMBER 28TH, 1993. THE SEASON IS: FALL. THE NEXT HOLIDAY IS: COLUMBUS DAY." When Papa was admitted 13 days ago, six days after his 88th birthday, the sign was off by two days. Tonight it is accurate.

Standing in the quad, I can hear faint moaning. Rock and roll plays through speakers mounted in the ceiling. Buzzers go on and off, and some stay on uncomfortably long. I see no one. The atmosphere is surreal, ghostly.

Out in my company truck, on the way home, I have thoughts about turning around, going back to pack Papa's things and take him home with me. I do not.

CHAPTER TWO

The Phone Call

Before I ever set foot in Littleton House, before my father was put in a nursing home against his will, I had no idea there would even be a *Papa's Tales*. And I certainly did not know I would be telling it now. Of course, despite my starting his tale with one specific visit at the nursing home, Papa's story doesn't begin there. So let me start again, about a year and a half earlier.

On a hot July night, I was lying in bed waiting for an expected phone call from Eleanor, my partner of the past 20 years. As I waited for the phone to ring, I was thinking about our most recent conversations concerning my father, my pre-Papa father. At that time, my father still lived with Donna, just 20 houses away from me, on the same street. They had not married yet.

For almost three years, during my mid 30s, I had shunned my father. Living in such close proximity to my father provided me with many opportunities to shun him. If I saw him enter a local store that I wanted to go into, I'd wait until he left. If I was already inside and he walked in, I'd walk out. Eleanor had put up with my attitude and behavior for a while. She understood much about my troubled childhood, but she could no longer understand my unwillingness to forgive and move on. Eventually I had given in, just a little. I had begun seeing him again, but without any forgiveness.

It was just after midnight, and the day's heat lingered as I contemplated and continued to wait for the phone to ring. Eleanor was away in Vermont for the summer, visiting with her elderly, snowbird mom. She usually called me after her mom and she had finished watching the late news and had their last cup of tea together. That night, her call was late. I wanted to get some sleep. It had been a long, sweaty day in the self-employed carpentry business.

Baby was nudging me, asking to get into my bed. "Not tonight. It's too hot," I told her and pointed to her own bed on the floor. Begrudgingly she did as I wanted and I said she was a good dog.

I kept thinking about how Eleanor wanted more from me. She wanted me to make more of an effort to reconcile with my father, to stop calling him "the Old Man." She didn't think it right that I hardly ever saw him. Eleanor was trying to teach me the importance of family connections, but I was a slow learner in that regard. Back then, if I saw my father at all it was only to keep the peace with her.

My thoughts continued like that for some time. I worked on what to say to Eleanor. I wanted to tell her I'd do better. And at the same time, I wasn't sure that I could. Eventually the phone rang, but it wasn't the call I'd been expecting.

"Oh hi, Richard. I'm sorry for calling so late, but Manny is upset. I've never seen him so mad."

There was no mistaking that voice. It was Donna, the real-life Edith Bunker, as I thought of her whenever she spoke. There was the same high, shrill voice. Sometimes I swore I was hearing "Oh, Archie" when Donna responded to my father with, "Oh, Manny."

"What's wrong?" I asked.

"He's very angry with me. Can you hear him?"

I heard my father in the background. And although I couldn't make out the words, I knew the tone from my childhood. The Old Man was angry, all right.

"Would you like me to come up and talk to him?" I offered.

"Could you, please?"

"Sure, Donna."

"You don't mind?"

"Of course not," I told her. That wasn't true. I did mind but saw no way out. My two brothers lived miles away. For me it was just a short walk down the street.

"Oh, thank you. You'll be here soon then? I just don't know what he'll do."

"Five minutes, Donna."

"All right. Thank you, bye."

Reluctantly I got up, pulled on the same damp shorts and tee shirt I had worn earlier. As I tied my sneakers I wondered what Donna and my father could be fighting about. Nothing came to me. I certainly wasn't thinking that Donna would put him away in a nursing home a year and a half later.

They had been lovers for a long time. Their affair began while my parents were still married and Donna's late husband, Ken, was still alive. After my parents had divorced, Donna and Ken moved into my father's house with him. Donna and Ken stayed married until his death. Ken had passed away at Littleton House nursing home just about a year before the phone call in question.

During the two decades or so of my father and Donna's relationship, I'd never heard him even raise his voice to her, never until that night.

CHAPTER THREE

Short Walk On A Dark Street

Out on the road, the air was still hot and humid. Baby wanted to come with me but I made her stay home. At that point, my dog already had a better relationship with my father than I had with him. Whenever he saw her he doted on her, which seemed strange to me since he had never liked my having pets when I was a child. For Baby's part, she gobbled up his attention. That night I didn't want the distraction.

Most of the neighborhood appeared to be asleep as I walked slowly past the darkened houses. Having lived on that same street for 30 years, ten of them as a child in my father's house and the rest with Eleanor, I was familiar with every house and which cars belonged in each driveway. As for the residents, I knew very few. Everyone knew my father or at least knew of him.

I felt as alone as I had ever felt. A sense of déjà vu began to come over me. Many times during my early teens, before I owned a car to escape in, I had walked my street alone at night. After leaving a friend's house I had often worried about what I'd find when I got home. Would my mother be drunk? Would my parents be fighting? Would I get in the middle and come to blows with my father again?

Would the neighbors call the cops again?

Mosquitoes bit at my ankles so I quickened my pace.

Up ahead, there was one house with all its lights on, but at least there were no police cars out front. I was somewhat relieved.

I got closer. At the bottom of the driveway, I could already hear my father shouting at Donna from inside the house. I froze, and just listened to the Old Man's voice. A voice that still scared me.

Finding the courage to walk up the driveway took a few more moments. Finally, I was able to move. Once at the front door I considered knocking for a second, decided not to, then opened the door and stepped inside my childhood home.

CHAPTER FOUR

The Interloper

When I closed the door behind me, the yelling stopped abruptly. My father was standing to my left, about ten feet away in the doorway between the dining room and the kitchen. He was in his underwear. Wearing a nightgown, Donna sat on one of the dining room chairs, the chair turned backward to the table.

At least I didn't overdress, I thought. "What's all the noise?"

"Oh, look who's come to see us, Manny," Donna piped in. Then she got up, stepped over to me and gave me a perfunctory hug and a quick peck on my cheek.

"Who is it?" Manny asked.

I knew my father didn't see very well, but I always found it odd that he never seemed to recognize my voice.

"It's your son Richard," Donna answered for me.

"Ah, Richard. What brings you here so late? It's kind of late, isn't it?"

"Donna called me. She said you were upset—angry."

"Well, no, not really."

"Okay, I'll go back home then," I said as I turned back toward the door.

Before I could get my left hand on the doorknob, Donna grabbed my right and stopped me. "He's mad at me for going away this weekend. I guess I left him alone too long."

"That's not the problem and you know it!" Manny barked back at her. Then he took a couple of steps toward us. His voice got even louder as he shouted, "Where did you go!"

"Manny, I told you I was going to Connecticut before I left," Donna answered, not realizing his question was loudly rhetorical. Then she turned back to me. "He forgets, you know."

"Shit, I forget! I know where you went and I know who you were seeing. That interloper! I should have thrown him out of here last week. Who does he think he is, worming his way in here?" Manny thrust both fists out in front of him. "Next time I'll knock him on his ass!"

Laughing nervously, Donna retreated behind me. "Oh, listen to him. See, he's really angry."

"You're God damn right I'm angry! Who wouldn't be? You bring another man into our home. What is he, your new swain?"

"What are we talking about?" I asked while I walked toward my father. When close enough, I tried to put an arm around him.

He pushed it away. His muscles were drawn up hard and tight.

I reached over to the dining room table, dragged a couple of chairs out and said, "Dad, sit down. Tell me. What's going on?"

"He means Bob Green," Donna interjected, still standing where I had left her. "I was …"

"Green, the libertine!" Manny interrupted her, and sprang back to his feet.

"I don't think you met Bob. Did you?" Donna asked.

I didn't answer. But I remembered meeting someone new a few weeks earlier. It was Father's Day and Donna was having one of her pool parties. I had stopped by with an obligatory card just to satisfy

Eleanor. While I was there, someone introduced himself as Bob. He seemed like a pleasant fellow. Gray hair, in his 60s, I'd guessed. At the time I just thought he was a mutual friend of theirs. There wasn't any sign of hostility then, or if there was I had missed it.

"Green, what can he give you? He's a beggar, you know," Manny informed her.

"Oh, Manny, he is not. He has a job and a nice apartment."

Manny shrugged his shoulders and threw his arms out to both sides. "Job! Apartment! What's that? He owns nothing. Two rooms on someone else's land. I own my house!" With his arms still out and his palms turned upward, he began circling the dining room, offering up all that was his. "Here you can do anything you want."

"I have needs, you know," Donna said, her eyes tracked Manny as he moved. Then she focused on her hands and nervously rubbed them together. "I can't always stay home and take care of you."

"Needs, what needs?" Manny asked.

"I can't always be here with you. I need to get out once in a while."

"I make no demands on you. So you drive me to the store and cook a few meals for me. That's all I ask. You have to eat anyway, don't you? A few meals for a whole house and you're free to come and go as you please."

Donna looked at Manny, then back at me. "He just doesn't remember what happens when I'm not here," she pleaded.

"What the hell are you talking about, woman?"

"You left the stove on and fell asleep." Donna moved to the table and sat down. "If I hadn't come home in time the house could've burned down," she reminded him, and then turned back to me. "You should've seen it. The whole house was filled with smoke. He put a knackwurst in the frying pan and then he went and took a nap. He didn't even know what he'd done when I woke him."

"Is that true, Dad?"

"I don't know—she's making a big deal out of nothing. I know what you're doing, woman, and I won't have it. Not in my house!" Manny moved right up to her chair. "You slept with him, didn't you?"

"Well, I have needs …"

"Needs, needs! You keep saying that. Just tell me what you want!" Manny demanded. Then, slowly, he moved back and sat down in the chair next to me.

"Donna, tell him," I said. "It's late and we're not getting anywhere like this."

"I'm not an old woman. I'm a lot younger than you and I still need to make love."

A lot younger? Only 30 years younger. What's 30 years among lovers? I thought.

Manny cocked his head. His white, bushy eyebrows rose up and out as he opened his eyes wide. "We don't make love?"

"Not anymore. Not for the last five years."

"No, that's not true. You're exaggerating. Five years? No, that can't be true."

"Yes. Might be even longer. I can't even remember the last time we had sex."

"Well, is there something wrong?" he asked Donna.

"I don't know. Is there something wrong with you? There's nothing wrong with me."

"There's nothing wrong with me!" Manny declared. Then he got up, beat his chest and danced a little jig. Stepping in front of Donna's chair again, Manny bowed, took her hand in his and kissed it. Then he said, "I stand ready and able at your disposal, Madam!"

We all laughed at this for several seconds. Then Donna spoke to me as if my father had left the room. "It's all in his head. He can't do anything anymore."

"What do you mean? I'll show you." Manny grabbed her arms and made her stand up.

"No, no, Manny. It's all right," she said in a patronizing manner. "You don't have to prove anything." Then she gave him a hug and sat back down.

"Well, if you don't want me, you must have someone else. Is Green it now?"

"Oh, I don't know, Manny. He wants me to marry him."

"Then pack your bags and get out! This is my house and I don't need you. I can take care of myself. See how long you last with him! He has nothing. He's a pauper."

"But, Manny, this is my house too. You want me to leave here? I like this house. All my things are here. And my pool—how could I leave my pool?"

"It's him or me. Him or me, baby." Like Cagney in an old gangster movie, my father flicked his thumbs back and forth. Then he said, "Is you is or is you ain't my baby?"

I was lost in his manner of speech. *Does anybody really speak that way?* Suddenly, I noticed he had stopped yelling at Donna and she started smiling and flirting with him. I felt like I was in Alice's wonderland. Like some strange ritual dance, things continued this way for several hours. One minute Donna talked of how trapped she felt taking care of my father. Then he'd get mad and threaten to throw her out. She'd become coquettish again, and the next thing I knew they were buddy-buddy.

"Remember when you used to cook for me, Manny?" Donna asked at one point.

"Yes, of course!"

"He used to make Hungarian goulash."

"Ah, my goulash. World renowned!"

"And he made paprika chicken."

"Oh, chicken paprikash! It was marvelous!"

"That's when I was still working full time. You remember, Manny."

"But of course, I was quite a chef!" My father turned to me. "You're hungry, aren't you, kid?" he encouraged, shaking his head up and down. Then he looked back in Donna's direction. "What have we got to eat around here?"

"See, that's all he ever thinks about now, food. The other night he got me up at three in the morning to make him hot dogs. Imagine, the two of us sitting here at three in the morning eating hot dogs. It's a wonder I get any sleep at all anymore."

I didn't have to imagine. It was close to three by then.

"Is there something else I should be doing?"

"You should be sleeping," she told him.

"Ah, but the night is for wining, dining and dancing!" He danced a tango and motioned for Donna to join him.

Instead she remained seated, and half smiling, half laughing, she shook her head from side to side. "You see? This is what he does. He's up all night and then sleeps all day."

"So, what's wrong with that? I have someplace to be?" Manny put one hand in the air and with the other behind his back, he snapped his fingers. Then he spun around an imaginary dance partner.

"No, but I do! I have to go to work."

"You're working now?" Manny asked, as he sat back down.

"Yes, part time," she answered him. There was an air of self-importance in her tone. "And then there are other things I need to do. I can't just lie around sleeping all day, like you."

"I see. You have engagements? You have to see your lover, I

suppose."

"Oh, Manny, stop that. He's not my lover. I love you. Remember before I moved in? When I used to come by after work and slip into bed with you?" Donna went over and sat on Manny's lap. Stroking her hand through his hair, she said, "We had some good times back then, didn't we, Manny?" Then she turned and faced me. Her eyes were warm and bright. There was a smile on her face as she remembered to me, "He used to be a really good lover. He was the first man I ever had an orgasm with. Isn't that so, Manny?"

Had I heard that right?

"What's that, my darling?" Manny asked. Apparently, he'd lost track of the conversation.

"Didn't I tell you I never had an orgasm before I met you?"

That answered my question.

"Well, I suppose you should know," Manny answered her as she climbed off his lap. Then he got up and started for the kitchen, and over his shoulder asked, "What's wrong? Has my performance declined so much?"

With disappointment in her voice Donna told me, "See, he still thinks he can get an erection." Her warm smile faded.

From the kitchen Manny shouted, "This is what you need, a good fuck! So go to him if he's so good!"

"He's not bad."

"Dad, Donna! Stop it! I've heard enough of this. More than I ever wanted actually." I got up to leave but lingered at the front door for a moment. Turning back I saw my father standing behind Donna with his arms around her waist. I had to smile. "What am I going to do with you two?" I walked back to them. "Sit down for a minute." I beckoned.

They did as I asked.

"Now listen. I've heard both of you. I understand the problem—

at least I think I do. We certainly can't solve this tonight—I should say this morning. I'll call Peter and Carl later—after I get some sleep. We'll set up a family meeting—and we'll see. Okay?"

They nodded in unison.

"In the meantime, try to be nice to each other. I need some sleep and I don't want to come back here today."

CHAPTER FIVE

Brothers in the Hood

Back in our old neighborhood, my brothers and I met in front of our father's house. I had called the meeting as promised. It had been years since all of us were there at the same time.

Peter and I stood waiting by the open door of Carl's blue 260Z. He needed time to assemble his wheelchair.

"Want any help?" Peter asked.

"I got it." Carl had the frame leaning against the doorjamb. One wheel was already attached. He reached to the back seat for the footrests, one armrest and the other wheel. His motion was smooth and well-practiced. He popped the second wheel on, hung the footrests and tossed the seat cushion into place. With a hand on the steering wheel for balance and the other grabbing the chair, he transferred in one quick jerk. The chair shuddered for a second as he landed.

"Another successful touchdown! Well-done," Peter said, with a smile.

"You never know. It's always a crapshoot," Carl responded. Then he reached back in the car for the second armrest. Once he had it in place, he tapped his hands twice and popped a wheelie with the chair. "Ready to rock 'n' roll!"

Although I'd seen this stunt many times, I was still impressed with my big brother's antics.

Carl went into his shirt pocket for a cigarette. Once the cigarette was lit, he took a long drag, tilted his head back and blew smoke straight up over himself. He watched as the cloud dissipated into the evening air, then he brought his head forward again and said, "So what are we going to do with the old geezer?"

"Hey, watch that! That's my father you're talking about," I pretended to be offended.

"No, that's my father you're talking about," Peter piled on.

Fully amused with our own wit, Peter and I laughed and chuckled for a time. Carl just shook his head.

"What time's the tribunal?" Peter asked sarcastically.

"Six o'clock," I answered.

"What's it now?"

Carl, the oldest and the most punctual one of us, looked at his watch. "12 minutes of," he told us.

I felt like we were all hesitant to face the task at hand. Several years earlier, we had been to a similar family meeting. It was when our parents divorced. Father needed money to settle. He presented us with a proposition. If we gave him what he needed to pay off our mother, when he died we'd own the house. All of us turned him down. When that failed, Manny made the same offer to Donna. She accepted.

Carl bent over and crushed his cigarette onto the driveway. Then he picked the butt up and put it back into the pack. "Should we go in?"

"I think we should have a plan first," I suggested.

"Yeah, what's the rush?" Peter asked. "We've got 12 minutes. We ought to be able to figure out the rest of Gramps's life with time to spare."

"Okay. I'll have another smoke then." Carl lit up.

I wanted one too, but I couldn't risk Peter's disapproval.

Peter walked away from Carl's smoke. I followed him. At the corner of the garage we stopped. Peter turned and shook his head. There was a bemused smile on his face.

"What?" I asked.

"Oh, I don't know. I was just thinking of some of the crazy shit we did around here."

"Care to be specific?"

"Remember that bomb we built?"

"Which one? There were so many."

"The magnesium one."

"Oh, yeah, the one that was supposed to be a rocket. It came close to blowing your hand off—if I remember right."

"That's the one."

Being only three years apart, my two older brothers were pretty tight growing up. I was the baby who came five years after Peter was born, so I missed out on many of their adventures when I was little. They didn't want their baby brother getting in their way and embarrassing them. Peter in particular never wanted me hanging around and only tolerated me when my parents insisted. When I was 15, Carl went into the Coast Guard and Peter lost his buddy. I became Carl's replacement and that's when we started setting off bombs together. But we never destroyed anyone else's property. We just put ourselves at risk.

"So—what about it?"

"Remember after it blew, Manny came running out the front door calling for us?"

"Yep!"

"You and I hid right over there." Peter pointed to a thicket of forsythia bushes at the edge of the driveway. Then he imitated Manny, "Boys, boys—what gives—sounds like the whole house is coming down!"

"Yeah, Gramps was pretty pissed with us that night. We must have spent 20 minutes there before we dared move. Then I think we drove around in your car for a couple of hours until we were sure he'd gone to bed."

Peter laughed. "Gramps," he repeated. "How'd we come to name him that anyway?"

"I'm not sure. But you know"—I looked over to make sure Carl was still out of earshot—"I don't think the bomb was the craziest thing that ever happened here. Killing Sergeant tops my personal list."

"Are you still beating yourself up over that?" Peter questioned. "It was just a dog. The dog was the crazy one! Get over it! I'm sure your partner in crime has."

I checked again on Carl's location. He was not aware of what had happened to Sergeant. If he knew about the dog, I feared he wouldn't understand how I could do such a thing. In a whisper I said, "I know Sergeant caused a lot of trouble. Shit, half the fights I had with Dad were over that damn dog. But killing him … I mean, don't you think that was wrong?"

"Get over it! It was just a dog." Peter sounded annoyed with me then.

But I couldn't get over it. I was about to tell him that, about to tell him that for years afterwards, I became scared of dogs. I thought every dog somehow knew what I had done. I used to love dogs. And I still did love them.

Carl wheeled over. "What's going on?"

I changed the subject. "We're trying to figure out when we started calling Manny 'Gramps.' How's your memory?"

"It sucks," Carl said. Then he fired up his third cig of the past ten minutes.

I touched Peter's shoulder. "Well, the way I remember it, you and I were holed up in your room and Dad came calling for us. I don't remember exactly what he was angry about that time, but he was mad as hell about something we had done. You started humming the theme from *Peter and the Wolf.* I joined in and after that he became 'Grandpapa.' I think we shortened it to 'Gramps' for convenience."

"I don't remember any of this," Carl said. "I must have been at sea."

"I think you were. The time's right for the Coast Guard," I excused him.

"So what are we going to do with him?" Peter asked.

"I don't know. I suppose it's up to me," I said reluctantly. "I live the closest and you all have families."

"No, that's not fair—you have a life too," Peter said empathetically. "Maybe we have to sell the house and put him in a nursing home."

"Donna owns part of the house, you know. Remember she gave him the money to buy Mom out when we turned Dad down," I reminded him.

"Is that in-law apartment still intact?" Carl pointed to the garage.

When Donna loaned our father the money to settle his divorce, she and Ken were living in the same neighborhood just two streets away. Ken suffered from MS and was severely crippled. Our father suggested they sell their two-story house and move in with him, in his single-story ranch house. The arrangement would be perfect for our father. They agreed. Manny got busy building himself a little apartment combining the family room and the attached garage.

After Donna's husband died, Manny moved back into the main part of the house with Donna and they rented the apartment for some extra cash.

"Yeah, the apartment is still there. They rent it to a single guy—I think his name is Jeff," I said. "But so what?"

"Well, maybe we can move Dad out there—and let Donna have the rest of the house," Carl suggested.

"Do you know if Jeff has a lease?" Peter asked.

"No, I think he's a tenant at will. The apartment isn't even legal. But I don't see how that solves anything. I don't think Dad can function by himself. Donna said he almost burned the house down about a month ago," I told them.

Peter spoke up again, "And you think she's done with him—I mean, what if we hired someone to come in and help? You think she'd agree to that—or has she already made up her mind to leave him?"

"I'm not sure. She said she still loves him, but it seems she also has another suitor. According to her, some guy named Bob wants her to marry him."

Devoid of emotion, Peter assessed the situation, "Then I guess we've got to sell the house—pay Donna what she's owed and find a home for Gramps."

"Whatever we do, we should go in now. We're late," Carl informed us.

CHAPTER SIX

The Announcement

Carl spun his chair around and headed for the front door. I braced myself for what I was sure would be coming next.

As Carl neared the door, he stopped abruptly. In front of him was a painted plywood ramp. The paint was peeling and the layers of plywood had started to delaminate. The incline was too steep for Carl to negotiate by himself. "You're going to have to pull me up," he said with disgust. "Technologically illiterate asshole."

"Do we really have to get into this again?" I asked, trying to deflect Carl's displeasure.

"You're a carpenter. What's so hard about one-inch rise to 12 inches of run? It's code, you know." Carl and Peter are both mechanical engineers. In their world, one and one always add up to two—every time, no exceptions—no excuses.

"I've told you what happened and you know how he is," I tried to defend myself.

"I'm sorry. I know it's not your fault," Carl apologized.

Our father must have heard something. The door opened and he popped his head outside. "There are my boys! We were getting worried about you."

"Yeah, right," Carl muttered under his breath.

"Let me get you in," Dad offered Carl his help.

"Keep him the fuck away from me," Carl responded.

"Dad, we've got it covered," Peter interceded. "Go in. We'll be right there."

I tipped Carl's wheelchair back and pulled him up the ramp backward. Once inside, I noticed the spread that Donna had laid out on the dining room table: fancy lace tablecloth, napkins, a platter of assorted cheeses, crackers, five long-stem wine glasses and a bottle of champagne on ice. A second later, Donna entered the room smiling and wearing a long dress. Then I realized something I'd missed just moments before; my father was dressed in a suit.

Perhaps sensing he'd be the most receptive, Donna made a beeline to Peter and said, "I've got good news. Manny asked me to marry him and I said yes."

"I guess I should consider this as gaining a mother instead of losing a father," Peter quipped.

Donna laughed. "Oh, Peter, you're so funny." She moved in for a hug.

The embrace lasted a little too long for Peter's liking. "Easy, Mom," he said.

Donna giggled as they separated.

I was speechless. I looked to Carl for support but couldn't make eye contact.

Donna proposed a toast. "I bought champagne to celebrate. Oh, Carl, could you open it? Everyone, take a glass."

Manny heard the pop and spoke up, "Ah, champagne! What's the occasion?"

"Silly Manny. Don't you remember, you asked me to be your wife?"

"I did? And what was your response?"

"I said yes, of course," Donna answered. "Champagne, everyone!" She went around with the bottle.

Peter lifted his glass. "Go forth and procreate!"

"Hey, what are you suggesting?" Manny questioned.

Donna joined the joke. "I think Peter wants a sister."

By then I was dumbfounded. I needed air and some space. The glass slider to the backyard pool beckoned to me. *Nobody would miss me if I went right away.*

At the edge of Donna's pool, I stood still for a few moments appreciating my newfound solitude. The smell of fresh-cut grass and a backyard barbecue mingled, blending together in the summer's evening air. Just below my feet, the pool pump quietly gurgled.

What just happened? I wondered. *That was insane. Why didn't my brothers speak up? How come I couldn't say anything? Getting married?*

I felt a touch on my shoulder and startled. I turned around. In front of me stood a man in his mid 20s. He had dark hair and wore glasses. His face looked familiar.

"Sorry, I didn't mean to scare you," the young man said. Then he stuck out his hand. "Jeff."

I shook his hand and said, "That's okay. I guess I was deep in thought—I didn't hear you coming."

"Well, just so you know, I wasn't trying to sneak up on you—or anything. Once again, I'm sorry."

"No, no, no, it's okay, really. I'm fine." I released my grip. "Actually, you and I already met a few weeks ago."

Jeff took a moment. "Oh, that's right! Father's Day, wasn't it?"

"Yeah."

"You brought your dad a balloon with 'Happy Father's Day' printed on it. All in psychedelic colors—I think."

"Yep, that was me. I'm surprised I showed up at all, but since I did I figured I needed to bring something. Picked it up last minute on the way over here."

"You guys don't get along?" Jeff questioned.

"You could say that."

"Yeah, I know how that goes—I don't even speak to my father anymore. All we ever did was fight. But your dad is so cool. I can't imagine anyone not liking him."

"I've heard that before—it's pretty much the prevailing opinion of everyone outside of family."

"So none of you has a good relationship—your brothers, I mean?"

I was a little uncomfortable with Jeff's questions. But his manner was disarmingly charming, and I felt almost compelled to answer. "Carl barely tolerates Manny—I have my moments—I guess Peter does the best with him. We're all still trying, though. That's why we came over tonight."

"I get it and I'm sorry if it seems like I'm prying—it's just that I like your dad so much. I don't want anything bad to happen to him."

"Well, thank you for that."

"Do you know what Donna is up to?" Jeff questioned me.

"I'm not at all sure anymore. This"—I pointed to the slider and the merriment still going on inside—"was supposed to be a family meeting to see how we could help her with my dad. I thought they wanted to separate—or at least change the living situation. Just last week she was complaining about how trapped she felt taking care of my father. It never crossed my mind they would marry each other."

"I don't think it crossed Manny's mind either," Jeff said.

"What do you mean?"

"It was Donna's idea," Jeff stated confidently.

"How do you know that?"

"Can we sit down? This might take a while."

We moved to the small patio table beside the pool. I sat and Jeff scooted a chair over close to me. Before seating himself, he angled his chair to provide a sightline of the glass door.

Almost in a whisper, Jeff began, "She wants Manny's house."

"I don't understand—she already owns part of it," I told him. "If the house needs to be sold she'll get her share. With interest too—we're not going to cheat her."

"She wants all of it for herself."

"How will marrying my father make that happen?"

Jeff sneaked a peek back at the slider, then answered, "Once they're married she's going to put him away."

"Put him away where?"

"In a nursing home—the same one in fact where she dumped her last husband." Jeff thought for a second, then ventured, "Ken, was it?"

"Yeah, but Ken was seriously ill when he went there."

"MS, right?" Jeff checked, and seeing me nod, he continued, "That's what your brother Carl has, isn't it?"

I wondered where he was getting all his information, but I didn't see any harm in answering. "Well, Jeff, there are a whole host of symptoms considered to be multiple sclerosis; hence, the name—*multiple*. My brother would tell you, 'Doctors'—neurologists, in particular—don't know what the fuck when it comes to MS.' He's had it almost 30 years now and none of them can really do anything for him. But my brother's condition is very different than Ken's was. Carl has what's called 'slow progressive.' From his waist up, he's strong—don't arm wrestle with him because you'll lose—I know, I have. Ken was frail. His disease affected him everywhere—

legs, arms, eyesight—he even had trouble swallowing. Toward the end he was skinny as a rail."

"Oh, I didn't know," Jeff said. He seemed embarrassed to have accused Donna so summarily. "When did Ken die?"

"About a year ago, at Littleton House—that was the name of the nursing home—in case you haven't uncovered that yet."

"I'm sorry. I'm being too nosy, aren't I?"

"You do ask a lot of questions for someone who's supposed to be telling me what Donna's plans are."

"It's just that since I've been living here, Manny and I have gotten really close. He's like the father I never had."

"That makes two of us."

"I'm not joking! If you guys don't give a crap about Manny, there's nothing I can do." Jeff got up as if to leave.

"Sorry, I didn't think you were. Please don't go."

Jeff sat down again.

"You seem very sincere but you have to understand, dealing with Manny is difficult for us. There's a lot of family history you don't know. When you say that you were always fighting with your dad, I assume you mean the typical: disagreements, arguments, maybe some yelling and just generally not getting along." I got no indication to the contrary from Jeff, so I went on. "When I say it, I'm talking about bloodletting brawls, usually ending with the cops being called. Not to mention the psychological shit that caused it all. So don't judge me too harshly—it's tough for me to see Manny the way you do."

Jeff took his time before speaking again. "Do you think Manny should be put away?"

"Not when you say it like that. I do think he needs help and I doubt he can live on his own anymore."

"Why—because of his eyes?"

"There's that, but the bigger problem is his memory. You must have witnessed it."

"Sure, sometimes he forgets my name. I don't think that means he should be locked up, though. And did you know that Donna is seeing someone else on the side?"

"It isn't really 'on the side' anymore—everyone appears to know about it—but yes, I know she's been going to Connecticut."

"Sometimes she's gone all weekend. I've been kind of hanging out with Manny when she's away. I read to him. And he's been teaching me all sorts of things. You do agree your dad is really smart, don't you?"

"So he tells me." I caught his look. "Yes—he's brilliant!"

"The way he talks, it's so inspiring—all that energy. He even has me reading stuff for myself. Ever heard of books called *Manhood of Humanity* and *Science and Sanity*?"

"Korzybski, yeah. It was required reading growing up here. I think I managed to struggle through them at least once. Isn't my thing, though; too much math, no characters and not much of a plot."

"Manny says the books are the foundation for general semantics. He's been teaching me about it too. I just love listening to him. He's fascinating. You can't put him in a nursing home. It would kill him."

"Nothing has been decided by us. We just came to see how we could help. None of us knew anything about the wedding plans."

"Manny didn't ask her to marry him. Donna put that idea in his head when she was scared she'd lose the house."

"I ask you again, how do you know that?"

"I just do. Up until a couple of days ago, your dad was still furious with her. He sure remembers who Bob is. But Donna's been working on Manny ever since. She's convinced him that if they get married, she'll stop seeing Bob. Your dad is a very proud man and . . ."

"She's coming," I said, as I saw Donna was heading toward the door.

Jeff got up quickly and stepped out of sight. "I'll talk to you later—there's more I need to say—you live down the street, right? I don't have a phone."

"Number four," I told him.

CHAPTER SEVEN

Jeff Again and Gone

Donna opened the sliding door. She couldn't see Jeff skulking around the corner. "Oh, there you are—we wondered where you went."

Jeff tiptoed away, leaving me searching for an excuse. "Champagne doesn't agree with me—it gives me a headache."

"I have aspirin inside," Donna offered.

I declined politely. Reluctantly, I rejoined the festivities. Quietly and separately, I urged my brothers to wrap things up so we could leave. The process took another hour.

Finally, when all the goodbyes had been said and the front door closed behind us, I erupted into a quick retelling of Jeff's allegations. We discussed. No conclusions were reached. But we all agreed that something seemed fishy.

Carl transferred back into his car. As he disassembled his wheelchair, he said, "Sorry, guys, but I've got to go. I'm really tired. Let's get together again—just the three of us."

Peter offered me a ride home and we left Carl to finish packing up on his own. During the short ride, Peter speculated about Jeff's motives. "I wonder what he's trying to get out of this. You know—I mean, he could have just kept quiet. Why would he want to get involved?"

"I don't know. He seems to genuinely like Manny—go figure."

We arrived at my house and Peter parked on the street in front. Before shutting the engine off, he ran the windows down. "What the hell are we going to do with them?" he said, as much to himself as to me.

I had no answers. We sat silently for a minute. Suddenly, we heard a clattering sound and then a loud thud behind the car, followed by a scream, and "Shit! Shit! Shit!"

Peter and I got out, and we found Jeff sprawled across the lawn with a bicycle lying half on top of him. We rushed over and helped him up. "Are you all right?" I asked.

Jeff looked at his arms and took inventory. "Yeah, just a little scraped up is all."

"You sure? Want to go inside and wash up—check for damages?" I offered.

"No, I'll be all right. But I need to look for my glasses. I only had one lens in them and I couldn't see the curb," he explained. Then he joked, "I guess I found it, though."

"Are these them?" Peter asked, as he picked up a twisted mess of wire rims.

"I'm sorry—Jeff, this is my brother Peter."

They shook hands and Peter gave back what remained of the glasses. "Uh-oh, now the other one's gone," Jeff lamented.

Peter got a flashlight from the Mercedes and the three of us looked for the missing glass. Once the lens had been retrieved, Peter said, "Why don't we sit in the car? You can pop the lens back in—and then tell us why you risked life and limb to come down here."

Jeff got into the back alone. Peter turned on a few lights. After struggling a bit, Jeff managed to reconstruct his optics. He looked around at the interior. "Nice car," he said.

Peter shut the lights off and started in on him, "So, Jeff, what is your involvement with our little family affair? My brother told me you think there's a plot ensuing."

"Well, after you guys left, Donna got real busy making plans. I could hear her on the phone inviting people to the wedding. While she was preoccupied I managed to talk with your dad. He seems pretty confused, if you ask me. Also, he said Donna wants a ring. Manny doesn't have much money left and if you're going to stop her, you need to act fast."

"Interesting," Peter said. "First of all, what makes you think we should stop them from getting married—I mean, assuming we even could? And second, how do you have knowledge about our father's finances?"

"I've been helping Manny write his checks. I know Donna's supposed to do it, but she's been spending so much time with Bob lately—and, well, sometimes your dad needs money—to go shopping and stuff. I couldn't help but notice that the balance is getting low."

"You better be careful," Peter returned. "Donna has a legal power of attorney—you don't. It's not appropriate for you to know Manny's business. And considering what you're accusing her of, you better hope she doesn't find out about the checkbook."

Jeff fired back, "Well, at least I care what happens to Manny and I'm not trying to steal his house!"

"From a practical point of view, how do you think Donna can steal his house?" Peter asked.

"She told me how herself. Once they're married she'll start the paperwork with Medicaid and after Manny qualifies, she'll put him in the nursing home. She said she knows just how to do it without having to pay. She was practically bragging about it to me. I guess her last husband gave her plenty of practice."

My brother continued his interrogation. "And if she had such a plan—why tell you?"

Jeff hesitated while trying to answer my brother's question. "I'm not sure why Donna told me her plans—it was late—Manny had gone to bed already—the two of us were sharing a bottle of wine and—I don't know—maybe she was a little drunk. It almost felt like she was flirting with me."

"Wow. Now you've got Donna chasing after you too. What's next?" Peter asked.

"I'm sorry if you don't believe me. Everything I've said is true. I don't mean any disrespect, but how did Manny and Donna hook up in the first place?"

"He stole from the sick and the weak," I offered.

"I'm serious—isn't he twice her age? I mean, more power to him, but it does cause problems. Don't you think?"

"Not quite twice—your point is well taken, though," Peter conceded. "All right, let's assume everything you're saying is true. Would you be willing to repeat what you've told us to a lawyer?"

"I don't know. I don't really like lawyers."

"Does anyone?" I posed the question.

"Not until you need one," Peter answered for all of us.

"It's just that my ex is suing me for support, and I've been having a rough time of it lately. I'm not sure I can stand many more questions about my integrity," Jeff said.

Peter softened his approach. "Okay, let's say we go to Manny's attorney and without mentioning you, we tell him what our suspicions are—what then?"

"What do you mean?" Jeff asked.

"Something has to be done with Manny. He can't be left on his own."

"Maybe so—still that doesn't mean you should put him in a nursing home. I'm no expert on the subject, but he's not ready for that. I can't imagine him playing Bingo. There has to be some other solution." Jeff waited for us to respond. Peter and I remained silent. "You know, if you got rid of Donna, I wouldn't mind watching out for Manny at night and on the weekends. Maybe during the day you could hire an aide or he could go to elder daycare or something."

"And what would you expect in return?" Peter asked.

"Nothing—maybe you could give me a break on the rent—money is a little tight for me right now. But nothing really—I'd be with Manny just for the joy of it."

"Okay, Jeff. Sorry you got dragged into all of this." Peter had heard enough. As if chairing a corporate meeting, he said, "How can we reach you if we need to?"

"I don't have a phone, but you know where I live—for now, at least. If this doesn't get resolved soon, though, I'm moving out. I can't stand watching what she's doing to him." Jeff got out of the car, climbed back on his bike and rode away.

Peter turned to me. "What the fuck was that? Where does Manny come up with these people?"

"I don't know," I said, not wanting to disagree. "I know Jeff seems a little weird. Still I really think he's sincere."

"Maybe so, but what does he want from all of this? It sounds like the guy is a bum. No phone—can't afford to get his glasses fixed—and he's filling out checks for Manny. I don't trust him. I think we should have a look at Dad's checkbook and see if anything's missing. Do you know where he keeps it?"

"Not really. I suppose I could find out," I told him. "Still, what about Donna? It doesn't make sense—her suddenly wanting to marry Manny. After all, just last week she was considering marrying

Bob. I don't trust her either."

"You're right. Let's confront her with what Jeff said and see how she responds," Peter suggested.

We began to say our goodbyes, and before leaving, Peter offered to call Carl and bring him up to date. I promised to look for Dad's checkbook to see if Jeff had written any checks for himself.

CHAPTER EIGHT

Anonymous Warning

During the next week I tried to look for our father's checkbook but to no avail. Donna's car was always in the driveway whenever I drove past. Apparently she really did stop going to Connecticut to see Bob Green and thus was home on the weekend as well. By the following Monday, I convinced myself that it didn't really matter. Jeff had already moved out. I was sure that if he had helped himself to any of Manny's money, Donna would have discovered it by then.

The wedding arrangements had been made for the end of August. It was not until the last days of July that we met again at my father's house. Somehow my brothers and I convinced Donna to just have a celebration and put the marriage plans on hold. We all pledged to help Donna with Manny's care. More champagne was consumed. A consensus had been reached, or so we thought, and I departed happy.

My happiness ended, two days later, when I received a message on my answering machine: "Donna is planning to elope and marry your father in front of a justice of the peace in two weeks, before you boys can find out about it."

In disbelief, I played it back several times. I could tell it was a woman's voice, but it seemed deliberately disguised and there was the sound of running water in the background so I couldn't recognize who had warned me.

I called my brothers again. We all agreed a lawyer was needed, and soon. Carl secured an appointment with the firm that had drafted Manny's power of attorney.

CHAPTER NINE

Meddling

On the day of the meeting at the lawyer's office, I was late. Already seated at the conference table were my brothers, Donna, Manny and the attorney. The lawyer got up, shook my hand and introduced herself, "I'm Attorney Toni Rafanelli. Please, have a seat."

I listened to a brief synopsis of what had already been discussed. I sensed the inevitable, but tried to present my case nonetheless. "I'm concerned that my father is being railroaded into this marriage," I began.

"What makes you feel that way?" Ms. Rafanelli asked.

I went over my father's recent forgetfulness. I retold what was discussed at the most recent family meeting. I couldn't bring myself to openly discuss my father's impotence and how that might affect a marriage with Donna. Instead I tried to get the message across by association. Looking over at my father, I could see he was ready to nod off. It wasn't until I mentioned the late-night phone call from Donna, and Bob Green's name, that Manny seemed present. Suddenly, his eyes were wide open and his head was erect.

Attorney Rafanelli asked, "Who is Bob Green and what has he to do with any of this?"

"I haven't seen him in a month!" Donna piped in. "It's all over with him."

The attorney turned toward Manny. "Manny, what is your understanding of Donna's relationship with this Bob fellow?"

"Oh, that guy again," Manny began. He seemed annoyed and embarrassed at revisiting the subject. "Well, you know how young girls are—they let their emotions rule them. It wasn't anything serious, I don't think." Manny turned and grasped Donna's hand. "Was it, my darling?"

"No, Manny. I told you I'm done with him."

"Well, there you see—easy come, easy go," Manny dismissed it. A big victory smile lit up his face.

"Is there anything else?" The attorney asked.

"Yes, as a matter of fact there is," I said. "What about Jeff's allegations that Donna already intends to put my father in a nursing home once they are officially married?"

"Great! Now we have another name thrown into the mix. So where is this Jeff? Do you have an affidavit from him, or is he going to show up late as well?" Attorney Rafanelli asked sarcastically, clearly losing her patience.

"We haven't been able to contact Jeff. He is a little uncomfortable about talking with you about this. But he told my brother Peter and me."

"That makes it hearsay, and hearsay from an unreliable transient you can't even find. Now listen, Donna and your father have had a long-term relationship. If they wish to marry, that's their right and their business, not yours. Anything else on your mind, Richard?"

It felt useless, but I responded anyway, "As I understand it, Donna is legally Manny's attorney-in-fact. I know this because I'm a signatory on the power of attorney document and I'm listed as her alternate. Since my brothers and I have raised questions about her intentions, it seems that allowing her to continue in that capacity unchecked is a little like letting the fox watch the chicken coop."

"What would you propose as an alternative?" She questioned.

"Well, if they are determined to wed—and for the record I want it noted that I think that's a bad idea—but if they are determined to do this, then I feel that my dad's power of attorney should be changed."

"First of all, this is not a court, so 'noting something for the record' is not relevant here," the lawyer in Ms. Rafanelli admonished me. "But in regards to changing the power of attorney, what did you have in mind?"

"I don't know. Obviously I'm not a lawyer," I acknowledged. "But it seems to me the power could be divided between the four of us."

"You mean your brothers, you and Donna?"

"Yeah, something like that," I answered.

She turned to Carl and Peter. "And you both feel this way as well?"

They answered affirmatively.

"Well, that hardly seems fair, now does it? That's three against one.

"It's fairer than leaving things the way they are, under the circumstances," I responded.

"I have a letter here from your father's doctor stating that Manny is of sound mind and perfectly aware of what it means to enter into a marriage. Would you like to see it?"

"No. I'm sure you have it or you wouldn't have mentioned it," I replied.

"You know, I think you boys are just meddling in your father's affairs. And I don't think you have any right to do that."

"Of course you can think anything you want," I addressed the lawyer's accusations, "but our reason for being here is not self-interest. We just want our father to be protected. And I don't want him placed in a nursing home at Donna's convenience. What if we divided the power four ways but made it by consensus—could such a document be drafted?"

Attorney Rafanelli took a moment to consider my latest proposal. "I suppose it could, but it would be difficult to construct. And I anticipate problems with implementing such a device. For example, in the event of an emergency, who would make decisions?" She addressed her next question directly to my father. "Manny, how do you feel about having your power of attorney divided between your three sons and Donna?"

He stalled for a moment, then said, "Oh, I don't know. I think we should keep things the way they are. It's simpler that way."

"Well, you heard it, gentlemen. If there's nothing else, I think this meeting is over."

CHAPTER TEN

"Who's the lucky woman?"

On Saturday, August 29, 1992, as the morning of Manny and Donna's wedding approached, I contemplated not going. Eleanor was still away with her mom, in Vermont.

I looked in the closet. A gray three-piece suit stared back at me. I tried it on. It was six a.m. and already hot. While I thought more about boycotting the wedding altogether, I considered which tie to wear. I knew I must go. It wouldn't be fair to my brothers not to. And of course, Eleanor would be disappointed in me again if I sat this one out.

Perhaps I was just brooding. I have always felt superior to Donna, both intellectually and in people skills. And yet, I couldn't convince anyone to stop the impending marriage. Donna had won and I had lost. My bad mood was probably more about that than some deeper concern for the Old Man.

I removed the suit from its hanger and neatly laid it over a wing chair by the front door. I thought of making some coffee. Instead, I went back to bed for a while.

A little before ten, guests were still arriving in front of the First

Parish Unitarian Church with the white steeple, in the center of Chelmsford. Outside, and within earshot of my father, I watched as Manny greeted the new arrivals. His best man, Oscar, a longtime friend and business associate, stood next to him.

The hot August sun had rewarmed the sidewalk. I felt the heat from the pavement penetrate the bottom of my thin-soled dress shoes. I continuously shifted my weight to help keep my feet cool.

Across the street, on the town common, I observed as Manny's grandchildren (my niece and nephew) and Donna's grandchildren raced about the lawn playing tag. They needed to burn up some energy, release some tension, before being asked to sit quietly and seriously with the adults. I wanted to run with them as a child again, without responsibilities, when the summer meant the sound of lawnmowers, the smell of fresh-cut grass, and the taste of pistachio ice cream at Skip's outdoor stand.

The last few guests approached. Harry, an old friend and fellow member of the New York Society for General Semantics, shook Manny's hand and asked, "So how does it feel to be getting married again?"

To this my father replied, "Married! Who's getting married? —I'm getting married? —Well, gee, who's the lucky woman?"

In the moment, all who heard this assumed he was joking. They laughed. I laughed too, but I wasn't quite sure he was kidding. Of course, with everyone laughing around him, Manny took credit for the joke by laughing along.

Someone from the wedding party came outside and called to Manny, "We're about to start and we need the groom. Come on."

"Where am I going?" Manny asked.

"Inside the church, please!"

"Oh, church. Sounds serious! I'll be leaving now," Manny said. Then he took a couple of quick steps in the opposite direction.

More laughter ensued. Everyone filed into the church. I found a seat by myself.

From my vantage point in the rearmost pew, I could see all in attendance.

Middle left, there was a group of former board members and investors of Foto-Cube Inc. I hadn't seen most of them for many years, but I recognized them from investment parties and business meetings held at my father's house. Even though all had lost money, some in significant amounts, none seemed to hold a grudge or feel cheated by my father. And after all, they were there.

My family sat to the right. Carl had his wheelchair parked in front of the first row. Carl's wife, the first Donna Ebner, was slightly behind and near his side. Their son, Brian, nine, had a small role in the wedding ceremony. He wasn't sitting with them at the start.

In the same row, Peter and his wife, Marsha, had their seven-year-old daughter pulled up close to them. Rachel was shaking her head back and forth. I couldn't hear from where I was seated, but my niece appeared to be upset and Marsha was trying to console her. I remembered something about Rachel having been asked to be a flower girl. *Maybe she's boycotting—good for her.*

Across the aisle, Donna's family was assembled. Robbie, her son; his sister, Dawn; and Dena, Robbie's wife, all sat together. I'm sure Dena and Robbie's children attended too, but I could never keep track of their names or how many of them there were exactly. Donna's parents were present as well.

Scattered about, I could pick out a few familiar faces from the neighborhood. I didn't recognize anyone else, but it was a pretty good crowd, 60 to 75 people, I guessed. More than I'd expected. Music started. The procession began.

Once the service started, I noticed my father's head drop as if he was about to take a nap. Then Manny would startle and straighten

61

up. That happened again and again.

It was too damn hot in there. I lost my focus and started to daydream. An organ piped in, church bells rang and suddenly it was over. My shirt was soaked from perspiration and my glasses were fogged. As for the exchange of vows, the placing of the ring on Donna's finger and the kissing of the bride, I must have missed it.

I waited for the newlyweds to finish their grand departure. Then I went home to change before completing my obligation to be at the reception.

At the hotel, there was a three-course luncheon, with white linen, provided for all the guests. Later, there was live music for dancing. I wondered who had paid for all of it.

Spoons began clinking against glasses. Oscar spoke. Donna beamed. Everyone applauded—everyone except Manny, for he had fallen asleep with his head on the table in front of him.

CHAPTER ELEVEN

Remodeling

Shortly after their wedding, Donna took a trip to England by herself. Other than that the year passed uneventfully in the marriage of Donna and Manny. That is to say, uneventfully from my point of view. There were no midnight phone calls to answer. No meetings. No meddling in my father's affairs.

I stopped in on occasion. Mostly when I knew Donna wouldn't be there. Usually Baby came with me. She gave us something to talk about and made the conversations easier. Sometimes during the day, we found my father resting on his self-made patio, at the rear of the house by Donna's pool, a straw sombrero over his face for shade. Often he was asleep. Baby helped out there as well. She was better at waking him than I.

When we talked about anything other than the dog, our conversations mostly centered on one of my remodeling projects. It never seemed to matter which one as my father asked the same questions about all of them, usually several times during any visit. When I asked how he and Donna were getting along, he always said everything was fine. Beyond that, he didn't elaborate.

Then suddenly everything changed. Three hundred eighty-one days after the wedding, I received my second anonymous phone message. Someone inside Donna's inner circle told of the impending plans for my father.

Once again, I couldn't determine who had called. I played it for Eleanor: "Donna intends to put your father in Littleton House tomorrow. I just thought you should know."

"Any ideas?" I asked her.

"I don't recognize the voice. But more important, what are you going to do about it?" Eleanor challenged me.

At first, I couldn't answer Eleanor's question. For it was also my question, and I had no answers for myself either. After a time, I responded with, "I'm not sure what I can do. Perhaps it's fate or divine justice or something. Maybe Manny needs to be in a nursing home. I don't know."

"What do you mean by 'divine justice'?" Eleanor asked, sounding annoyed and disappointed with me.

"Maybe his own past insensitivities have come home to roost. You've seen how he carried on with Donna right in front of Ken. We've talked about it before and I know it bothered you as well."

"And how is that justice for anyone? It's not justice for Ken; he's dead and buried. Your father? Somehow you think his being put away in the same nursing home where Ken died is justice? I don't understand you!"

"I'm sorry. I'm at a loss right now. I don't know how to respond, what to do, or what to think. I tried to stop the wedding—you know I did. My efforts failed. Donna holds all the power and I feel totally ineffectual. What more can I say?"

Eleanor grabbed me and held on for a very long time. Then she said, "Think about it, sweetie, and when you're ready I'm here for you."

Later that same day, we decided to confront Donna. With Eleanor by my side, I felt more empowered. While walking up the street to my father's house, Eleanor and I discussed how to approach things.

Outside the front door, we encountered a bathtub, two sinks and a toilet lying on the grass. Neither of us would have been that surprised to see Manny lying there as well among Donna's other discarded objects.

We knocked. Donna answered. "Oh hi. Manny's asleep right now. Did you come to see him?" She seemed startled by our presence.

"Doing a little remodeling?" I asked, sarcastically.

"Oh, Manny's bathroom. Yep, I'm having a new tub put in. A Jacuzzi. Would you like to see it? Come in," she finally invited us.

We stepped inside to go look at Manny's new Jacuzzi. The noise of our arrival awakened him and Manny headed up the hallway as the three of us turned to walk down it.

"Who is it? Who's here?" Manny asked.

"It's Richard and Eleanor, Dad."

"Richard, my boy! Oh, and Eleanor, I haven't seen you in ages. How are you, my darling?"

"Hi, Manny. I'm fine. How are you?"

"Well, I have no complaints. You know I'm a man of leisure now." My father had been retired for about ten years by then, but he never missed the opportunity to remind working people that he was free from such burdens.

The four of us remained compressed in the small hall for a short time. Eleanor and Manny hugged. Donna started in to get things moving again. "They want to see the Jacuzzi, Manny." We all crowded into the bathroom.

After some chitchat about the installation job, I asked my father how he liked his new tub.

"Well, well, you know me. I like everything. The old tub was fine, but anything to keep my little darling happy," he said. Then he gave Donna a squeeze.

I kept looking for any indication that my father knew where he was headed in the morning. But judging by Manny's last comments, it seemed obvious he did not.

Donna invited us into the dining room for coffee. When it was ready, I asked my father directly, "Do you know where you are going tomorrow, Dad?"

"Going? No. Am I going someplace?"

Donna shook her head and her eyes beckoned me to stop.

Without hearing an answer to his questions, Manny turned to Donna and asked, "Are we going somewhere?"

Donna's head continued to shake from side to side and her eyes became fiery mad. Her angry eyes remained fixed on me as she answered, "No, Manny, we aren't going anyplace."

"You haven't told him, have you?" I asked and waited. "If you don't, I will."

"He knows, he knows! He just forgets."

"I know what? What am I forgetting?"

"Donna, tell him!" Eleanor demanded.

As we waited for Donna to reveal herself, Manny stirred his coffee round and round with a spoon in one hand, while he drummed his fingers nervously on the table with the other.

The wait became longer. "Donna! You need to tell him. He needs to hear it from you," I insisted.

There wasn't any response.

"Will somebody tell me what's going on here?"

I'd had enough. I answered my father's question: "Donna is taking you to a nursing home tomorrow. It's all been arranged."

The room became silent. Manny looked at Donna. She didn't

return his gaze. Instead, her eyes focused into the air where they could not be reached.

"Donna?" Manny beckoned for a response.

She looked ready to cry.

In a softer, quieter tone, Eleanor said, "Donna, Manny is talking to you and you need to respond to him."

Finally, Donna replied with, "What, Manny?"

"What is this talk about a nursing home? Are you putting me away? Am I sick?"

"No, Manny, you're not sick." Donna avoided his first two questions by answering only his last.

"You didn't answer him!" Eleanor snapped.

"What do you want me to say?" Donna retorted.

I weighed in to back up Eleanor, "Answer all his questions! Are you putting my father in a nursing home?"

"Yes, he's going to Littleton House tomorrow," Donna finally admitted.

"Littleton House, but that is a nursing home. If I'm not sick why are you taking me there? Are we visiting someone?"

Again she didn't answer. I couldn't hold back any longer. "No, Dad, you're going there permanently, to live."

"Wait a minute now! What are you telling me? I live here. This is my house!" he declared. His voice became louder and his face redder with each protest.

"It's my house too, Manny," Donna began to defend her position, "and I just can't take care of you at home anymore."

"So where are we going to live?" Manny asked.

"I'm going to live here. You can stay at Littleton House and I'll come visit you."

"No, no, this is my home! I paid for it, didn't I? I'm not leaving my home! Donna, what are you saying—do you want a divorce?"

"No, Manny. I just think I can take better care of you in Littleton."

"You're coming with me then?"

"No, but I'll visit you and I'll still be your wife."

"Visit me, shit! I'm not going, I tell you! This is my house. I own it! You go live there if you want to!" Manny shouted at her. His face became fully flush. The veins in his forehead bulged.

"Now see what you've done!" Donna directed her venom toward Eleanor and me. "You've gotten him all upset and for nothing too. Who asked you to butt in! He could have a heart attack, for God's sake!"

Consumed with self-righteous anger, I shouted back at her, "Who asked me! He's my father and I'm his son. I don't have to ask anyone, let alone you, to talk to him."

"Well, sometimes you don't act like it. You never come to see him and pretty soon he won't know who you are. He won't even recognize you anymore. I've seen it happen as a nurse, you know. Plenty of times, I have. You just don't have any idea what Alzheimer's does to them."

Sometime in the future, I might be able to see some truth in Donna's words. Not that night, however. Then I felt only rage and disdain toward her. I couldn't understand how she was prepared to put my father in a nursing home without first preparing him.

If I could have thought clearly, I might have realized that what I did was not any better. After all, the circumstances then were not so different from those of the previous year before they had married. That year, and the night of Donna's midnight phone call for help in particular, I had been willing to facilitate. This night, I was a one-man wrecking crew intent on causing Donna as much grief as possible, even if it hurt my father more.

Somehow, I did manage to put my feelings aside for a moment.

I offered to go to the nursing home with Donna and my father. Donna accepted and agreed to stop by and pick me up in the morning.

There was nothing more Eleanor and I had to say. We left Donna to deal with my father's continuing agitated disbelief.

CHAPTER TWELVE

Just Visiting

In the morning, Donna did not pick me up. Instead she carried out her plan undeterred by our attempted intervention. Since Donna had worked as a nurse at Littleton House for several years, Manny had been there many times with her in the past. They had often visited her late husband, and after he died, Donna and my father would go there just to see some of her former coworkers. It probably seemed perfectly normal to stop by after breakfast. Not remembering the previous day's confrontation with Donna, my father most likely had no idea he'd be staying there for lunch and every meal thereafter.

Peter and I arrived at Littleton House while Donna was still completing paperwork. Our father talked with one of the aides and didn't notice us when we came in. Unannounced, we entered the admissions office where Donna had just signed a DNR (do not resuscitate) order for Manny.

Clearly startled by our presence, Donna put her pen down and pushed the document to the side. "Oh, Peter and Richard." She got up to greet us. Then she introduced us to the director by saying, "These are Manny's sons. They've come to help with his transition."

Both of us let the misrepresentation of our intentions slide at that moment. Instead, I swiped the DNR document off the desk and asked, "Donna, did you forget we decided we weren't going to sign one of these just yet?" I tore it in half. Then I turned to the director and said, "In case you were unaware, Donna and I share my father's health proxy and he was pretty clear about not wanting a DNR. And anyway, his stay here is only temporary. My brother and I are looking into a more suitable placement for him."

Perhaps not wanting to cause a scene, Donna didn't contradict me. The director offered my brother and me a tour of the facility. Donna left to find our father.

Our tour guide walked us past the activity room. "And here is where our residents get together and have fun playing games and singing songs and such," she tried to sell us, with a smile.

Through a pair of glass double doors, I surveyed the room. There was a large TV at the far end. It was on. The room remained devoid of any human life forms. In my head, I renamed it the *inactivity room.*

My carpenter's eye assessed the materials used to construct Littleton House, the building. I saw cinder block walls, asphalt tile floors over poured concrete slabs, dropped ceilings. *Circa mid, to late '70s,* I thought. *Doesn't look anything like a "house."*

Also, I didn't see any provision for central air conditioning, no visible ductwork. There were window air conditioners in the main offices. *Curiously, I wondered what they did with all 125 elderly residents when it was in the 90s and oppressively humid. They couldn't fit all of them in the four small administrative offices. I remembered how debilitated my father used to get in the hot weather. He often said, "Give me cold over heat. The cold I can dress for. When it's hot there is only so much you can take off and then you just die." My father could die here next summer. He could die here before then.*

72

We came to the end of the main corridor where the three other hallways that led to residents' rooms connected to form a quadrangle. In the corner stood an easel with a placard. It read: "TODAY IS: MONDAY; SEPTEMBER 13TH, 1993. THE SEASON IS: FALL. THE NEXT HOLIDAY IS: COLUMBUS DAY." I pointed out the sign to Peter and asked, "Today is Wednesday, isn't it?"

"That's what I've got. Maybe they know something we don't," he offered.

Heading down the hallway toward my father's room we passed the nurses' station. And across from the nurses' counter there was a row of metal folding chairs lined up against the wall. Several residents dressed in hospital gowns occupied the seats. Scanning the row, I saw heads attached to bodies whose muscles could barely hold the weight of bone and skin, let alone support a skull. Hollow, emaciated faces, with eyes pointed downward and inward, showed no recognition of us passing by. Some of the residents were engaged in what sounded like an ancient conversation with themselves. They muttered sounds, a kind of ritual chant. When I walked past I could recognize the verbalizations of a name and pick out a word or two. The director didn't introduce us to anyone and my brother and I didn't say hello on our own.

When we reached my father's door, the director opened it. "Whoops!" she said, and promptly closed it again before we could step inside. Not fast enough, however, to prevent the smell of human feces from wafting out into the hall. "They're doing a little cleaning right now. Why don't we go down and look at the family living room? They should be done in there momentarily."

We walked past five more doors. "This is one of our three family rooms. There is one for each wing. It's a nice space to enjoy some private time with your loved one. No need for reservations. We just ask guests to be respectful and wait to go in if another family is using the space," the director informed us.

A dark blue couch with matching wing chairs, end tables with lamps, a small wooden desk in one corner and the ubiquitous TV filled the 12-by-12 room. With wallpapered walls and drapes with tiebacks, this was the only space I'd seen so far that in any way resembled a *house*.

When we got back to my father's room, the odor of bodily waste had been replaced by the smell of disinfectant cleaners and air fresheners. There were two hospital beds in the room, separated by an opaque plastic curtain hung on an aluminum track mounted to the ceiling. Across from the end of the beds, there was one small dresser for each occupant. A shared three-foot-wide closet was built in next to the bathroom, and a small quantity of my father's clothes had already been moved in. There appeared to be no space left for anything more.

Our tour guide got paged to go back to her office. The director left with her apologies.

I checked out the bathroom. The doorway looked too narrow for a wheelchair. Inside there was not enough room to turn one around, so I supposed it didn't matter anyway. Sink, toilet, mirror, that was all.

I rejoined my brother in the room. Peter had a picture of our father's brother, Alfred, in his hands. It was in one of the plastic frames Manny invented and sold to Polaroid when he was the president of Foto-Cube Inc. "Look what I found on top of Dad's dresser."

Taking a closer look, I saw Alfred dressed in his SS uniform. "That's not cool," I said. "We can't leave that here."

"Agreed!" Peter put the frame in his pocket.

There didn't seem to be much more to see, so Peter and I decided to leave. We didn't offer to help with our father's "transition," as Donna had put it. At that point, dealing with Manny's realization of what had happened to him was her problem alone, once again.

CHAPTER THIRTEEN

Preparing for Action

In the next days, I spent much of my time considering what options I had to help my father. I researched other facilities, and learned there were places called "assisted living centers." After visiting several, I came to understand how they differed from nursing homes. Most of the residents, while maybe forgetful or somewhat physically impaired, were still very aware cognitively. They could come and go on their own. Some still even drove and had reserved parking spaces. There were no wristband monitors with alarmed doors to make sure residents didn't escape, as was the case at Littleton House. One of these assisted living centers in particular, Sutton Hill, seemed like a much better fit for my dad.

On the phone, I talked with a representative of Beth Israel Deaconess Medical Center in Boston and asked about its dementia evaluation services. I also spoke with someone from Elder Services of the Merrimack Valley. There I found out that Donna had started the evaluation process for my father but that it was never completed. Although as Manny would say, "Never is a very long time that hasn't happened yet."

I continued to talk with my brothers about creating some sort of action plan to get our father out of Littleton House. Carl told me he was willing to help make phone calls, but he couldn't visit. The nursing home environment was too frightening for him. Suffering with MS and being confined to a wheelchair left Carl feeling he might be institutionalized sooner than the rest of us. He didn't want to be reminded of that by visiting Manny at Littleton House.

Peter's time was limited. He ran a business with several employees and had a family to attend to. But he agreed with me that Littleton House was not right for Dad. He said he would look at an alternative placement with me once I narrowed down the field. I told him about Sutton Hill. We agreed to ask Donna to go with us to visit, figuring that if she liked the place it would be the fastest and easiest way to get our father out of Littleton House.

I called Donna's lawyer to see if, now, we might change the power of attorney. Her lawyer was still resistant to the idea, but agreed an evaluation seemed appropriate. Attorney Rafanelli told me she would contact Donna and set up a meeting for the family. Thus far, I hadn't heard back from her.

Most important, I committed myself to visiting my father often, if not every day. I felt it was really up to me to try to right this wrong. But I realized that in some ways it was up to Manny himself. I could understand why other people thought him demented. When meeting women for the first time, or what he thought was the first time, he often took their hand, bowed down, kissed it, clicked his heels and pronounced, "Emanuel Carl Maria Ebner von Eschenbach, at your service." They probably thought he suffered from delusions of grandeur. But that is his full name. As far as the bowing and kissing, he'd been doing that for as long as I could remember so I did not see it as a sign of recent dementia. In fact, lately, perhaps because he was so angry that his blood flowed stronger, my father seemed much more aware than I had seen him in a long time. He was confused for sure. And his memory was not reliable, but no one's is totally reliable really. During our most recent conversations, however, my father appeared to be in touch with the reality of his situation as long as I reminded him of the facts. I'm no professional in the field, but he didn't present himself to me like someone who was demented.

The last time I visited him, we talked about ways he might be able to improve his memory. I wanted him to think about his life from before I was born. He even agreed to make that his homework, when I wasn't there.

One day, I tried calling the doctor who is on staff at Littleton House. I tried several times during the morning and later in the afternoon, but I was always told he was with patients. I left messages. He didn't return my calls. Just before five I called again and his answering service told me he had left for the day. For some unexplained reason I called again. I don't know if he came back for something he had forgotten, or if he was expecting another call, or what, but he answered. When he heard my last name he said, "Shit!" Then he composed himself enough to listen.

I told him how my observations of my father's condition differed from Donna's. I raised my concern that no psychological screening had been completed prior to his placement at Littleton House. And that I didn't feel a nursing home was the right environment for Manny. I asked if perhaps his heart medication could be contributing to his memory loss.

The doctor listened to all I had to say and then responded with, "Your dad seems like a nice fellow, but you need to face the fact that he is crazy as a loon."

Very professional, I remember thinking to myself. It was useless to go on.

I needed a plan, something or some way to help keep my father focused and as sharp as possible. My hope was that if I could get him a proper evaluation, then perhaps a geriatric specialist would see what I saw. Manny was eccentric for sure, but that was nothing new and not a result of his recent memory loss. He was not "crazy as a loon."

Although had anyone said that to me only a few years earlier, I would have enjoyed hearing them say that about him, especially considering what my relationship with my father was at that time. During a short visit with my dad, most people might easily think that he was crazy. And the way doctors are overworked and so tightly scheduled, I don't imagine that this doctor was allowed the time needed for a thorough examination. Just as I didn't know why the doctor even answered the phone that day, I also couldn't know what pressures, constraints and stresses he was under.

Also, I wasn't totally clear what was motivating me. That I cared at all perplexed me. I thought about the times when Manny used to travel a lot for work. One night in particular that I remember, my mom and I prayed his plane would crash and we'd be rid of him. I was ten. Decidedly, this was a strange activity for a mother and a son. Perhaps stranger still, my mother was a devout atheist so praying seemed out of character. Both my parents were atheists who never missed the opportunity to let others know that fact. For most of my life up to that point, I had invested much energy toward hating my father. And I usually tried to convince all who knew him that he was a phony.

Lately my attitude had softened. I began wanting people to see beyond the surface, as I never could have before. I was not sure whether the times Baby and I spent with him this past summer gave me a new appreciation of my father or if I just felt empathy because of his situation. His acceptance of Baby, but more than that, his genuine love of my dog, surprised me and had moved me to tears.

And yet, I wondered if I just wanted to be right, if I wanted to prove to the lawyers, the doctors and Donna that, even though I'm just a carpenter, I knew more about my father's condition than they did. Furthermore, I was so mad at Donna for lying to me repeatedly that I was willing to do most anything to get back at her. Revenge was a strong motivator. I didn't want her to get away with this.

CHAPTER FOURTEEN

The Plan

Baby and I pulled into the parking lot of Littleton House at 3:30 p.m. on a Friday. She was leashed, not that she really needed to be. The leash was for the humans that might be scared of her just by her size.

I had left work early to spend time with my father and to present my plan to him. Earlier in the day he had called me and he seemed very agitated.

As my dog and I came up to the entrance, I noticed something new. There was a large banner strung across the columns that support the front overhang. It proclaimed, "Fifteen Years of Loving Care." If the banner was at least partially true, then my guess on when the building was built had been correct (1978).

I had advance permission for Baby to visit with me. The staff had been having such a difficult time keeping my father calm that anything that helped with the cause was much appreciated. And they had already seen Baby work her magic.

At the nurses' station we were both greeted warmly and told that Manny was in his room napping. I unhooked Baby's leash and said, "Go find Papa!" She started down the hall to his room.

Strange. That was the first time I had ever called my father "Papa." Nonetheless, Baby seemed to know whom I was talking about. Of course the logical part of me assumed all she needed to hear was "go find." But there is a metaphysical side that made me think my dog was connected to the universe in ways which I was not. She had always known my father was my Papa, and she had just been waiting for me to figure that out for myself.

When I got to Papa's room, Baby was already nudging him with her nose. For humans this would be an ill-advised technique. Manny had been known to lash out quite forcefully when his sleep was disturbed.

Baby used her long, square Great Dane snout to nuzzle under the blankets until she located his head.

"Hey, what's going on? Leave me alone." Papa swiped a hand across his face. Undaunted, Baby persisted. "Stop it, damn you!" He opened his eyes. "Who's this?" Papa took another swipe and came in contact with one of the dog's tall, straight ears. "Oh, it's my doggie. My doggie's come to see me. Hello, doggie, doggie, doggie."

Once Papa is fully awake, he's a perfect European gentleman. But during the process, some of the nurses and aides have complained that waking him has been a dangerous assignment. I've tried to teach them my techniques—speak softly, don't rush and never touch him before he acknowledges you. Unfortunately, around here, those who aren't doing time never have enough of it. And so far, they don't have a dog to send in first.

My father swung his legs over the edge of the bed and sat up. Baby backed off.

Manny's roommate was nowhere to be seen, so I slipped into the bathroom for a second and left the door open.

"Well, if you're here, my sonny boy must be around somewhere," he said, while patting Baby's head.

"In the bathroom, Papa."

He turned toward the sound of my voice and asked, "What did you call me?"

I stuck my head out of the bathroom door and told him, "Papa, Dad."

"I don't remember you ever calling me that before."

"Well, this time it's not your memory. I never did call you Papa before just now. And other than to Baby, I haven't ever even referred to you as Papa."

Papa smiled as he told me, "That is what I called my daddy."

I finished up and stepped back into the room. "Really? I didn't know that, but then you've shared very little about your father."

"I didn't have him for that long. You know I left Austria when I was only 15?"

"That I did know. Hey—I want to hear more about my grandfather—just let me get Baby settled." We always traveled with a foam pad or her beanbag bead. Great Danes are bony and they don't do well on hard tile floors.

"Oh, your daddy brought your bed for you," Papa talked to Baby while continuing to scratch behind her ears. "Is he good to you? You can tell me." Baby spun around and rested her hindquarters on Papa's lap. "Hey! You big oaf, what are you trying to do? Look at her. What does she want from me?" he asked, as if this were the first time it had happened.

"She's already got what she wants. Didn't you know Great Danes are lap dogs? It's what they do."

"Lap dogs—good God, she must weigh over a hundred pounds, for Christ's sake."

"135 pounds to be exact, Papa." Then I knew he was truly awake and what would be coming next. *How much does she eat? She must …*

"Man, the size of this beast," he said, stroking down the length of Baby's body and then lifting up her tail with his hand coiled around it. "She must eat you out of house and home. How much do you feed her?"

I answered Papa's questions and a minute later he asked them again. That might have continued if my dog was a smaller breed.

"You're getting kind of heavy, my friend," Papa finally complained.

"Baby, get off." She did as asked. "Say, Papa, let's go to the living room to talk. It's more comfortable there and I want to hear what it was like growing up in Austria. Also, I want to tell you about my plan."

"Your plan," Papa repeated my words.

"Yes. I have an idea that might help with your situation."

"My situation," he said and a quizzical look came to his face. "What is my situation?"

"Stuck here against your will! Stuck in a nursing home, remember?"

"Oh, yes, yes, of course."

"So I have a plan …"

"You have a plan," Papa interrupted.

"Stop that!"

"Stop what?"

"You keep repeating everything I'm saying."

"I do? Oh, I'm sorry. That must be very annoying," Papa apologized and wagged a finger at himself. "Shame on me," he said.

When I was growing up in his house, my father would often use techniques from his general semantics training to let people know he had heard them accurately. Repeating back what someone said was one of those techniques. He was always engaging others in discussions. It didn't matter whether you were family, a business associate or the plumber come to fix a leak, all would be exposed to the teachings of Alfred Korzybski, according to Manny. Conversations would begin and then a lecture would break out. As a child, I hated that, and never really felt heard or listened to, no matter how precisely my words were thrown back at me.

Right then, I wondered if Papa was repeating what I said just in order to help him remember. And I felt bad about reacting with annoyance. *Must resist letting the past trigger my responses,* I chastised myself.

"Papa, I'm sorry for sounding annoyed. You have nothing to feel ashamed about. In fact, I remember you always telling me that shame, jealousy and guilt were unproductive endeavors. 'A set of useless emotions' I think you used to call them. Let's go to the living room. I've got something to show you."

When we got there, Baby wanted the couch, but settled for her bed on the floor, next to the wing chair Papa had plopped down into. I seated myself in front of him. Then I pulled my micro recorder from my pocket and placed it on Papa's lap.

Papa asked, "What-cha got here?"

I handed it up to him. "It's a mini-tape recorder."

"A tape recorder, but it's so tiny." He turned it over and over. "Where's the tape in this thing?"

I reached across, popped out the cassette and put it in the palm of his free hand.

He angled his head sideways and moved the tape to within an inch of his eye. "But I can barely see the thing, for Christ's sake. And you say there is recording tape in here?" Papa shook his head in disbelief.

After retrieving tape and recorder, I said, "Let's do a test." When reloaded and ready, I gave it back to him. "Say something, Papa."

"How do I do it—is there a button?"

"No, just talk. It turns itself on when you speak."

"But how does it know?"

"Technology."

"Amazing!" Papa put the recorder right up against his lips.

"A little too close. Let me help you." Together we adjusted the distance. "Okay, now say something."

Papa arched his back, stuck his chest out and tilted his head up. With the recorder at arm's length out in front of him he was ready. "Emanuel Carl Maria Ebner von Eschenbach," he announced dramatically, then added, "Something!"

When we played it back, Papa roared with laughter. After he stopped laughing he asked, "Do I really sound like that?"

"Technology doesn't lie. Now, Papa, the last time I was here I gave you a homework assignment. Do you remember anything about it?"

"Absolutely!" he said. "I remember nothing."

"That's okay, no tests. I asked you to think about things from before I was born. So here is my plan. I want to interview you about your life. I have kept notes about recent events and I will read those back to you. I need you to tell me about stuff that happened before I was born and/or that happened when I was too young to remember. If we put our memories together I think we can keep you sharp enough to get you out of this place."

"I hope you're right. I can't stand it here much longer."

"So what was life like when you were little, back in Austria, and how did you come to America?" I began.

"By boat," Papa responded instantly and casually.

I waited for more. "That's it—by boat—that's all you can say about coming to this country?"

"Did you ask for more? I have no secrets, but you need to be specific. Details, man, details."

"Okay, when—where—why?"

"Now you're talking, kid. What was the question again?"

"America. How come we're speaking to each other in English and not in German?"

"*Sprechen Sie deutsch?*"

"*Nein*, Papa. You never taught me. English, please."

"Well, it was after we lost the war—my father was sent back to Vienna."

"Details, Papa. Which war?"

"Oh, WWI. My father was a highly decorated officer—a colonel in the Austrian Army—I remember he used to say his one regret was that his chest wasn't big enough to display all the medals he had won."

"You said you were sent back to Vienna. Where were you before that?"

"Sopron."

"*Sopron?*"

"In Hungary. I was born there, you know. Ah, we had it good in Hungary. To be an Austrian officer was almost like being a member of Royalty. My father was schooled in art, history, literature and music. Back then officers had to have culture as well as tactics. And to be assigned to the diplomatic corps as my father was, now that was the height of achievement in the military."

"Is that where you learned Hungarian and was that your first language?"

"I had two first languages—Austrian German and Hungarian," Papa said proudly. And he added, "Well, three really when you count High German, but that's more like the difference between British English and American English."

"So, you said things were good for your family in Hungary. How so?"

89

"We had a grand house, with servants—lots of them. And I had a governess to teach me things. We were part of the aristocracy."

"And when you moved back to Vienna all that changed?"

"Oh, yes! There wasn't even enough food for my brother, my three sisters and me. My father was reassigned and put in charge of—," Papa paused, then came back in German, *"ein Krankenhaus—eine Nervenheilanstalt* – a hospital — a mental hospital. He hated it and felt as though he'd been demoted. And we lost all our benefits—no big house, no servants and no governess either."

"So your parents decided to ship you off to America?"

"Not right away. I went to military school for a while, but when that didn't work out, my mother decided it would be best for me to go live with relatives in New York. She pretty much ruled the house. First she sent me to Holland for a year."

"How come?"

"I think I was too young to travel and immigrate by myself."

"How old were you?"

"14 or maybe 15? I think I needed to be 16."

"And so you had a year or so to learn your fourth language?"

"Yes, but once you know German, Dutch is pretty easy to pick up."

"What did your father think about sending you away? You were his first son, right?"

"I was the eldest. He never talked about my having to leave, though. I remember my father being very quiet most of the time. After supper he'd go to the living room and smoke his pipe." Papa curled his fingers and put his thumb in his mouth to create an imaginary pipe. Then he pretended to puff on it. "He always fiddled with that thing. Tapping out the burnt ashes, carefully cleaning it, then packing it again. Sometimes I'd watch him in secret from upstairs. He'd sit in the dark, constantly relighting and puffing away. I can still see my father surrounded by clouds of smoke, his face lit by the glow from the bowl. But I never figured out why this interested him so. He spent more time with that damn pipe than he did with me."

So that's how you learned to be a father, I thought. As a young child, I wanted my father to play ball with me. But Papa felt sports were a waste of time. Instead, he'd spend hours in his various woodworking shops creating all of his inventions that ultimately went nowhere. After his day job was over, and after supper, I could hear the sounds of table saws ripping and routers spinning long into the night. The weekends were no different.

On the few occasions when he was willing to play badminton with me in the backyard, it never lasted long. Just about the time I was having fun, running and sliding to make a difficult shot, my father would become concerned that we were ruining the grass. Then he'd end our game and go back to one of his projects. By the time I was eight, I gave up asking him for anything.

"I'm sorry your dad was so distant. It must have been hard not having him to talk to about being sent away—especially so far away as America."

Papa responded thoughtfully, "Yes, I suppose it was." His voice was wistfully sad as he added, "Once I left home, I never saw my father again."

An alarm went off out in the hall. *Another attempted escape.* I shut off the recorder. Most of the residents wore wristbands that activated a buzzer if they got too close to an exit door. My father had one on for the first several days and he set off the alarms many times. I told the director I'd talk to my father about not trying to leave. It seemed to have worked and his wristband was removed.

I got up, closed the door and sat back down across from my dad. After turning the recorder back on, I asked, "What do you remember about your trip here?"

"First I went by train across Germany and then from Rotterdam by boat to Liverpool."

"Weren't you scared?"

Papa took a moment to think about that. "No, more excited than anything else, I think. I always loved to ride the trains. They were all steam engines back then." Papa moved his hand off the dog's head where he'd been resting it. Then, bringing both arms to his sides, he began moving them like the cams and pistons of a locomotive. Simultaneously, he also imitated the sound, "*Sh, sh, sh, sh, sh, shhhhhh—woo—woooo!*" Baby startled, raised her head and banged it on the end table. "Oh, my poor little doggie. What happened—did my engine scare you?" He comforted the dog.

When she settled herself again, I got Papa back on track. "After your year in the Netherlands, you went to Liverpool and got on a ship to America. Do you remember the name of the boat?"

"I have no idea." Papa shook his head. "That was a hundred years ago. I do remember it had two funnels."

"Funnels?"

"Smoke stacks, you probably call them. Oh, it was a pretty big ship—20,000 tons maybe and at least a couple of football fields long."

A sports reference, now that is a surprise.

"There must have been a few thousand passengers. Most of us traveled third class and we were kept separate. They didn't want us to mingle with the rich folk."

"So you crossed the Atlantic and when you got to Ellis Island, what year was it? I assume that's where you landed?"

"Ellis Island, well, of course, that's where everyone came," Papa chided me for questioning the obvious. "It was the summer of 1921, July, I think, or maybe August. I wasn't quite of age yet—

and—ah—there were a couple of months involved. So rather than go back to Vienna—which I could have—I stuck it out on the island. Hah, hah, hah."

"What was that like?"

"Good God! Don't ask me." Papa shook his head and soon his whole body got involved.

"That bad?"

"Terrible. There was absolutely no—there wasn't anyone who could talk English."

I thought Papa meant German, but I decided not to correct him.

He went on, "Obviously that made everything worse. I learned every ferryboat that came in and out. That was the only amusement I had."

"Where did you sleep?"

"Barracks. The beds were all in tiers."

"Bunk beds?"

"Bunk beds, that's right—in stacks of three. I slept above someone and under someone else, I think. I remember the place was filthy, especially the bathrooms. And crowded—you couldn't breathe. Kid, you have no idea!"

"Sounds awful. You said you were there a couple of months—could you go outside at all?"

"No. They didn't like you to wander around."

"So you watched the ferries from a window?"

"Yes. I spent all my time at that window. It was the only thing I had to do."

"Could you see any of the other people as they entered?"

"No, I don't think so. Just the boats from a distance."

"And after you were old enough to leave—what, 16?" I checked.

Papa nodded.

"Where did you go?"

"To my sponsor's—my aunt's. She had paid my passage. You had to have a sponsor to enter the country. They wouldn't let anyone immigrate without one."

"Did your aunt come to get you?"

"She sent my cousin. And you know, that was a pretty funny scene as I remember it."

"How so, Papa?" I asked, while I watched a little grin grow larger on his face.

"Well, it was summer—August, I think—no, maybe September—yes, it must have been September. Anyway, it was hot as hell and I was wearing all the clothes I owned."

"Didn't you have a trunk or a suitcase or anything?"

"Oh, sure. I must have had something. But I remember not all my clothes fit in the bag—I think it was too full with pictures of my family—so I wore the rest. It was so hot. I was sweating like a pig when my cousin first met me. He took me to the subway and told me, 'Now listen, you stay on this car to the end. Wait for me at the last station—don't move. I might be there already, but if I'm not, just stay put until I come to get you.' Then he took the train to Mount Vernon, got in his car and picked me up at the end of the subway line—241st Street I think it went to at the time."

"How come he didn't just ride with you—on the subway, I mean?"

"I'm not sure. I think he was embarrassed. I wore all those clothes—was sweating—and I still had my sign on."

"What sign?"

"The sign that said: 'Deloused in Liverpool.' Hah, hah, hah."

"No wonder your cousin didn't want to be seen with you. Who put the sign on?"

"The eastern part of Europe was plagued with lice, you know—

of course Austria wasn't really affected—but everyone was checked for lice before we left England. So they put that sign on me and told me not to take it off or else I'd be in big trouble."

"Was it in English? Did you even know what it said?"

"I had no idea. I only knew not to remove it."

"So you wore it the whole time you were on Ellis Island then?"

"I guess I must have, because it was on me when my cousin came to get me. Hah, hah— 'Deloused in Liverpool,'" Papa repeated several more times, smiling and shaking his head with each repetition.

The door to the recorder popped open, indicating we had run out of space. I heard myself telling Papa, "Hold that thought," before wondering if he was capable of doing what I had just asked.

CHAPTER FIFTEEN

A Chicken and a Chick

I flipped over the tape and asked, "You said that before you were sent away to America you went to military school. What was that like?"

"Things were pretty tough at home back then. Austria still hadn't recovered from the war."

"Just after World War I, right?" I asked, despite knowing the answer.

"That's right."

"How old were you again?"

"*Eins, zwei, drei,*" Papa counted aloud in German using his fingers to help keep track, then translated the answer, "… *funfzehn,* I must have been 15 or 14. I'm not really sure."

"I'm sorry, Papa. It doesn't matter. Please go on."

"They never fed us enough. Usually a small dish with noodles and a piece of stale bread is all I got." He formed a circle with his hands to indicate the size of the plate. "They rarely gave us any meat. I was always hungry, it seemed. And they worked us very hard during the day too."

"What did they make you do?"

"Oh, military exercises. Drills and formation, that sort of thing." Papa sat up very straight in his chair and mimed marching with a rifle over his shoulder. "And then of course, there were the classroom studies. Hah, hah, I was always getting in trouble in class." From his expression he seemed quite pleased with himself about that.

"How so?"

"Well, you know—I was always challenging the authorities. Our instructors wanted us to see enemies." Papa thrust his arms out in front of him and made a fierce look, as if charging in battle. After a few seconds, he dropped his pose and said, "I didn't see enemies. I only saw other people. And once you see people it's very hard to want to kill them. I was a big disappointment to my mother. I never just did what I was told. 'Why can't you be more like Alfred?' my mother always asked me. My brother, Alfred, was perfect." Papa stiffened and made what I assumed was an Alfred face. "He always did what he was told without question. I remember him saying to me, 'There is no greater honor than to die for the Fatherland!' My poor brother got just what he wanted too."

"He was killed in World War II?"

"That's right."

"You know the only photograph I ever saw of him was in one of your Insta-Frames on your dresser here. Donna put it there for you, but Peter and I removed it. In the picture he was in uniform and we didn't think it should be displayed publicly."

"That would be Alfred. He was very proud to be an SS officer. The dope!"

"Do you miss him?"

"I never really knew him growing up. When I got older and settled in over here, I wrote to him and tried to convince him to come join me. But he was a Brown Shirt by then. Completely brainwashed. I still don't understand it." Papa shook his head again.

"Was he in military school too?"

"No, not then. He was too young. After I got kicked out maybe. I don't really know."

"So why did you get kicked out?"

"Well, one night we were sitting on our bunks, my friend and I. It was after supper and the two of us were still very hungry. So I suggested we get ourselves a chicken to top off our meager meal."

"Were you in barracks or tents?"

"No, no, barracks. The cadets were housed in barracks, but the commandant—he had a house. And in his yard he had chickens for laying eggs. So we snuck out, jumped over the fence and snatched one."

"And nobody heard you?"

"No, not at first. We were pretty quick about it. I could move a lot faster back then, you know. As soon as I grabbed one, I held its beak closed so it couldn't squawk." He acted out the scene from his seat.

"So how did you cook it, or did you eat it raw?"

Papa made a disgusted face. "Oh, no! We cooked it, but we had to kill it first. I sent my friend Iresch to one of the classrooms where there was a fine steel sword hanging on the wall. If I remember correctly, I think it was the commandant's own blade. Anyway, while I waited for Iresch to return, I hid with the poor thing behind some bushes. Once the sword arrived, we chopped the chicken's head off over a stump. Oh, the thought of it still gives me shivers." Papa wrapped his arms around his body, giving himself a hug. "Blood splattered everywhere! And then, when we plucked it—my God, there were feathers all over the woods and hanging from the branches of the trees."

"So how did you think you would get away with it?"

"I suppose we didn't think at all. We were hungry, that was it! And at the moment all we thought about was how to get the bird cooked so that we might eat."

"And how did you cook it?"

"Well, while Iresch finished plucking, I went back to the barracks. I removed one of the steel stays from under my mattress and grabbed a couple of wooden chairs. When I got back to Iresch, the chicken was naked. He held it and I plunged the sword through lengthwise. Then I pushed the metal rod in where the sword went." Papa acted out the whole scene in front of me. "We found some rocks and placed them in a circle, broke up the chairs and our barbecue pit was ready. After we lit the fire, Iresch and I took turns—one of us would rotate the chicken while the other remained on lookout duty."

"You were worried someone would see the fire?"

"Yes, yes. We had gone pretty far into the woods, but still we didn't know if it would be visible back at the school. Apparently it was, because our sergeant saw it, but we didn't see him lurking behind some trees." Papa pretended to be his sergeant for a couple of seconds, and then continued with the story. "I don't know how long he was watching us—it took quite a while for the chicken to cook. We had to gather more wood as the chairs burned up pretty quickly. Eventually we decided it was done. It smelled heavenly. Our mouths were watering as we sliced off the first piece with the sword. And then, just as we were about to bite in, my sergeant jumped out from behind the trees and shouted, 'Halt *genau dort an.*' It scared us half to death!"

"So that's how you got in trouble. He reported you?"

"Oh, yes! First I tried to bribe him with some of the chicken, but he must have been eating better than us for he never even gave it a thought. He just marched us back to the barracks and placed us under arrest. The next day they court-martialed me."

"And how'd that go?"

"It was awful, especially for my parents! In the main hall, in front of all the other cadets, they had to watch as the commandant grabbed my stripes and tore them right off my shirt, first the red one and then the gold. They were humiliated. For the son of an Austrian colonel to do such a thing was unthinkable. My father never really spoke to me after that. And my mother, she cried. Oh, how she cried! 'Emanuel,' she kept saying as she wept."

Baby got up, pawed at my feet and growled softly.

"What does she want?" Papa asked.

"She needs to take care of business. Let's go for a walk."

"All right." Papa got up. "Do I need a jacket?"

"No, I think you'll be fine as you are. It's not really cold."

"I never know what it's like outside anymore."

On our way out we stopped by the nurses' desk to let someone know we were going for a walk, but that we'd be remaining on the grounds. Once out the front door I released Baby and told her, "Up in the woods." She bolted across the expansive lawn and disappeared behind the tree line.

"Oh, this is nice!" Papa said as he felt the sun on his face. He was wearing navy blue sweatpants, a matching sweatshirt and sneakers. There was little or no wind. The temperature remained in the low 60s. It was perfect for him to get outside for a while.

We walked across the lawn toward the direction where Baby had gone out of sight. Near the edge of the trees, but still in the sun, there were a couple of red picnic tables with benches. Papa and I sat down on the same side, next to each other, facing the woods with the sun on our backs.

After a time, Papa asked, "Will she be all right? She won't run away and get lost, will she?"

"Not a chance. She knows where she is and her favorite people are right here."

"I just thought she might wander—chase a squirrel and lose track."

"She'll be fine," I reassured him. "She just likes her privacy."

"I'm with her!" Papa agreed.

"We'll call her in a few minutes if you're still worried, but we probably won't have to. While we're waiting, I'm curious …"

"Yes?"

"You said that after military school you were sent to America to live with your aunt. When we left off, your cousin put you on the subway, told you to ride it to the end and wait for him. Did he show up?"

"He must have. I'm here, aren't I?"

"Okay then, your cousin picked you up and took you to your aunt's."

"That's right, Aunt Emily, 20 North Terrace Ave., Mount Vernon, NY."

"Any chance you remember her phone number, Papa? Just kidding—go on. So, you were at your aunt's. What was it like? Could you understand each other—did she speak German?"

"Yes, yes. Her German was better than her English, I think. We understood each other all right, but I didn't much like what I was hearing."

"What did she say?"

"I was told that it cost a lot of money to bring me here, that she had paid all my expenses and I must work very hard to pay her back."

"What did she want you to do?"

"Shovel shit! My aunt owned a chicken farm—an egg farm, really. It had been my cousin's job before me to clean up after the chickens—and—well, the way things were when I got there, I'd say he'd been slacking off. There were droppings everywhere—six inches deep in places. I had to scrape chicken shit off everything in the barn. And boy, did it stink!" Papa screwed up his face and pinched his nose.

"Sounds awful! How long did you tough it out there?"

"Only as long as I had to, and that was too long, I think. I'm pretty sure she lied about how much I really owed. But I had no way of challenging her. I do remember quite clearly the day I refused to shovel shit for her anymore. That morning one of the chicks— some of the eggs were allowed to hatch to keep up with the hens that died or weren't laying—anyway—that day a new baby chick got out of its pen. The little thing ran about in circles, and as I was trying to catch it, it ran right under my foot." Papa let out a squeal. "I crushed the poor thing. After that I couldn't even go into the coop anymore. I told my aunt, 'Send me home if you want to, but I'm not cleaning any more chicken shit for you.'"

"How did she respond?"

"She was very angry. She told me I had to pay back every cent she'd spent on me."

Baby emerged from between the trees and at an all-out run she made a beeline for Papa. "Oh my!" Papa exclaimed as he braced for impact. Of course, being a civilized beast, Baby pulled up at the last second. The love fest resumed with the dog's tail thumping Papa's legs and Papa saying, "Here's my doggie. I was beginning to worry about you. Oh, you're such a good doggie. You came right back to me, didn't you?" Her tail thrashing got a little too intense and Papa cried out, "Ouch! That thing's like a whip."

"Baby, easy girl. Go lie down." As usual, she obeyed.

And then Papa asked, "Is Donna my wife now?"

"Yes. You've been married a little over a year."

"How can that be? If I'm married to her, why am I not at home with my wife? Why am I here in a nursing home?"

"For the moment this is where Donna thinks you need to be. I don't agree with her and I'm working on changing her mind. And you can help with that by trying to remember things if you can. Also, the more cooperative you are with the staff, the better our chances of getting you moved to someplace nicer."

"I want to go home to my own house. My house is someplace nicer. I want to sleep in my own bed and sit in my own yard. Not on some public bench. I worked hard for that house and that's where I want to be." Tears filled his eyes.

Suddenly, the shrill cry of a broad-winged hawk projected down from the top of a pine tree. Papa couldn't see it, but he heard it, all right. "What was that?" he asked.

Looking up and pointing, I said, "It's a hawk, Papa. He's in the top of that pine tree. Up there!"

Baby sprang to her feet. Then another quick shriek could be heard, before the massive bird took flight, swooped down to the edge of the grass, picked up an unaware chipmunk and disappeared into the tree line beyond the woods.

"Whew!" Papa exclaimed. "What did he get?"

"Dinner, I think."

"What was it?"

"A lowly chipmunk."

"Oh, poor thing. Just enjoying the day and now he's that beast's supper."

Shamelessly, I seized the opportunity. "Speaking of supper, Papa, I think they're serving inside soon. We should go back, but Eleanor and I want to take you out shopping with us tomorrow."

"Shopping? Do I need something?"

"No, but we need your opinion. We want to get a new dining

room set and we thought with all your furniture experience you could help us find something that is well made."

"Whatever I can do. What time is this excursion to take place?"

"How 'bout we pick you up around 8:30 and we'll go out to breakfast first."

"Marvelous! I'll be here at the ready."

I walked my dad back across the field. Before going in, I let Baby into my truck. Then Papa and I headed to the cafeteria-style dining room. His preordered fish sticks, french fries and overcooked, gray green beans were already waiting for him.

CHAPTER SIXTEEN

A Different Dog and a Different Father

**Warning: this chapter contains graphic
descriptions of animal cruelty!**

When I got back, Baby was curled up in a tight ball on the passenger's seat. I started the truck and drove out of the parking lot onto Foster Street headed toward Littleton center. Once past town, we got onto the highway going north. In 20 minutes or so we would be back home in Chelmsford.

In my head I started going over the most recent visit with Papa. And as I thought about it, I realized it was actually the very first visit with him as my Papa.

I felt like his memory was better. Initially at least, the plan seemed to be helping. But I tried to remain guarded about the process and not expect too much. I had already seen that my father could be sharp one day and dull the next. His mental awareness was at its best when he was either angry or excited about something. I preferred trying to focus on the excitement side of things.

Traffic was light on I-495, especially for a Friday evening. That was fortuitous, as it allowed me to think without putting others and myself in terrible danger.

From the passenger seat I began to hear snoring, Baby's one bad habit. Well, maybe one of three. Right then, I would have allowed her most anything. Unexpectedly for me, I had become witness to a mutual love affair between her and my father. That my dog saw the good in Papa, and that he returned her affection, had already begun to change my perception of him. It made it possible for me to begin forgiving my dad and ultimately myself. An important first step, and something I knew pleased Eleanor.

It was a very different dad, and a very different dog relationship, that had continued to fester hatred in me for so many years. Sergeant was a stray German Shepherd that had wandered into our yard when I was about 14. I kept the dog for a year and a half. During that time, life was even more miserable at home than usual. My father and mother constantly argued about the dog. She wanted to let him in at night. Manny would not allow it, and said if I was to keep the dog at all, it must remain outside.

Sergeant barked incessantly. My father would yell at me, "Shut that goddamn dog up or I will!" Sometimes I'd sneak him into the house after my father was asleep. Usually he'd catch me sneaking him out again in the morning and then I'd be punished. Sometimes I fed him spoonful's of peanut butter just to keep him quiet.

During the day, Sergeant lifted his leg on my father's bushes and pooped on his lawn. If I missed one and my father happened to see it—or worse—he stepped in it, I'd be punished. Many times the dog broke free from his chain and ended up at the pound. My mother and I continually paid fines to have him released. By the winter of 1967-'68, life with Sergeant around had become unbearable.

One afternoon that winter, while my parents were at work, my friend Roger and I got to talking about what a pain in the ass my dog was. Roger was a couple of years older than I. There were rumors in the neighborhood that he was dangerous. Whenever I asked if any of the stories about him were true, he wouldn't confirm or deny them. He'd just smile and say, "Sometimes rumors are true and sometimes not. That's why they call them rumors." He was so cool and mysterious. I looked up to him. And his parents had bought him a brand-new car, a Camaro. What more could a teenager want in a friend?

"Let's get rid of him," one of us said.

We thought about options, like letting him go in another town, but figured he'd probably find his way back, or just get picked up by the dog officer. And knowing my mother, Judy, she'd drive around to every pound within 50 miles to find him.

Somehow we started to entertain the idea of killing Sergeant. I'm not sure who first suggested it. It could have been me or it might have been Roger. We had already killed one of my pets together. We had put my canary inside a cardboard tube and said, "We'll fire one gunshot at the tube, and if it misses we will let him live." It missed, but we claimed the bird moved, so we fired several more rounds until we hit him.

I do remember that I didn't want to shoot my dog, so Roger suggested we gas him.

He said something like, "Gas is perfect. Think of the irony. He's a German Shepherd."

"Maybe I should just run an ad in the paper and see if someone will take him," I remember saying.

"You think your mom would go for that?" Roger questioned. "Whenever I've been around, she seems pretty attached."

Roger was right; my mother had become very attached to keeping Sergeant. But as I reflected on that, I thought her need to keep the dog had more to do with not giving in to my father. If we gave Sergeant away my dad would have won. Judy hated to lose, especially to my father.

Roger and I continued talking about killing and after a while it didn't seem like such an outrageous idea to me. It was just a dog. Something flipped inside me and I agreed to do the deed.

"Okay—but how would we do it? The gas, I mean."

"We need a hose," Roger said. Then he began looking around my garage. Nothing looked promising. The garden hose was too small. Suddenly he had it. "The dryer hose. It's perfect. Get Sergeant and put him in the back of my car. I'll take the hose off the dryer and get some duct tape from my trunk. We'll put everything back just as it was when we're done. Nobody will ever know."

As I undid his chain, Sergeant slipped free from me and began running in circles through the snow. I made a few feeble attempts at catching him, and then headed to the refrigerator for a bribe. With a package of luncheon meat in hand, the type speckled with red pimentos, I coaxed my dog back to me. While Sergeant wolfed down the bait, I grabbed his collar.

When we got to the car, Roger was already there. "What took you so long? Everything's all set." Roger had attached one end of the dryer hose to the tailpipe with the other end passed through a side window. Tape closed all gaps. He placed an old blanket down to protect his seats. The gas chamber was ready.

Roger started his car. At first, Sergeant seemed to think he was going for a ride. He stood on the rear seat and wagged his tail. I began having second thoughts about going through with our scheme.

After a time, it became so smoky inside that I could barely make out the dog's shape. Eventually we heard a loud thud as Sergeant collapsed between the seats. "That should do it," Roger said slickly.

We opened all the doors and my partner in crime turned off the motor. When the smoke cleared, I checked for any signs of life. "He's still breathing!"

"Man, that sucker's tough," Roger said. There was a tone of appreciation in his voice. "Maybe we should let him go."

It was not to be. As with the canary, we found a reason why the dog deserved to die.

A moment later, Sergeant lost his lunch. Partially digested meat splattered beyond the protection of the blanket. Still recognizable pimentos stuck to the back of Roger's seats, leaving sticky red rings around where they landed.

"Fuck!" he yelled. "That does it! He's dead!"

Roger told me to put the hose directly over my dog's mouth. I did as he asked.

Then he restarted his car. It took only a few minutes for Sergeant to succumb to the exhaust. "He's dead," I pronounced.

Once again, Roger shut off the engine. Then we had a body to get rid of.

"What are we going to do with him?" I asked frantically. "My mom will be home from work soon." I was panicked about being caught. Too panicked to feel anything about what I'd just done.

"Don't lose your cool. I know a place," Roger said.

We disconnected the hose from the tailpipe and reconnected it to the dryer. Then we jumped into the car and headed for New Hampshire. Although it was cold, for most of the ride we left the windows rolled down. Not a word passed between us.

At the end of a dead-end dirt road, just out of view of the lone nearby farmhouse, we stopped and dragged out the still-warm body of my lifeless dog. The snowbanks were a few feet high. Roger held the rear feet, I the front.

"Ready? On three," he said and counted.

I let go of my end at two. As a result, Sergeant's body didn't make it up over the bank, but rather, fell clumsily, sliding back down into the road.

"Screw it!" Roger said. "Let's get out of here."

Roger turned the car around and we drove like maniacs back to the paved road. The vomit smell that we had begun to ignore became overwhelming again, and once more we rolled down the windows.

With the cold winter air blowing in our faces, my friend began to laugh. "Did you see the way he landed? That was fucked up. Why'd you let go?"

"I was nervous."

"Too nervous to wait one more second. Well, anyway, the deed is done."

"Oh shit!"

"What?"

"I forgot to take his collar off. His tags are on it."

On the way back to the scene of the crime, I remember thinking that this must be how criminals get caught. I wondered what else I had overlooked.

During the next few days, I endured the torture of searching for Sergeant with my mother. As Roger had predicted, Judy drove me to all the neighboring dog pounds. We made lost dog posters and stapled them to countless telephone poles. And we cried together, but our tears didn't express the same, shared loss.

As my exit came up, I was forced to leave my remembrances and concentrate on driving. Baby had felt the truck slowing down and awakened from her nap. I reached my hand over and patted her head. "I'm so, so sorry," I told her. I still felt the need to apologize for murdering one of her kind.

CHAPTER SEVENTEEN

An Emotional Breakfast

Saturday morning, Eleanor and I got to Littleton House around quarter to nine. Papa was at the nurses' station, dressed and ready to go. I was impressed.

"Good morning, Manny," Eleanor greeted him and gave him a hug.

"Ah, Eleanor, my darling. You're a sight for blind eyes, but beautiful as ever, I imagine."

"Thank you, I think? Ready for breakfast?"

"Oh, Manny Ebner is always ready to eat! What are we going to have?"

"Anything you want. Let's go get in the car."

"Hi, Papa," I said, feeling a little hurt and ignored. Aside from Baby, Eleanor has always been the biggest champion of my dad.

"Hello, sonny boy," Papa answered me and turned to Eleanor. "Do you hear what he calls me these days?"

"Yes, Manny, and I think it is wonderful. It's wonderful you're spending so much time together. And overdue."

For breakfast, Papa ordered scrambled eggs, rye bread toast, home fries, sausage links and coffee with cream. After he bit in, he told us it was the best meal he had had in a couple of weeks. And then he said something odd, or maybe not so odd. "How could Donna put me in that place without my knowing what she was up to? Do I have … oh, I don't remember the name of it … what is it called again?"

"Alzheimer's, Papa?"

"Yes, yes—that's it. Do I have that?"

"The short answer is no. I don't think you have Alzheimer's."

"And I don't either, Manny," Eleanor agreed.

"Then how could Donna get away with this? Why would I let her take me to a nursing home?"

"I think she tricked you."

"Tricked me, how?"

"The night before, when Eleanor and I confronted her about her plan to put you in Littleton House, you were there with us and very much aware of what she was intending. But by the next morning you had forgotten. And since Donna used to be a nurse at Littleton House, she probably said she wanted to visit someone there. You just went along for the ride never knowing it was a one-way trip."

"What a thing to do to somebody." Papa shrugged his shoulders. "I just don't understand her anymore. We were so close."

"I know you were."

"But if I don't have … if it's not …"

I sensed Papa's frustration so I filled in the word for him again, "Alzheimer's."

"Alzheimer's! Alzheimer's! Alzheimer's! Why can't I remember that?"

"It's okay, Papa. Alzheimer's is the disease everyone tries to forget."

"Maybe so, but I feel you're keeping something from me."

"No, Papa. I tell you everything I know. Unfortunately, that's not always very much. Until Donna suggested you had Alzheimer's, I didn't have a clue what it was really. Since then I've done some research. From what I understand, the only sure way to know if you have Alzheimer's or not is to do an autopsy of your brain. Since you're still very much alive, I think that's not a very good option just now."

"I'm glad to hear you're always looking out for me," Papa said, with his most serious face painted on. "So if not Alzheimer's, what? Why do I forget?"

"I don't know the answer to that, but there are doctors more qualified to make a diagnosis than the two you have seen so far. And I am working on it. We will get you a proper examination and evaluation. This I promise you."

"And what can I do in the meantime?"

"Be nice to your caregivers, the nurses and staff at Littleton House. And try not to worry about the memory thing. I see improvements. Not a very scientific assessment on my part. Certainly not up to your standards of analysis. And yet, anecdotally at least, I'm witness to you being sharper of wit than you were when you decided to marry Donna."

"I agree with him, Manny," Eleanor said.

"I suppose I should consider this as good news?" Papa questioned.

"Take it any way you want to. I certainly think it's better than hearing you have a life-ending brain disorder that will leave you completely debilitated in a short time. Donna's prediction of your imminent demise has been greatly exaggerated, I think."

"You know, I've been sitting around much of the time without anything to do, so I've been thinking a lot about where I went wrong with Donna. And it seems it all goes back to my trying to teach her general semantics."

"How so, Papa?"

"Well, I think I figured out where Korzybski went wrong too—where he missed it," Papa began. Then he reached for his empty cup.

"More coffee, Manny?" Eleanor motioned to the waiter who happened to be walking by with a pot.

The waiter poured. Manny took a sip, swallowed and considered. "Korzybski tried to analyze human interaction by using the science of mathematics, logic and critical thinking, but he never addressed the human emotion. You see, humans are not always logical when it comes to behavior. To try to define and explain the human dimension and overlook emotions is to leave out a key element in the equation."

Said by the man who always preached you must be in command of your emotions and not let them rule you. I was stunned. And not by his lucidity. That seemed to come and go without any good explanation. What was flooring me was this crack in his defensive shell. I had waited for it for so long, gave up expecting, and resolutely concluded I'd never see it. Now that it was there, I was speechless.

Eleanor came to my rescue by saying, "But you always said how affectionate Donna was."

"Yes, she was—but I realize now how emotionally immature she is. Her affection is like that of a teenager or a dog—always needing physical contact and reassurance. Unlike your dog, it doesn't seem to matter where she gets it. She falls in love with anyone who shows any interest in her. I don't think it is something she can control."

"You think that's why she started seeing you, even though she was still married to Ken?" Eleanor asked as tactfully as she could.

Papa paused. "Perhaps," he responded. Without acknowledging

his own role in their affair he went on, "When Kenny got too sick to be any use to her, she got rid of him. And now she has done that to me. Maybe I should call her. Do you think she's home?"

"I don't know, but you said you'd help us shop for furniture. Can we call her after that?"

"Oh, yes, yes. I'm sorry. But let me pay the bill. Did it come yet?"

"Here, Papa." I started to hand it to him and then realized he wouldn't be able to read it. "$21.46," I told him.

He reached for his wallet and pulled out a lone dollar bill. Handing it to me he asked, "How much is this? You know I don't see so well anymore."

"It's a single, Papa."

"A one dollar bill?"

"Yes."

"Well, that won't do it. Here"—Papa passed his wallet to me—"see if there's any more … I usually keep a Ulysses in one of the credit card sleeves just for emergencies. Should be a 50 in there somewhere."

I pulled his wallet apart and took inventory: Social Security card, Medicaid card, a card from Guild for the Blind, a slip of paper with his name, address and phone number handwritten on it, a photo of Donna and an empty gum wrapper. I removed the wrapper and put the rest back in order. "No, Papa, no money." I gave his wallet back to him.

"How can that be?"

"It's all right. I've got it. You can treat next time."

"I know, but that's not the point. I need to find out what's happened to all my money."

For my father, living in America meant saving enough to own a home, paying your bills on time and always taking care of your share. I felt his embarrassment. "We'll look into it, Papa."

At the furniture store, despite being legally blind, Papa managed to wind his way around the numerous displays of lamps, chairs, tables and tchotchke without bumping into anything. He asked the salesperson to turn over any of the items Eleanor and I seemed interested in, including the dining room table itself, so that he might inspect the hidden elements of the construction.

In my various homes growing up, from our apartment in Flushing, New York, to the two rented houses in Massachusetts and finally our only purchased home in Chelmsford, at least 50 percent of the furniture was built by my dad. He made end tables he called "butterfly tables." I tended to think they looked more kidney shaped, but nonetheless they were unique and very useful. His Mondrian cabinets, whose doors consisted of variously sized square and rectangular panels, with each panel painted in bright contrasting colors of red, yellow, blue and a single white one, could not be found in any furniture stores.

The majority of what he built was for our home use, but he always had ideas about marketing some of his pieces. Most of his designs were very creative and clever. I know my dad sold a few items, but nothing really took off to the point of any viability for commercial manufacturing.

After considering my father's recommendations, Eleanor and I chose the set we wanted and placed an order to have it delivered. We had Papa back at Littleton House in time for lunch. He forgot about wanting to call Donna and I didn't remind him.

CHAPTER EIGHTEEN

"I'm something of an intellectual, you know."

Time to stop revisiting the past. Must stay in the moment, as Papa would tell me. Today is Wednesday, September 29, 1993, and there is work to be done. I call my brothers. Peter and I decide to see Donna's lawyer unannounced. I have gotten tired of being stalled for an appointment and Peter suggested we just show up without one. Carl can't join us, but I am so glad to have Peter's support in matters dealing with lawyers. He is much better than me at such things. Give me a pile of wood and tell me what you want built and I'm fine. Put me in front of an attorney and I can never figure out what they want aside from money, of which I have very little.

With both of us agreeing Dad should be involved in such a meeting, I pick him up and meet Peter at the lawyer's office in Chelmsford. We are all there by nine and told that the attorney will "try to clear some time for you all by around 10:30."

We go out for coffee. While enjoying a cup, Peter presses our father.

"We are about to see a lawyer on your behalf," Peter begins. "So, does Manny know what Manny wants?"

I feel the question is harsh, but still, what do I know? I'm no expert on how to best help my father. I let it be.

"Well, I don't want to be where I am," Manny responds.

"Okay, fine. That is what you need to tell the attorney," Peter says. "But you can't be wishy-washy about it. If you are inconsistent with your responses, then you are likely to remain right where you are."

We finish. Papa tries to pay once again with the same lowly one dollar bill that has occupied his wallet ever since being incarcerated at Littleton House. Peter pays for all of us.

Back at the law office we have a short wait before the receptionist announces, "The attorney will see you now."

Attorney Toni Rafanelli greets us at the door and reintroduces herself. Then she asks, "How're you doing, Manny?" She offers her hand.

Manny takes it, kisses it and asks, "And how do you know of me?"

"Manny, we've met several times."

"We have? I see—I see. And was it good?"

We all laugh nervously. Ms. Rafanelli doesn't answer him.

Inside the conference room a four-by-eight-foot table fills the space with barely enough room for chairs. The attorney makes her way around and sits facing the door. A yellow legal pad, a pen and a telephone share the surface of the otherwise empty table.

Peter and I seat ourselves across from her. Manny takes a place at the far end. This seating arrangement troubles me from the start. I can see my father's face but I'm not sure he can see me. And worse, I'm not close enough to touch him.

Just as I'm about to suggest a change, the lawyer tells us, "So you are aware, I've put a call into Donna and she's running a little late, but should be here soon. I think we must wait for her."

Peter speaks up, "Before she gets here, I have a question for you. Are you representing our father or Donna?"

"I represent both of them as a married couple," she answers without hesitation. But her face and voice reflect a degree of perplexity.

"And under the circumstances, you're comfortable with that? You feel it's ethical?" Peter continues his questioning.

"Yes, I'm comfortable. I've been their attorney in family matters for the last several years. What's your point?"

"It seems to me that Manny's interests and Donna's are in direct conflict with one another. So I wonder how you can protect our father if you also represent Donna." Peter's delivery is direct, dispassionate and matter-of-fact, perhaps perfected by his experience in high-level corporate meetings. Once again, I am glad to have him here with me.

"I really think we must wait for Donna," Toni deflects the questions, her tone now a little annoyed, a little nervous.

Some general conversation passes the time. Coffee is offered. There are moments of awkward silence. Donna arrives.

After greeting Peter and me, Donna maneuvers herself around to where Manny is seated. She bends over, kisses him on the cheek and continues past the next few chairs, finally sitting next to her lawyer.

Peter begins, "We are here on Manny's behalf. Toni, are you aware of our father's situation?"

"That depends on what you mean by 'situation,'" she counters. "I'm aware that he's currently staying at Littleton House nursing home, if that's what you mean."

"Do you know what that place is like? Do you know how unhappy my dad is being there?" I ask.

Donna speaks before the attorney can answer. "They're all

unhappy at first. It's called the 'adjustment period.' I've worked in this field for years and I've seen it all before. Nobody likes having to go to a nursing home but they get used to it."

I think, *Like your last husband got used to it before he died there.* "Well, they don't have a lot of choice, now do they!" I snap. "And furthermore, he is not 'they' and he is not 'nobody.' He is a person. He is my Papa. And he's sitting right over there in the room with us." I point and add, "Remember, you just kissed him on the cheek."

"To answer your question, Richard, no, I've not been out to Littleton House personally, but I understand it is a licensed Level III facility," Toni says calmly. "As far as your dad's feelings, we've not talked in some time." She shifts her focus. "Manny, what do you think of the place you're living at?"

"It's not for me."

"What don't you like about it?" she follows up.

"Well, I have no freedom. And it's boring. There's no one for me to talk with. I'm something of an intellectual, you know. Those people have nothing to offer. I ask them a question and I get no response, just blank stares."

Picking up her pen, Toni asks, "Is there someplace you'd rather be?"

"I don't understand why I can't be in my own home. I'm not a harm to anyone."

"Now, you see! He has no idea what it's been like at home with the two of us," Donna interjects. "He forgets everything that happened over the summer."

"What do you mean?" Manny asks. "What happened?"

Donna turns sideways in her chair. Speaking directly to Toni, she says, "He would sleep all day and then get up in the middle of the night. He'd run the tub, then go to the refrigerator. I'd hear him, get up, shut the water off and try to get him back into bed. That's when he'd get angry and physical with me. I really started getting scared at night."

"So why didn't you ask for help?" I question. "Before you insisted on marrying him, you weren't shy about calling me late at night to come down. I still live just up the street. So why didn't you call me? Instead, you put my father in a nursing home without even telling me."

"You have no idea what it's been like this last year. You never came to see him," Donna defends herself.

"That's not quite true. I'll grant you I didn't see my dad as often as I should have. But I saw him more often than you know about."

Donna looks directly at me now. "What, two or three times in the whole year?"

"No, more like two or three times every couple of weeks. I would stop in during the day when your car was gone. When I was sure you weren't there."

Donna turns back to Toni. "You see? His sons hate me!"

I soften my tone. "I don't hate you, Donna. But I can't have a good talk with my dad when you are around. You're always interrupting. When I try …"

Donna interrupts, "Everything's my fault! My fault!"

I try again, "I'm not saying it's your fault. I don't think you can help yourself, but when I would ask my father a question, you'd always answer for him. This doesn't allow …"

"If I didn't take care of him he'd have nobody. You boys don't care what happens to him! You're never any help! I've taken care of him all these years. And where were you? Nowhere! That's where!"

Toni puts her hand on Donna's arm to get her attention. "Donna, easy, easy."

"This is what I mean," I begin again. "She continually interrupts and she doesn't listen to what I'm really trying to say. I can't …"

As if to prove my point, Donna talks over me. "I don't have to listen to this! I won't listen to this! They think they're so great! Well, they can take care of him! I'll just walk away from the whole thing if that's what they want. I don't …"

"Donna, shush!" Toni commands. Donna does what her lawyer tells her.

We all shush for several moments.

The sound of knuckles cracking breaks the silence. That would be Papa.

Peter speaks first. "It's obvious that Donna can't handle the situation on her own. We are here to make sure our father is well taken care of. And it is our contention that Manny is not getting what he needs at Littleton House."

"Well, you know, quite frankly I think Donna is right," Toni begins. "You boys only seem to get involved in the eleventh hour. Donna has been complaining about the situation with your dad for some time now. She has told me that you guys don't come to see him, and don't offer her any help."

"That's so inaccurate!" My irritation now manifests. I go on, "If you'll remember, we were here a year ago. I told you then, I couldn't see how their getting married would work. I even said Donna planned to put my father in a nursing home."

"I don't understand you," Toni reacts. "You seem to think Donna planned this all out. Like she had some great scheme in mind. I mean, honestly! They've had a 20-year relationship, for God's sake. She has just come to her wits' end with your dad. That's all."

Donna gets up abruptly. "That's right, we had 20 wonderful years. Didn't we, Manny?" She walks over to him, leans against him and begins running her fingers through his hair.

Manny warms to her touch. He relaxes his hands, puts an arm

around her and says, "And we'll have 20 more!"

Toni smiles. Peter smiles. Reluctantly, I smile. Donna giggles. Manny looks altogether pleased.

I'm not sure if Donna employs some deliberate stratagem, but her actions definitely affect Papa. Some body contact, a few kind words, a stroke of her hand and Manny is ready to forgive her anything. I conclude she is dangerous, and a greater adversary than I'd assumed.

"I'm not saying she had some grand plan to steal his house and put him away 20 years ago, when they first met. But last year, in these same offices I informed you about what the young man living in their house had told me."

Peter breaks in, "What reason would …" He looks to me for cuing.

"Jeff," I remind him.

"Why would Jeff lie? And if he did, it's an interesting coincidence that everything he predicted has since happened," Peter postulates.

"He was no angel, you know," Donna counters. "I could tell you some stories about him all right!"

"Could we get back to the point," Toni says. "We're not getting anywhere like this."

"That is the point!" I contend. "You said yourself that Donna has been complaining for some time—that she was at her wits' end. They've only been married for a year and her problems with Manny didn't just start this last summer. It seems to me she was at her wits' end a year ago before they married. And yet, she married him anyway."

"Oh, but he got much worse this last year," Donna pleads. She looks to Toni for support. "Toni can tell you. Remember my phone calls, Toni?" Donna laughs nervously. "I didn't know what I was going to do. I even thought about giving him a pill and ending it all."

The office gets silent for a moment. Peter and I exchange glances, then he comes back with, "Let me understand you Donna. Are you saying you had intentions of poisoning our father?"

Still standing next to Manny, Donna answers, "I wasn't sure what I was going to do, but I thought about it." At the other end of the table, the lawyer cringes.

Manny pulls his arm free, leans back and looks at Donna. "Hey! What are you saying? You want to snuff me out."

"No, not really, Manny." She tries to reach out to him, but he pulls back farther. Slowly, Donna moves along the table and reseats herself next to her lawyer.

"Were you aware of this?" Peter asks, looking directly at the attorney.

Toni responds, "I only knew she was upset. That's why I've been helping her with the legal and financial aspects of your father's placement."

"Well, I think her comments about wanting to kill our father are proof positive that she has no business acting as his power of attorney," Peter states.

"Now look, people say those kinds of things all the time. It doesn't really mean anything. It doesn't mean they're actually going to do it," Toni says

"She didn't just casually say it, twice now. She said she didn't know what to do and that she was thinking about killing our father. This demonstrates an unstable mind," Peter insists.

"I am not unstable! That was several years ago and I got cured."

Peter and I look at each other with puzzled expressions. I'm not sure of the exact reference for Donna's latest revelation.

"Thinking about murdering people doesn't sound like 'cured' to me." Peter digs in a little deeper, maybe just to see what comes of it.

"I told you that was when Manny was home and he pushed me around! And I had a prescription for the Haldol too, but I never gave him more than I was supposed to. You can ask the doctor if you don't believe me!"

"People, people, please!" Toni pleads. "This is not helping. Blaming and accusing isn't going to get us anywhere. Peter, why don't you tell me what you boys want here."

I think, *I want you to stop calling us "boys."*

Peter lays down some demands, "We want the equity in our father's house to be used for him—to provide him with a good environment—someplace where he can make friends and at least have some chance of being happy. Where he is now is just unacceptable."

"You have someplace in mind?" Toni asks.

"We already took Donna there on Monday. Sutton Hill in North Andover," I tell her. "Donna said she liked the place—that it seemed a better fit for my dad. She even agreed to have Manny transferred and started filling out the paperwork. Then she changed her mind without telling me. I had to find out from the admissions director at Sutton Hill." I look directly at Donna. "When I asked you if things were all set for his transfer you told me yes. You lied to me!"

"What do you boys expect?" Once again Toni comes to her defense. "You gang up on her, intimidate and threaten her! Of course she's going to say anything to get you off her back."

"When did we threaten her?" Peter asks.

"You told her she'd have to sell the house. That you'd make her sell it."

"That's not a threat. It is a fact," Peter tells the lawyer. His eyes are trained on hers. His hands remain motionless, folded on the table in front of him.

"You see, that's what I mean. You're threatening again."

"How's that a threat? My father has equity in his house that should be available to him. If she is unwilling to use it for that purpose, then I must do what I must do. And if that means hiring a top-flight lawyer, I'll do it!" Peter says emphatically.

"You have to realize what you're saying," Toni begins her response. "That house belongs to both of them. You can't ask her to sell her home. She needs a place to live also."

"What is her equity in the house?" Peter asks.

"She owns half."

"In title?"

"In title and as spouse."

"When was title transferred? Before or after they were married?" My brother is leading somewhere, but as of yet I don't have a clue where. I look at Papa. He's paying attention intently. But I feel this is all too much for him. *It's too much for me.* I have the urge to go to him, to touch him, hold his hand and let him know I'm still here. I hesitate and the opportunity escapes. I remain seated.

"I don't see how that is relevant," Toni responds to my brother's last question.

"If title transferred before they married, then Donna had a capital gain and she owes taxes on her equity." Peter shifts his eyes to Donna. "Did you pay capital gain taxes?"

"I pay my taxes," she replies.

"I didn't ask you that!" he barks at her.

"And I don't think she needs to answer you," Toni interjects.

"Well, wait till she is forced to answer an interrogatory, under penalty of perjury!" Peter loses his composure, just a little. I think it might be deliberate. He opens his notebook and writes. I can't see what he's writing.

"There you go again with the threats!"

"No threat! You need to understand something here. I am worth several million dollars. If I have to use my resources to make her do what's right, I'll do it. No threat. You can count on it!"

To this latest barrage, Toni asks, "If you're worth all that money how come you haven't offered any financial support for your father?"

"None of them ever help me with the expenses," Donna piles on.

"That's not the point. I am willing to help my father, but there needs to be controls." Without looking down, Peter begins writing in his notebook again while continuing to speak. "I'd have to know the whole financial situation and where my money would be going. I'm certainly not going to write a blank check so she can go off to England with her boyfriend." My brother makes reference to that trip Donna took soon after she and Manny were married.

"I didn't go with my boyfriend. I went alone. I don't have a boyfriend!" Donna shouts. Her face is red and I know the look on it. She'll be crying soon.

"You didn't go with Bob?" Peter presses her.

I catch a puzzled look from Toni. "My brother means Bob Green. He's the man Donna was seeing in Connecticut just before she married our father. We mentioned him to you at that meeting a year ago."

"I haven't seen Bob in over a year! I went alone, I tell you. I don't care if you don't believe me." Now Donna is crying. She gets up from her chair, fumbles for her handbag and through her tears declares, "And I don't have to take this any longer. I won't take it, I tell you!" She works her way behind Manny without looking at him and bolts for the door. "Adultery—adultery! So what! I'm not the only one!" she shouts to no one in particular. Donna flings the office door open and slams it behind her as she leaves. The bang is loud. The wall shakes.

"Wow! What's got into her?" Papa asks.

When I heard that Donna was on her way and would be joining us for this meeting, I didn't plan on trying to drive her away. I don't think that was Peter's intention either, but now that she's gone I have to admit I'm glad. Perhaps without her here my brother and I can make some progress with the lawyer.

"I wish she hadn't left like that," Toni begins. "How can we resolve this without further conflict?"

Now you want to compromise? "Isn't it amazing the difference a year makes? Last year, right here in these offices, you were an advocate for my dad's right to run his own life without our interference. Our 'meddling,' I believe you called it. You supported his decision to get married without any safeguards. Now you seem to think he has no rights. And you accuse my brothers and me of not getting involved to help," I begin to speak my mind.

"First of all, I'm not saying your dad has no rights. Of course he has rights! But things have changed since then. With no disrespect for your father," Toni gives a quick glance in Papa's direction, "Manny has gotten worse during the last year."

"If you mean his memory, I disagree. A year ago he had trouble remembering who he was going to marry—so now he has trouble remembering he got married—I don't see a big difference—except he was better off before. At least then, he didn't have to contend with a wife consumed with putting him away in a nursing home." Toni tries to interject but I don't let her. "Furthermore, my dad does not need full nursing care. He can dress himself. He's not incontinent and he still walks more spryly than his wife, despite her being so much younger. If Donna was at wits' end trying to take care of my father, she should have gotten professional help in determining what was causing his condition. Had it been determined that my father needed to be in a nursing home—which I think he does not—but if that was the consensus, she might have spent time preparing my father for such a change instead of tricking him and just dumping him there. And rather than having you help her with his 'placement,' to use your word, she should've involved us. The way things have been handled, my father is being treated like he's crazy and has no choices about how and where he wants to live."

"Well, I'll tell you …"

"No, I'll tell you," I interrupt. I don't know where my strength is coming from but I'm on a roll and not to be messed with. Not today. Not this time. Not in the moment. "I've sat here twice now in the last year and listened to you say, 'Well, I think—.' Well, you know—it's time you listen to what I think!"

The attorney puts her pen down on the pad in front of her and folds her arms. "Go ahead, speak your mind."

I feel I'm getting the Missouri look. "Sure my dad has a memory problem. I never disputed that. He has trouble remembering simple things that we all take for granted, like what he had for breakfast or who he last spoke to on the phone. But these are the same problems he had a year ago. Back then you didn't see them as an obstacle for him to marry. Now suddenly they're reason enough to put him away. Where's the justice in that?"

"It's more serious than not remembering breakfast. Did you know he almost burned the house down?" Toni asks.

"I know Donna keeps saying that. She brings it up every chance she gets. But did you know that this supposed event also happened before they were married? So it isn't evidence of my dad's worsening condition," I tell her.

The lawyer avoids my question and changes tack. "Donna tells me she has been in contact with Manny's doctor and he agrees your father's situation has gotten worse." She shrugs her shoulders.

"What can I do? I have to defer when it comes to medical decisions."

"Are we talking about the doctor assigned by Littleton House?" I ask.

"No, I'm referring to your dad's family physician."

"The same doctor who gave you a letter saying my father was capable of deciding to marry Donna a year ago?" I ask for clarification.

"Yes, that's right, the same doctor that has been his family doctor for the last 20 years. Who better for me to rely on?" Toni states and questions with impunity.

"Well, actually my father has never really had a family doctor. In general, he doesn't put much faith in doctors—and I'm beginning to understand why. This doctor we're talking about is really Donna's."

"Oh great! Now I suppose you're suggesting there's a conspiracy."

"The only one in this room who has ever mentioned conspiracy is you and I'm tired of the insinuation. All I'm suggesting is that there's no long-term history of this doctor knowing my dad. To say he's been his family physician for 20 years is a distortion. How much time has he spent with Manny over the last 20 years? That would be a better question." Toni doesn't respond verbally. Instead she shrugs her shoulders again. So I go on. "As you well know, just like attorneys have specialties, so do doctors. It is my understanding that this doctor you rely on is a general practitioner. What are his qualifications in determining competency? Does he have any special training in geriatric medicine or memory dysfunction?"

"I don't know the answer to your questions," Toni admits. "But we can't change the past. What would you like to see happen at this point?"

"I want my father evaluated by a specialist in memory loss and related elderly issues."

"I understood such an evaluation was already underway," Toni contends.

"You mean Elder Services?" I ask.

"Yes, that's right. I seem to remember Donna saying they came to the house and interviewed your dad."

"They did. They started an initial screening but Donna never waited for them to finish the process. Apparently a bed became available at Littleton House and perhaps Donna didn't want to lose the opportunity," I tell her.

"So when will the evaluation be completed?"

"Never. Not that one anyway."

Toni takes a deep breath, puffs her cheeks just slightly and releases the air in one short quick burst. "What do you mean?" she asks. Her voice is strident. Her expression reflects exasperation.

"As you may or may not know, Elder Services is a state agency. I called the nurse who started my father's evaluation and was told their mandate is to perform prescreening only. Once Donna placed Manny in Littleton House they were forced to drop the case. I guess she just jumped the gun, so to speak."

"Terrific!" The attorney in Toni is having trouble keeping her annoyance in check. "So what now? Won't the nursing home do an evaluation?"

"They had Donna sign a waiver."

"One of their nurses already told us this is the worst case of elder abuse she's ever seen," my brother re-enters the conversation.

Upon hearing Peter's comment, Toni's eyes get wide. "The worst case of elder abuse?" she repeats, questioning what she's just heard. "That's a serious allegation. You best be sure of what you're saying."

"I'm quite sure. That's what she said."

Toni picks up her pen again. "What's this nurse's name?"

"She asked to remain anonymous and I've got to respect that," Peter tells her.

"Now you can't just go around making unsubstantiated claims like that," Toni warns.

"They're not unsubstantiated," I tell her. I heard it too. In fact, four of us heard it. My partner and my brother's wife were there with us when the nurse said that."

"Well, this is serious. I'm going to call the home right now and get to the bottom of this." Toni picks up the phone.

"Before you call," Peter catches her attention. Toni delays. "Understand, we're not saying the staff at Littleton House have been abusive to Manny. Quite the contrary, they've been very helpful and caring toward our father. The nurse's comment related to his being there in the first place and not how any of the staff were treating him."

"All right, but I still feel I should inform them." Toni completes the call and puts the phone in conference mode so we can all participate.

We speak with the admissions director, whom my brother and I met the first day, and with the director of nursing. They press for the name of the nurse. We protect her identity. Eventually the topic shifts to my father's evaluation and they confirm what I had told the lawyer. My father's right to a prescreening evaluation had been waived. Donna's signature is on the waiver.

After hanging up, Toni asks, "So where do we go from here? I don't have a clear sense of what you boys want. It would be nice if we could work this out in a spirit of cooperation."

"It would be nice," I agree. "But cooperation implies both sides. It also requires trust. Right now I have very little trust in Donna. She has lied and deceived me too many times."

"Well, someone needs to give ground here or we'll never solve anything. Make a suggestion—one of you—please!"

"I want my dad evaluated as soon as possible. I promised him that." Looking over I can see Papa is wide awake and paying close attention even though he's remained silent for a long time now.

"All right, I'm sure the nursing home has had to deal with similar circumstances before. I'll call them back and ask for a referral." Toni reaches for the phone again.

"Unacceptable!" I state.

She pulls her arm back. "Well, don't just tell me it's unacceptable. I haven't heard either of you offer any alternatives."

"I've done a little research," I begin. Actually Eleanor helped with the research. She located two major teaching hospitals in Boston that perform just the kind of evaluation we need. Today I'm armed with their names and numbers. "Deaconess or Brigham and Women's. Either is acceptable."

"Okay, I'll get the numbers and we can set up an appointment right now," Toni says. I reach into my pocket and hand her a paper with all the contact info. She smiles as she says, "I guess you did your homework."

When the attorney calls, all the key people are in meetings. She leaves her number. It's agreed that she will follow up and let me know as soon as she obtains an appointment.

We get up and move toward the door. Before he opens it, Peter says, "One more thing before we go. My father's power of attorney—we'd like to change it."

"I don't think I can do that."

"Why not?"

Toni is now standing inches away from my brother, sandwiched between the two of us. Papa stands by his chair. "Well—I mean— under the circumstances, your father's condition being what it is and all. I don't think it would be appropriate," she stammers.

"Although I've not seen the document itself, it's my understanding that they're typically written to only take effect after someone has been deemed incompetent," Peter postulates. "Since no evaluation has been done, my father should still be considered competent. And he told us he wants to change it. Ask him."

"Well, that's exactly my point. There is a question about competency and therefore I think we must wait for the evaluation." The lawyer gives my brother the same answer she gave me when I spoke with her on the phone last week.

"Donna didn't wait to put him away," I say. "But now my Papa has to wait in Littleton House against his will. That's due process, all right!"

"I'm sorry. My hands are tied in this matter. I must wait for a medical determination," she insists.

"Can I at least get a copy of the document? I'm a signatory on it and I never received one," I tell her.

"Certainly, no problem. I'll have my secretary make you a copy right now."

"Oh, and a couple of other things," I begin. "We know that Donna had been giving my father Haldol over the summer. From speaking with her at the nursing home, she herself said it was not very effective and the side effects were awful. I know that on the 17th the nursing home gave it to him. I have asked that they call me before using drugs to calm him down, and so far they have been honoring my request. However, I would like it in writing that he is not to be given antipsychotic drugs."

"Once again you are asking me to step out of my area and make a medical judgment. I simply can't do that."

"All patients in nursing homes or their legal guardians have the right to refuse antipsychotics. It happens to be the law in Massachusetts. Look it up. I did. And since Donna is, at least temporarily my father's guardian there should be no issue about this being put in writing."

"I'll check into it," Toni promises. "You said a couple of things. What is the last thing? And it needs to be the last as I have clients waiting."

"My dad has only one dollar in his wallet. I want him to have at least 50. My father likes to offer to pay when we go out. I don't mind treating him, but it's part of his identity to be able to contribute. And it's humiliating for him when every time he opens his wallet there is only a single inside. Since his autonomy has been stripped in most all other areas, the minimum Donna could do to show good faith is to let him have some of his own money."

"I'll speak with her about that, but perhaps not today," Toni suggests.

"Understandable. Timing is everything," I acknowledge.

Peter and I thank Toni for her time. And at 2:30, four hours after first sitting down, we are finally done with lawyers, for now.

CHAPTER NINETEEN

Reading Nurses' Notes

A few days later, Eleanor and I are at Littleton House again to take Papa out. It's later than I wanted it to be, around 8:30 at night. With all the time I've been spending with the lawyer, on the phone with doctors and visiting Papa, my carpentry projects have gotten behind. Today I had to work late just to catch up a little.

I stand at the nurses' counter waiting for the sign-out book. Eleanor is in Papa's room keeping him company while he gets ready to come with us. There are no nurses in sight. This procedure of signing my father in and out is still uncomfortable for me, although I do understand why it is necessary.

After a while, I look over the counter to see if I can spot the book for myself. I don't see it, but another notebook with my father's name catches my attention. I reach over, grab it and begin reading to myself:

"ADMISSION and DISCHARGE RECORD, Date: 9/15/93, Patient ID Number: 901, Primary Diagnosis: Dementia 290.10—PROBLEM ORIENTED MEDICAL RECORD: Senile, Blind—PHYSICAL EXAMINATION, Assessment of Mental Capacity: Poor, Estimated Length of Stay: long term—SOCIAL SERVICE

ADMISSION NOTE: Durable Power of Attorney: Mrs. Donna Ebner—PREADMISSION SCREENING, Responsible Party Signature: Donna M Ebner: 9/15/93."

I think about being ten years old and remembering my dad telling my mother he was going to have her locked up. He said it during one of her drunken rages. She had just spit in his eyes. At the time, I thought all my father had to do was call someone and they'd take my mother away. It scared me. I didn't know about due process back then. But I know better now. You can't do it over the phone—you have to come in and fill out a few forms first.

I skip ahead several pages and continue reading:

"Date: September 28, 1993. Dear Resident, Family Member or Legal Representative: The purpose of this letter is to notify you that Littleton House nursing home will be discharging you on or about 10/4/93. We are discharging you for the following reasons: Per your request to transfer to Sutton Hill.—UPDATE: 9/29/93. RE: Manny Ebner. At this time, it appears Manny will be staying at LH until further notice—there will be no discharge on Monday—10/4/93."

Eleanor and my dad walk up next to me. "What are you looking at?" Eleanor asks.

"Manny's records. They were sitting right out on the desk."

"Is that about me?" Papa asks.

"Yes, Papa. They're the daily nurses' notes. Want me to read them to you?"

"Well, of course! I can't read them myself."

I flip back a page. Eleanor moves in closer and reads to herself as I read aloud to Papa:

"9/26/93—Resident pacing up and down the hallway today. Keeps asking to call his wife and son Richard. He finally reached Donna at 1 p.m., and spoke with her for half an hour. She told me that when he was out with his son yesterday, he got away from his son's house and somehow walked to Donna's house. She was quite concerned about this. She said that the family is looking at another facility in Andover tomorrow that is more assisted living. Manny is going out with his son this afternoon."

"Am I moving?" Papa asks.

"Not right away. You were supposed to, but Donna changed her mind. Now we have to wait for your evaluation. Remember my plan, Papa?"

Before he can answer me, a woman's voice behind us shouts, "What are you doing?"

I turn, still holding the notebook. I see a woman staring at me with an angry expression on her face. I don't recognize her, but I think her voice sounds familiar. "Who wants to know?" I respond.

"I'm the director of nursing here," she informs me. "What are you doing with a patient's chart?"

"I'm reading it."

"You can't do that! You can't just read someone's chart—that's confidential."

"It's not just someone's chart. It's my father's, and I'm reading it to him."

"But you can't do that!"

"Excuse me, but these are my father's records." I hold up the book and point to my dad. "Here is his chart and there is my dad." I begin reading aloud again: "9/30/93—Wandering about all day, agitation noted." I close the book for the moment. "Now, there you see—I've read to him from his records—so I guess I can do it," I tell her. My voice is calm, monotonic.

"That's not right! It's illegal!"

"Call a cop," I dare her. I'm bluffing, but part of me hopes she will call the police. Itching for a fight, I'd love to get it on the police log that I think my dad has been kidnapped and is being held against his will.

"You've got to give those back to me!"

"When we're finished reading you'll get them back. And you really should keep them in a safer place—leaving them out like that, anyone could just come by and read them. They're supposed to be confidential, you know." At this last comment she walks away in a huff, muttering something barely audible as she leaves. *That's why her voice sounds familiar; she was on that conference call with the lawyer the other day. Just doing her job. And I've been telling Papa to be nice and cooperate with the staff. So much for heeding my own advice.*

Eleanor takes the records from me, as I turn to talk with Papa for a moment. I want to make sure he knows what just happened. From his responses, he seems to understand perfectly. Now Eleanor nudges me with the record book. "Look at this"—she puts her finger on an entry—"they've drugged him!"

I read to myself again:

"9/17/93—Resident very agitated, he apparently found his roommate sleeping in his bed, picked him up and threw him on his own bed, scaring the other resident. When his wife came in about 3 p.m. he was very upset with her, asking her why he had to stay here. Called attending physician and he ordered psych. Consult and Haldol 0.5 mg."

I look up at Eleanor. "Yeah, we already knew about this, remember? I told you I asked the nurses to call me first, instead of just giving Manny Haldol when he's upset. I think if you read through all the notes, you'll find that's the first and only time they gave it to him. And I brought it up with the lawyer the other day. Even Donna knows Haldol doesn't work for him." I hand the chart back to her.

When I learned that my father had been given Haldol, I didn't know what it was or what it was for. So I looked it up. From what I read: Haldol is a brand name for haloperidol, a butyrophenone that was developed in the 1960s to suppress the hallucinations of the mentally ill, like schizophrenics, and thereby reduce the aggressive and violent behavior that can be associated with such illnesses as schizophrenia, mania and dementia. Some of the curious side effects of the drug are: drowsiness, lethargy and in rare instances a high fever causing confusion.

"Are they giving me drugs?" Papa asks, having heard my conversation with Eleanor. "I don't want to be given drugs!"

"That's what Eleanor is checking on, Papa. You were given a drug called Haldol, but we think you only had it once since you've been here."

Eleanor begins reading aloud to both of us:

"9/18/93—Wife in to visit 10 a.m. Patient upset with nursing home placement. Son in to pick up for lunch—due to return for supper. Son said he would like to be called before his father is medicated with Haldol for agitation. He feels he could calm his father down and avoid medication." She skims a few more pages.

Papa and I talk. I tell him what I know about Haldol. Again he insists he does not want to be given any drugs.

Finding another section to read to us, Eleanor puts a finger in the air and begins:

"9/24/93—Very agitated—feels that he is in the wrong place— states that he 'functions at a higher level' than the other residents— feels he could get violent if he has to stay. Wife arrived. Seen by social worker—wife also asked for Haldol order to be changed as she feels that Haldol does not help her husband." Eleanor closes the book. "She wants the order changed. That means they could be giving him something else."

"Not without an order from the doctor, and that would be written down in his records."

"Are you sure?"

"Pretty sure. There are guidelines the nursing home has to operate under. I don't think they'd risk violating them just to please Donna."

"What about admitting Manny without an evaluation ever being done? Doesn't that violate guidelines?"

"Apparently not when they have a signed waiver from someone who has the legal power of attorney. I saw the form with Donna's signature on it. I don't think they printed the form just for her."

"That stinks!" Eleanor says in disgust. "And another thing—how does Donna know about how Haldol affects your dad?"

"She had a prescription for it and gave it to him over the summer."

"You knew about that?"

"We talked about it here one day when our visits overlapped and it came up again at the lawyer's office."

"How're we going to make sure they don't start giving it to him again—or something else?"

"We'll just keep reading his records every chance we get."

"You know, since Manny has not been deemed incompetent, he has every right to see his own records. That's the law—I know it is. And since he can't see well enough to read them himself, he should be able to assign someone to read for him." Eleanor takes Papa's hand. "Manny, do you want Richard to keep reading your chart to you?"

"Of course! I need to know what they're doing to me—and I don't see too well, you know."

"You should tell the lawyer what your dad just said—make her tell the nursing home they have to let you see his records whenever he wants you to."

"I will call Toni."

"Get her to put it in writing if you can," Eleanor suggests.

The director of nursing comes back. I hand Papa's records to her. "Now we need the sign-out book," I tell her.

"Don't you think nine o'clock is a little late to be going out?" she questions.

"No, I don't," I answer. Turning toward my dad, I ask, "Papa, do you think it's too late to go out?"

"Oh, no. I'm not tired and I need to get out of here for a while."

In the kindest tone I can muster, I say, "I understand this is unusual, but my dad is pretty unusual. He really needs a break."

"Well, I still think it is late, but it is up to you." Reluctantly, she produces the book. I sign it. We leave.

CHAPTER TWENTY

A Book is Born

Five miles, one town over and 15 minutes later, Eleanor, Papa and I pull into the parking lot of the Old Oaken Bucket in Westford. Once we're inside, a waitress we've gotten to know acknowledges us with a smile from the other side of the bar. She looks across to our favorite table, sees that it is unoccupied and motions for us to seat ourselves.

I discreetly place my hand on Papa's shoulder to help guide him down the two steps leading to the casual sunken eating area. Cushioned love seats, on three sides, surround a coffee table style-serving surface. A gas log fireplace, not currently lit, is situated across from the open end of the table. The space is semiprivate, cozy and perfect for this moment.

Papa is hungry again so he orders a hamburger with fries. Eleanor and I are not. We order coffee instead. While we wait, Eleanor says, "So, Manny, Richard tells me things are going well with your recording project."

"He thinks so? Well, yes, I suppose—that little recording machine is amazing."

"I think you are amazing. Richard transcribed some of your

recordings and let me read them. It must have taken so much courage to come here at 15 all by yourself."

"Not really. They just put me on a boat and off Manny went." In one quick slap, Papa slides one hand off of the top of the other. "I didn't have any choice in the matter."

"Choices are exactly why we need to continue working on your memory, Papa," I tell him. "We need to get you more choices in how and where you want to live."

I don't know much about how they evaluate someone for competency, but I assume a lot of it revolves around memory and an awareness of where one is in time and space. Papa's long-term memory seems intact to me. With very little cuing he is able to tell stories about his past that are coherent, engaging and filled with details. As for his short-term memory, that's not so good. At Eleanor's suggestion, I've been writing down what's happened to him lately and combining that with his recorded remembrances from long ago, the condensed story of his life, if you will. My hope is if I keep reading it all back to him, some of the more recent events may stick in different parts of his brain. Of course, Manny would question the scientific efficacy of my approach.

Food and coffee arrive. Papa digs in. I let him have the four or five minutes it takes him to devour everything before engaging in more mental exercise.

"So, Papa, I've been writing about you," I begin.

His bushy white eyebrows go up and his eyes widen. "You have?" The tone of his question sounds like he's suspicious. "Is that it?" Papa asks, noticing the thick, white, three-ring binder I have already placed on the table.

"Yes, this is your story, or as you would more precisely say, it's one story about you." I pick up the notebook and put it on his lap.

"Wow!" Papa lifts the manuscript up and down seemingly

calibrating the weight of my writing. "How many pages are here?"

"I'm not sure." Leaning over, I open to the last page. "Two-ninety," I tell him.

"Three hundred pages! Good God, man, that's a book. When do you find time to write?"

"Mostly early in the morning before work. But it's all just handwritten. I'm probably the only one who can read it, so I don't think it qualifies as a book." I lean back.

"The weight of this thing!" Papa raises the binder up and down a few more times. "This must be more than a bag of sugar, for God's sake."

"Maybe we can sell it by the pound, Papa."

He laughs, and then gets very serious. "So you're going to publish then."

"I don't know. It's not even finished yet."

"And if it's published, you think anyone will be interested in me?"

Eleanor chimes in, "I'm sure your sons and your grandchildren will be interested, Manny. It doesn't have to be a commercial venture." Eleanor knows almost as well as I that everything my father involved himself in became a commercial venture eventually. All with mixed success.

"Okay, let's assume we will publish," I tell him, hoping this will motivate him. "As for anyone other than family being interested, I think they would. You're a very interesting subject."

"Oh, I'm a subject, am I?" Papa pretends to be insulted.

"I'm sorry, a very interesting person. You certainly lived an unconventional life."

"You think so?"

Papa is fishing for praise and I'm in the mood to give it. "I do, creator and president of Foto-Cube Inc. Holder of several patents."

Papa sits up a little taller and uses his hands to turn out imaginary lapels.

"Longtime member of the New York Society for General Semantics, and contributing author to their magazine *Etc.* I've read a couple of the articles you wrote for *Etc.* and your writing skills aren't too shabby either."

"Keep it coming, kid."

Eleanor shakes her head and smiles.

"All right, dance instructor, self-taught piano player, gymnast, Harley rider, speaker of several languages, clock designer and electrician. Oh, I almost forgot iceman. Not exactly your 'go to the same job every day for 40 years and then retire' kind of dude, I'd say. And I suppose I should mention atheist, but it might cost us a few billion readers."

"Yes, I guess I was quite eclectic, wasn't I?"

"Humble too, I see. And speaking of patents, how 'bout all those inventions?"

"Inventions?"

Now he's toying with me. "I remember what I think was the only child's toy you invented. You called them Jiffy Joiners." Manny made blocks of wood that could be joined together using ¼ inch dowels. The blocks were a uniform 1 inch on four sides and then cut to length in increasing 1 inch increments, with the largest being 12 inches long. He drilled ¼ holes, evenly spaced, through all sides. With a supply of ¼ dowels of various lengths, I could build almost anything. They were a cross between Cuisenaire rods and an Erector set. "I think your Jiffy Joiners were my introduction to carpentry," I suggest.

"I always contended that learning should be hands on. Jiffy Joiners taught you math, my boy!"

"I know, Papa. But I don't want to forget those Butterfly Tables,

Mondrian cabinets, Cubed Art, Magna-Frames, Foto-Cubes, Insta-Frames, or even better, your domes."

"My domes, yes." He pauses to reflect, then continues, "I based my design on Bucky, you know." He means Buckminster Fuller, the architect and inventor. "I just changed the geometry a little so I could get more altitude in a smaller radius. I didn't want the things to get too big."

Papa looks pleased with himself. *This feels good. He looks happy.*

"So you remember my domes then?"

"I remember lying in the hammock and looking up at the stars."

"That was my favorite thing about them too," Eleanor says and adds, "that and no mosquitoes."

"Now you see, that's why I put the screening everywhere instead of having a roof." Papa moves the manuscript back to the table in front of him. "Your conventional screen house is too confining. You might as well stay inside!" He is animated now, talking with his arms and hands fully involved. "I wanted people to experience it all! The total outdoors—just without the bugs. Nature can be beautiful—but it can be a bastard too! Did I tell you I met Bucky once?"

"No, I don't think so."

"Yes, at a lecture on Bauhaus I think it was. Oh, I'm not sure. God I haven't thought about that in years. It must have been 50 years ago. How old am I—no don't tell me."

While Papa ponders his age, I reach over and snatch the manuscript. "So you see, I think we've got some material here."

"Maybe." Papa scratches his head. "Too bad none of them worked out though."

"Hey! What do you mean? That doesn't sound like the Manny Ebner I know. I thought the process was just as important as the result. Think of the fun you had—never a dull moment at our house."

"I suppose you're right. It's just that I wanted us to be free from the slavery. I always hated what capitalism does to the masses. It robs the time needed to evolve and it stifles the creative process." Papa pauses, shifts his weight and continues. "Animals must work almost every second just to survive. Did you ever watch a bird? It's a pitiful sight. They must flit about all day just to eat or keep from being eaten. We humans don't need to behave that way. We just haven't figured that out yet."

"So what are you proposing, communism?"

"Certainly not Stalinist Communism," Papa asserts. "That kind of communism might be worse, even for the ones on top. At least the entrepreneur has a chance of maximizing the human experience, unless his success blinds him to it. When money is the object instead of a vehicle to higher awareness, then life becomes a meaningless game. It's easier to be an oppressor when your stomach is full."

I've heard this speech before. And I've told others, that as a child and a teenager, whenever I tried to have a conversation with my father, I'd get a lecture instead. I hated it. When I reached adulthood my response was sarcasm. Eleanor has experienced the Manny lecture circuit as well, but without my negative reactions. Right now those reactions have been replaced with a warm sense of appreciation. Now I'm bathing in the sound of his voice. Never mind the meaning of the words, this I still don't always get or agree with, but that he can construct thoughts at all is a good thing. And I'm struck by the mystery of his brain, of all our brains. Is this really the same Papa who half the time can't remember where he is or how he got there? The same man that doctor called, "… a nice fellow, but crazy as a loon?" I wish the doctors could see tonight's Papa.

"It sounds like you're saying it's a good thing that we never got rich from any of your inventions. Otherwise you might not be so highly evolved."

With a stern expression, Papa looks down his nose at me. "You're amusing yourself at my expense I see."

"No. I'm sorry, Papa, conditioned response, I guess." I reach out, touch his leg and pull back. "I'm really just delighted that you're your old self tonight. And I think you had some great ideas for products. Some of it's just luck and timing." I reach over again. "Do you remember when you asked me if I wanted to join the business?" Papa shakes his head no. "I think I was 16 or 17—anyway it was just after I dropped out of high school."

"You dropped out?" Papa interjects.

"Yah, but I went back and finished."

"You dropped out of high-school and this is the first I hear of it. Where the hell was I?"

It is refreshing to hear Papa admit he should have been more involved as a father, even if he excuses himself by misremembering. But it is also unsettling for me to have such an advantage over him. Finally, because of his memory loss, I am perceived as smarter, more competent than him. More competent I may be, but smarter, still not.

"You were busy with the Insta-Frames, I think. But I'm sure you knew about my quitting. That was the whole point in asking me to help you. I didn't have a clue about where I was going or what to do next—typical teenager. Anyway, what I want to say is I wish I'd said yes. Maybe if I had we could've made a go of it."

"Well, I certainly could have used the help, and the encouragement. You know I tried to involve your mother, but she was always so negative. I never seemed able to please her."

"I'm sorry I was so negative too. A father and son business

sounds pretty good right now."

"You think so?"

"I do."

A quizzical smile forms on Papa's face. "Yes, I can see it," Papa frames a rectangle with his hands, "'Ebner and Son' on the door." With a broad sweep of his arms he continues, "Our names emblazoned ten feet high on the side of tractor-trailers. Can't you just see all the trucks leaving the warehouse — delivering our products to the proletariat? Then we'd sit back and become wealthy capitalists — ready for self-actualization."

Eleanor laughs. I'm chuckling.

Papa smiles. "Perhaps?" he considers. Then his arms drop and his smile dissipates. "Ah, but too late. I have no resources anymore. I don't even know where my wallet is." He reaches to his back pocket. "No, nothing. Have you seen my wallet?"

"No, Papa, but you don't need it. You don't need money to tell your story. What did you always say to me—the past you can't change—the future you can't know—always live in the moment. So in the moment we'll work on this book together—better late than never—right?"

"What are we calling it?"

"I don't know—how about 'Saving Papa's Tale'?" I suggest.

"Saving my what?"

"Your tale, your stories. The stories of your life."

"Oh, my t-a-l-e," he spells back to me. "I thought you meant my t-a-i-l."

"I guess you could take it either way."

"Ah yes, I see, a double-entendre. And so that's the title then."

"A working title anyway. We can change it to something else if you prefer."

"No, no. It's fine."

I think about what Papa's just said and a thought comes to mind. "You know, Papa, when I proposed the title just now, it didn't occur to me there could be a double meaning. You're the semanticist, why do you think it occurred to you?"

"That is both the beauty and the beast about language, my boy. It's beautiful for the reader, or in my case the listener, that we can all have our own special interpretation of what's being told. But for the writer it's a beast to be precise. I always reread books many times to see what other meanings I could squeeze out."

"Well—you just gave me a great idea."

"I did? Well, good for me! What was it?"

"Let's write two books together, one about your life, your tales and one about your situation or your tail."

Papa considers for a moment. "Sounds pretty ambitious—two books. I'm willing, but you're the one who has to do all the work. I only hope I can last that long."

"I don't mean two separate books with two separate covers. Rather, two story lines inside the same book. For structure and interest, you know?"

"I suppose so. You're the author."

"No, Papa. We are coauthors. I'm giving you equal billing."

"Thank you so much. But I just don't know what I can do."

"You can remember, and stay alive, at least until we get published," I tell him.

CHAPTER TWENTY-ONE

The Iceman Cometh

It is Columbus Day. I know this because it says so on that placard in the quadrangle. Baby and I have come to give Papa what I hope will be good news. I am carrying my own placard of a kind, a homemade, one-month calendar with large numbers written in bold black magic marker. I've also brought my tape recorder and the first few chapters of our book collaboration, now neatly typed.

It has been a productive week dealing with Donna's lawyer. When I called to check on the status of Papa's pending evaluation I was told the attorney hadn't gotten a date yet. Feeling like I was being stonewalled, I asked if I could handle setting up the appointment, was given permission to do that and now have a date, October 22. Also I have been cleared to read my father's chart without interference.

The evening nurse is at her station when Baby and I reach the desk. I request Papa's records. I'm handed his notebook politely and without question. I thank her and tell Baby to lie down for a minute. My dog circles several times, then reluctantly lies down next to my feet, giving out a displeased sigh as she settles.

I put my things down and remaining standing as I begin reading to myself: "10/4/93—4:40 p.m.—Stated, 'there's not enough petting around here.' When asked what he meant by petting he stated, 'touching, you know, caressing.'" *I wonder if his words will be used against him—used to further insinuate he's demented and just a, "dirty old man."*

I skip to the next entry: "10/04/93—6:10 p.m.—This writer received a phone call from Mr. Ebner's wife Donna Ebner. She will write a note giving permission to allow her husband Emanuel Ebner's son Richard Ebner to read Mr. Ebner's chart." *Kind of a convoluted way to write it down, I'm thinking. But at least they got the message. Mustn't argue with progress.*

I continue reading: "10/7/93—7:15 p.m.- Resident out with son due back around 8:30 p.m. Very pleasant this p.m.—confusion—agitation noted."

"10/9/93—10 a.m.—Wife, Donna Ebner, in, brought consent form—release of medical record to Deaconess Hosp. Boston."

"10/10/93—Pt. up walking halls all night. Did not sleep at all. Very concerned why wife has left him here. Says she has other men at home. Says he doesn't want to be here." I close the notebook, hand it back to the nurse and thank her again.

"Baby, heel!" The blue Great Dane gathers herself off the floor, steps to my left side and waits at attention for my next move. I turn, and as I do I'm facing that familiar row of chairs. Bodies fill all of them, just waiting, waiting for nothing it seems. *How could I have missed seeing them when I walked in? Have I gotten so, "used to this place," as Donna might say, that I don't even see them anymore?*

One of the bodies cringes at the sight of my 32 inch tall, 135 pound canine standing next to me. But some appear pleased to see her. Eyes that never changed their focus for me suddenly widen and look brightly at the dog. Long forgotten smiles form on some of the faces of the bodies. One woman struggles to reach her arms out in front of her, beckoning Baby to come closer. I ask her if she would like to pet the dog. She nods her head enthusiastically. Others join in.

After adding to the level of petting, touching and caressing in the halls of Littleton House, Baby and I head off to look for Papa. We find him sitting on his bed. His head is down. Both hands rub back and forth over his knees and I hear him quietly sobbing to himself. Baby pushes past me and races over to him.

"Oh, my doggie's here!" he exclaims. He puts his arms around her and hugs her. "How did you get here, my little doggie?"

"She came with me, Papa." I sit on the bed next to him. His roommate is out, occupying one of those chairs down the hall.

"Oh, my son, my son. My son has come to see me," Papa talks exclusively to the dog, "and he brought you with him."

I place my hand on my father's shoulder, close to his neck. The tension is obvious. "How are you doing, Papa?"

"I'm bored to tears," he says. "I don't understand what I'm doing here."

I move my other hand up and begin massaging Papa's neck and shoulders. I say nothing.

My father continues petting Baby and talking to her. After a time, he says, "That feels so good—what are you doing back there?"

"You scratch Baby and I'll scratch you," I say. Papa chuckles. I'm glad to see his mood change. "I have lots of good news to tell you."

"And I could use some, anything. What?"

"We have a date for your evaluation. You have an appointment on October 22nd, at Deaconess Hospital in Boston."

"In Boston? But how will I get there? You know I don't drive anymore."

"I'll take you of course! Maybe we'll ride the train together." These are the kind of responses from Papa I worry about. I'm fearful that if he says things like that at the Deaconess, they will, find him senile. When he was declared legally blind, over a decade ago, he continued to drive his VW Bug until his license expired. When questioned about the safety of that he'd say, "I don't go very far and my car knows the way."

"The 22nd you say. Where are we now?"

"I'm glad you asked me that." I get up and grab the special calendar from where I left it leaning against the doorjamb. Turning it and holding it close enough in front of Papa, I say, "I made you a chart so that you can keep track of the days." I put my finger on the 11th. "This is today, Columbus Day, and here is the 22nd, a Friday," I tell him while circling the date with my magic marker.

"Two more weeks in this place. I don't think I'll make it."

"Ten days, Papa! Not two weeks—think positive. Remember, you're retired now—you can't count five-day weeks—all seven must be used, and you're two weekends shy of two weeks." I feel like a cheerleader at a high school pep rally.

"And you say we'll go by train?"

"If that's what you want, sure."

"Yes, I'd like that. Haven't been on a train in years. You'll be with me, though? I don't think I could negotiate such a trip by myself."

"Of course, Papa. I'm here for you all the way, whatever you need. And I have more good news. Just let me post your calendar and we'll talk." I pin his calendar to the wall over his dresser with the thumbtacks I brought with me, and then X out all the days leading up to today. "So, Papa, I've been working on our writing project and I've brought the recorder you like so much. If you give me more material, I'll read to you what we already have. Deal?"

"Sounds good to me. Anything is better than just sitting around in this place."

Not wanting to be interrupted when Papa's roommate comes

back, we move to the living room. I put the recorder on the table in front of us. Papa is on the couch. I sit across from him in a wing chair. Baby settles on a corner of the rug. I forgot to bring her bed this time.

"So, Papa, when we left off you had told your aunt that you weren't going to clean the chicken coop anymore. What happened with that? Did she kick you out?"

"No, I continued to live there for some time—she had a room in the attic for me, but when I refused to clean the coop she insisted I pay her to stay there. So I got a job."

"Doing what?"

"I became an iceman's helper—delivering ice. Although I remember, pretty soon I was doing most of the work."

"Ice for iceboxes?"

"That's right. Electric refrigeration wasn't really there yet, and the ice business was huge. The demand for it in the city was endless. My aunt knew this old-timer that had been in the business since the 1800s. Boy, the stories he could tell."

"Where did you get the ice?"

"From icehouses. There were lots of them around—I think Mount Vernon alone had two or three of them, enormous buildings right by the edge of the water. They had huge conveyer systems that went down into the ponds or the river.

"The Hudson?"

"Yes, well, further upstate, the Hudson—maybe in Poughkeepsie—I think the river was still too salty down where we were. And also there were barges that took ice into the city. Now that I think of it—most of the time I think we took the empty wagon into the city and got our ice at the docks. But back in the day, my boss did it all—harvesting, cutting, and delivering. By the time I worked for him he was too old to keep up that pace."

"When—1923—'24?"

"Yes, yes—sounds about right."

"And how big were the blocks?"

Papa shows me the dimensions with his hands. "Three-foot cubes," he says. He looks at his hands and moves them in a little closer together. "Well, maybe just a little smaller—perhaps two by two. But boy were they heavy, at least 30 pounds, I think."

"So the blocks were already cut to size when you got them, but how did you move them? They must have been slippery, especially in the summertime."

"Yes, by then the whole thing had been figured out—it was big business and the ice was sized to fit in all the common iceboxes. My boss—why can't I think of his name? Oh well, anyway, my boss used to cut all his own ice from much larger blocks, sometimes right from the pond, but that was before me. He had a cache of special tools: large-toothed saws, ice gaffes, picks, tongs—many of them he had made himself. I remember one time when he showed me how it used to be done." Suddenly Papa pulls one of the couch cushions out from behind him and places it between his legs on the floor. "He'd look at that block like a jeweler examining a diamond in the rough," Papa says, staring at the cushion for a few moments. "Then he'd grab an ice pick, make some holes, take his chisel and a hammer, and a few whacks later that ice cracked in half just where he wanted it to." With imaginary tools in hand Papa acts out the whole scene while talking me through it. "'Emanuel! Load it in the wagon,' he ordered me."

"So how did you load it in the wagon and what was the wagon like, horse drawn?" I ask.

"Yes, yes, horse drawn. It was made of wood, had sides and a roof, with doors at the back. The old guy would make two depressions with his pick on each side of the blocks, then I'd use ice tongs to lift them over my shoulder like this." Papa gets up quickly and nearly steps on Baby's tail. She retreats to the other side of the room. Now Papa pretends to lift a block of ice, placing it at the end of the coffee table as if it were the wagon." He sits back down.

"When the wagon was full where did you go?"

"We had many regular customers in the city."

"Manhattan?"

"Probably or Brooklyn, one or more of the boroughs. You know, I remember the darn horse knew the route better than he did. Sometimes the horse would just stop outside a building for no apparent reason. The old geezer would crack his whip and yell at Stoney to get on, but the horse wouldn't budge. Then he'd fumble through his list of customers. Pretty soon he'd shout at me, 'Emanuel! One for 4-B.' I'd carry the ice up while he waited for me in the wagon. When I got back the horse would start walking to the next customer's house without us saying a word."

"Smart horse that Stoney. So you remember his name better than your bosses."

"Yep, the horse was nicer to me. He was lucky to have him. I think the old guy was losing his memory."

Could happen to any of us. "Didn't you offer to help him with the lists?"

"I couldn't. I couldn't read English yet—could hardly even speak it at that point."

"You're getting much better at it," I say jokingly.

Papa smiles. "You think so?"

"So how did you speak to the customers? Or did they speak German?"

"Oh, no. Well, some of them might have—I don't really remember. But we didn't need to talk. They were expecting the ice and it was obvious that I was the iceman. I'd knock—they'd let me in and show me to the icebox. As I left they stuck money in my hand and I'd bring it back to my boss."

"You never had to make change?"

"No, I don't think so. I guess they were always ready for me. Most people got ice three or four times a week."

"Do you remember how much it cost them?"

"Not much—fifteen cents a block maybe. Papa smiles and says, "Funny."

"What, Papa?"

"Well, I remember as I got to know some of the customers better they began giving me things."

"Like what?"

"Underwear."

"Underwear?"

"Yes. Handmade underwear."

"How come?"

"I'm not sure really. As a tip maybe, or perhaps they thought I needed it. After walking up four flights with thirty pounds of ice on my back, I was soaked by the time I got to most peoples' doors." Papa shakes off an imaginary shiver. "Weekends and just before holidays were the worst. Many customers ordered two blocks to see them through. That's when I got most of the clothes. I guess they felt sorry for me and thought I needed something dry to put on." Papa chuckles. "I remember I ran out of space in my little room for all the stuff."

"Do you remember how much you got paid?"

"Not much—less than a dollar a day."

I notice Papa is looking tired and figure this might be a good place to stop for now. "Would you still like me to read to you tonight or are you getting sleepy," I ask him.

"A little reading would be nice. I don't sleep very well in this place anyway."

"I know and I'm sorry about that. The nurse said you were up most of last night pacing. But you need to get your rest. It's an important part of keeping you alert for your evaluation." I get up and put the cushion back behind him. He settles in. I sit back in my chair, open the notebook and begin reading aloud from Chapter 1, "I find my father pacing in front of the nurses' station. His fists are clenched. His face is red. Mustering the brightest greeting I can, I call out ...."

CHAPTER TWENTY-TWO

"It is what you say it is ..."

At three in the afternoon on Wednesday I'm back at Littleton House for an unexpected extra midweek visit. It's rainy, drizzling and I have no indoor work scheduled. Baby is with me and since we find Papa napping, I let the dog do her magic to wake him.

Once awake and the first 15 greetings have been completed, Papa asks, "To what do I owe this honor? I wasn't expecting to see you today—or was I?"

"This miserable rain—it won't let me get any work done."

"Well, it is what you say it is," Papa responds with another phrase I've heard so many times before.

"There you go again. As many times as you've said that I still don't know what it means."

"You don't? Gee and you're so smart too. Well, it's really quite simple, you know. You say the rain is miserable and yet there is nothing intrinsically miserable about rain—or any other form of precipitation, for that matter. Children don't mind rain and snow; in fact, they love to play in it. It's only when Mommy projects her own fears onto them that they stop enjoying the experience—

'you'll get your clothes all wet … you'll catch a cold.' So you see, the only thing that makes rain miserable is you and your labeling it thus."

"But I can't do my job," I complain.

"So you get to take a day off—and you have the time to come see me. Is that such a bad thing?"

"No, Papa, it isn't. It's a good thing." *I get it.* "Want to go out and play?"

He looks at me as if I'm crazy. "I thought you said it was raining. Why would I want to go outside when it's nice and dry in here?"

I arrived only five minutes ago and already Papa has me chuckling. I'm not positive he recognizes his own inconsistencies, but I think his tongue is mostly in his cheek. *God, I love the rain.*

"Well, if you don't want to go out and play in the rain, how about I read to you?" I ask.

"That would be nice."

Baby is curled up on her beanbag. Papa looks comfortable ensconced in his bed. The roommate is nowhere to be seen. We will stay right here for now.

I help Papa prop up his pillows, take out our book and sit on the edge of his bed. Everyone looks more comfortable than I, but it's nice to be close enough to touch Papa when I want to.

I pick up where we left off last time and read to him from Chapter 2. He pays close attention. When I finish I say, "Want another chapter?"

"Well, of course! You can't leave me hanging like that, man. I need to know what has me so riled up."

"Okay." I read Chapter 3. "Out on the road, the air was still hot and humid. Baby wanted to come with me but I made her stay home. At that point, my dog already had a better relationship with my father than I … I got closer. At the bottom of the driveway,

I could already hear my father shouting at Donna from inside the house. I froze, and just listened to the Old Man's voice. A voice that still scared me.

Finding the courage to walk up the driveway took a few more moments. Finally, I was able to move. Once at the front door I considered knocking for a second, decided not to, then opened the door and stepped inside my childhood home."

"That's it. Probably needs some editing." I close the notebook and look up at Papa.

He is speechless. There's a troubled look on his face. Perhaps sensing Papa's distress, Baby gets up and solicits a pat on her head. "You and I fought?" Papa asks, while petting Baby.

"Sometimes."

"I mean, physically?"

"Yes, Papa, we did."

"What the hell was wrong with me?"

I place both hands on his blankets and press down over his legs. Baby backs away and let's me take over. "It's not like you beat me every day, Papa. Things just got out of hand once in a while," I try to reassure him. "I was no angel either."

"Yes, I know—but you were a child—to fight with your children—a parent should never fight with their child." Head down, Papa shakes it from side to side.

This is the closest he has ever come to apologizing. *Time to accept it.* I move closer, place my hand under his chin and raise it so that we are face to face. "Papa, it is over with. I promise you, we will never fight again." I give him a kiss on his forehead. He starts to cry. I take both of his hands in mine and say, "Papa, you know I'm always encouraging you to remember things—well, this is something I want you to forget. I forgive you. So, *fu-ge-da-bout-it.*" I say this in my best mob voice.

169

It must be good enough because Papa begins to laugh while still sobbing. Sobbing turns into sniffling and finishes with a runny nose. I get him a tissue. Once he has composed himself I tell him, "You've been getting a free ride today. Now I'm going to make you work. You need to do your part in this book-writing thing or you'll lose your billing." He gives me his famous raised eyebrows and now I know he's okay. I push the notebook to the end of the bed and take the recorder out of my pocket. Placing it on his lap between us, I ask, "So, Papa, how long did your career as the iceman's helper last?"

He thinks for a moment, then responds, "Oh, not so long. My boss got too old to work the wagon anymore and he retired. I could have gotten a job with another ice company, but there wouldn't have been any future in it. I knew refrigeration was on its way in. Besides, it was lousy work anyway—I was always soaking wet. Eventually I asked my aunt for help and she found me a new job."

"Doing what?"

"She got me an entry position at Ward Leonard."

"Any relationship to Montgomery Ward, the department store?"

"Oh, no, at least I don't know of one. Ward Leonard was an electrical supply house and manufacturer of high-temperature resisters and electric motors and such. The founder of the company was a brilliant electrical engineer and inventor. An MIT man, Henry I think was his first name, but don't quote me on that."

"Duly noted. Did you ever meet him?"

"No, no, he was dead and gone by the time I got there. But everyone had heard of him. He had hundreds of patents, even worked for Thomas Edison for a time."

"So what did you do there?"

"I serviced the girls—brought them whatever they needed to fill orders. It paid better than the iceman too."

"Do you remember how much you made?"

"No. I never saw my check. My pay went directly to my aunt and she doled out 75 cents a week to me—just enough to buy three sodas."

"Ice cream sodas?"

"That's right. American sodas were strange to me. And I loved the one with real pineapple in it—not syrup, but chunks of pineapple." Papa smacks his lips. "That was my favorite."

I'm confused and wonder if he is also. "Was it a soda or a sundae?" I ask.

"No. It was a soda—it was a glass with liquid in it."

"And ice cream?"

"Yes, there was some ice cream floating around on top, and you could have syrup if you wanted, but it was those nice chunks of real pineapple that I loved. The soda shop had these canisters at the counter and you could choose what you wanted. I always pointed to the pineapple."

"Next time we go out we'll have to see if we can get you one—but around Boston they might be called *floats*—a regional thing, I think."

"Oh, I'd love one. I could eat one right now!"

"I don't think we can manage that just now, but would you like some water or something?"

"Ginger ale would be nice."

As if ordered from the heavens, a nurse pokes her head into the room and says, "Hi, Richard. I saw you and Baby come in. Thought you might want a snack and something to drink. Ginger ale and Fig Newtons. I know Manny loves them. I'll just set them over here on the dresser."

"Thanks so much!" *Whatever your name is?* I am disappointed with myself and I must work on remembering names. There is no excuse for me not to, especially when all the nurses have name tags on. People like having their names remembered.

"Food and drink, Papa." I get up and serve us. "Here, Papa, take this." I hand him a small wrapped package of Fig Newtons and place the plastic cup of ginger ale on the lamp table.

"What's this?"

"Sustenance."

As he works the wrapper I ask, "How did you learn English? Did you just pick it up or did you study? Because you know—listening to you speak, most people wouldn't be able to tell it was your second or third or fourth language, or whatever the number is. I forget now."

Papa pops a fig bar into his mouth. "Ah, Newtons." Papa exclaims, "My favorite!" He tears at the cellophane for another one. "I'm sorry—you were saying?"

"I was asking how you came to speaky the English so good. I was wondering if you took classes or just picked it up."

"Oh, no, I studied. Studied very hard—well, I suppose I learned some from my surroundings—at work and such—but I knew that wouldn't be good enough. Language was a barrier I felt would hold me back. And I wanted to become a citizen. That was very important to me."

"So where did you study?"

"I'm not sure, but I think my aunt knew someone who gave lessons—in her home—at night. And I had formal classes when I joined the militia." Papa eats another Newton.

"Want some ginger ale to wash that down?"

Papa nods yes. I reach the cup over to him. "You said you joined the militia. Was that like the National Guard?" I wait for him to swallow.

"Probably. I'm not sure what they called it back then, but it was a military unit of some sort."

"Why did you join? You've always said you hated the military."

"It was required, I think—or maybe I thought it would be easier that way, to become a citizen, I mean. Anyway, I didn't mind it. This country had given me so much. I suppose I figured I owed something. As long as I didn't have to shoot anyone I was okay."

There is a knock at the door and a nurse comes in hand-in-hand with Papa's roommate. "I'm sorry to interrupt but Mr. Johnson needs to use the bathroom," she says.

I look outside to see the rain has stopped for now. "That's all right. I think we'll go out for a little walk—give you some privacy."

Baby hears the word *walk* and springs to her feet. "Are we moving?" Papa asks.

"The rain stopped. Let's get some fresh air. I'll find your sneakers." Papa gets up slowly and sits in his chair. I help him put on his sneakers. He doesn't really need the help but I know he likes the contact—the touching. I like it too. I get his parka from the closet and grab Baby's leash. This sends the confirmation signal to her—shoes, coats and leash equal walk. Baby begins wagging her tail.

We stop at the nurses' station to resupply with Newtons. It's almost five now and most of the bodies have gone to the cafeteria. A nurse hands us the fig bars and seeing our coats on says, "I'll get you the sign-out book."

"Do we need that?" I ask. "We're just going for a walk."

"You'll stay on the property?"

"We wouldn't think of leaving—would we, Papa?" My father makes an exaggerated side-to-side shake with his head. "We're just going to walk around the parking lot—get some fresh air into him." I pat his chest. Papa takes a deep breath, exhales and fakes a coughing spasm.

The nurse startles for a second, and then laughs as she says, "Manny, you're such a joker!"

As we make our way to the front doors, a stray body follows us. When we get to within a few feet of the exit, a loud horn sounds.

"What the hell is that?" Papa asks at a yell while covering his ears.

"The escape signal," I shout back at him. Baby folds her ears inward.

A few more seconds pass, and a male and a female nurse round the corner of the quadrangle, shouting, "Stop right there!" as they run to catch up with the escapee.

"Who are they screaming at?" Papa asks.

"This woman," I answer him. "She's trying to get out of here, but she has a transmitter on her ankle."

"Am I wearing one?" he asks.

"No, Papa. You had one on for the first couple of days, but you promised to be a good boy, so they took it off."

"Well then, let's get out of here. What's stopping us?"

The nurses arrive and redirect the woman. The alarm is shut off.

The three of us step out into the cool damp October air. Papa takes another deep breath, holds it in, and then slowly exhales. I don't hear any coughing this time. "Feels good, doesn't it?" I ask.

"Feels good just to get out of that damn building."

"I undo the dog's leash and give her some freedom. "Okay, Baby, go!" She races out about ten feet, then turns to see if we are coming. This process is repeated several more times across the parking lot until she reaches the edge of the driveway. There she stops to wait for us. If you have ever seen Great Danes bound across open spaces, you know they move much as wild horses do. It's beautiful to witness.

Papa and I follow and once reaching her, we continue walking down the long, straight drive toward the road. Littleton House was built at the top of a gently sloping hill that used to be an orchard. Along the drive many of the trees remain, forming a line to both sides of us. Although the drizzle has stopped, fog has rolled in and in the mist these untended fruit trees, their leaves dropped now and with their gnarled, craggy branches, look mysterious and somewhat foreboding. A few dried-out apples remain hanging and stare back at us like old shriveled eyes. Many more apple eyes cover the ground beside us.

We walk silently for a while. Baby wanders in and out of the trees seemingly unaffected by their presence. She stops often to sniff here and there and then quickly catches up, never losing sight of us.

After a time, I say to Papa, "Inside you were telling me you joined the militia and I was wondering if that's when you started gymnastics."

"Ah, you know about my athletic prowess!" Papa sucks his stomach in, sticks his chest out, pulls his shoulders back and with arms swinging, breaks into a brisk march.

I catch up to him. "Papa, slow down! It's hard to have a conversation at this pace."

"It is," he agrees, as he returns to a more normal walking speed. "And just what were we conversing about?"

"Your athletic prowess—gymnastics. Remember?"

"Oh, yes. Well, I became quite good—especially on the high bar. Near Olympic material, according to one of my coaches." Suddenly he stops walking altogether, puts his arms above his head, and jumps straight up. "The bar was pretty far up, you know. I remember I loved to do giant swings. Round and round and round—then just as you reached the peak of your arc—freeze—and now you are in a handstand at the top of the bar. Oh, what a feeling. When you hit it just right, there was nothing like it—perfect! Of course, sometimes I missed, and then it probably looked pretty clumsy."

"Do you remember falling off?"

"Not specifically any particular fall—but I must have fallen a hundred times or more while training. There was a critical point— everything in bar work relies on timing—and I remember crossovers were very tricky. For an instant you don't have either hand on the bar. If your timing is off, down you go onto the floor. Boom!"

"They didn't have mats back then?"

"Oh, of course, there was some padding and we had lookouts, but they didn't always do their job."

"Spotters, you mean?"

"Yes. Usually a couple of your teammates would stay on both sides of the bar, to help break your fall and keep you guided over the pads. But sometimes they weren't paying attention. If you overshot and hit the floor, boy, that hurt! The hardest thing was getting back up on the bar after a fall."

My father's obvious love of gymnastics makes me think about one of my passions—basketball. At least once a week for the past 15 years, I've played hoops with the same group of guys—and some women too. Since my father's incarceration at Littleton House, I haven't played. I miss it. "So how come when we were kids, you didn't let us play sports?" I ask, realizing I've never brought this up to him before.

"I stopped you from sports?"

"Yes. I remember when we lived in Sudbury, Peter and Carl had to sneak out to play baseball. They even kept their bat and gloves at a friend's house so you wouldn't know about it. They thought if you found them, you'd make them get rid of them."

"Oh well, baseball—I thought that was a game. You call it a sport?"

"It's a game, sure, but most people also consider it a sport. Anyway, what difference does it make?"

"Well, there's so much focus on games in this country. I guess I just wanted you kids to have a more complete experience. Art, music and dance offer more to the soul. Sports are one-dimensional. A competitive thing—always out to get the other guy."

"Does 'it is what you say it is' sound familiar? The friends I play basketball with are very supportive of each other no matter which team they are on. And there's a whole social side to the experience. I play with kids, men and women of all ages and different backgrounds. We've got college students from India, a Korean guy, a Syrian dad and his son—black, white, yellow—we've got it all. A lot of cultural exchange goes on during our games and especially during breaks. Plenty of times we don't even keep score."

"Okay, okay, so you've managed to hoist me up by my own petard. I'll make a mental note of this. Being the good general semanticist that I am, it won't happen again."

"See that it doesn't."

"Are you still playing basketball?"

"Yep. Once a week—sometimes more, although I haven't been lately."

"Well, as long as you enjoy it."

"I do, and it keeps me in shape. But you know I also enjoy music and art and dance, although I can't dance to save myself. Still, I don't see why sport and art are mutually exclusive. My best friend Glenn Foden, who you've met, is an artist and a cartoonist. He's the one that illustrated that first attempt of mine at writing a book. I met him on a basketball court. So if it weren't for basketball we'd probably never have known each other."

"Glenn? I think I remember him—a big guy. Didn't he work for you?"

"That's right. Very good, Papa. He did work for me for a short time—but that was before his cartooning career took off."

"He's making a living at it?"

"Yep—no longer needs a second job." Another artist with a second job comes to my mind, so I add, "I'll venture to guess you don't know that there is a famous basketball player, Tommy Heinsohn, who's also a very accomplished painter—and I don't mean house painter."

"What does this Heinsohn guy paint?"

"Landscapes, portraits, all kinds of things. I've seen some of his work and I find it exceptional. He wasn't too shabby as a professional player either."

"Interesting," Papa says and then he surprises me by asking, "So what became of your writing—what did you call it again?"

"*Staying Stoned.* Nothing really. I pitched it in California actually, but I got turned down. A copy is in a box somewhere but I haven't looked at it in ten years or more. I think Glenn's drawings were much better than my writing at the time."

"And it was about drugs?"

"Yes."

"I remember your going away that winter to write—up in the mountains somewhere I think. But I never understood—you and drugs? I thought you were too smart for that stuff."

"Addiction has nothing to do with intelligence, Papa. In some ways being smart only makes it worse. Mother is the smartest woman I've ever known and yet she continues to drink herself to death. We clever ones feel like we are above it all. And I didn't go live by myself in a cabin in the woods for three months just to write. I went to stop using. It worked too—I haven't dropped acid since I was 24."

"'Dropped acid.' You sound like a hippie."

"Papa, I was a hippie!"

We come to the end of the drive where it meets Foster Street. "Want to turn around now?"

"I don't want to, but I suppose we must. Wouldn't want to get you in trouble."

I'm assuming he's referring to our promise to stay on the property. I am amazed by this, by his remembering Glenn and by his being able to return to places in our conversation that I felt would surely be lost for him. It exceeds his usual two- or three-minute short-term memory capabilities. If it's not just a fluke and he can build on this, then his evaluation should go well. I must remain guarded in my hopes, for my own protection, but I am pleased in this moment. No evidence of Sundowning this evening.

On our way back up the driveway, I ask, "How come when we moved to Chelmsford, you let us build that basketball court in the side yard? What made you change your mind about letting us play sports?"

"I did?"

"Yes. Carl, Peter and a friend of theirs built that concrete court. They dug it, mixed the cement and poured it all by hand. They even built the pole and backboard. The rim I think you bought for us. I remember watching them for weeks and hoping they'd hurry up and finish before you changed your mind again and we'd never have a place to play."

My father looks puzzled. He doesn't respond.

"You remember your patio, don't you?"

"Ah, yes, my patio."

"That patio was at first our basketball court." After we grew up and moved out, our father took the pole down and repurposed the 15x25-foot surface for an outdoors entertainment area. He built a large, round wooden table (almost eight feet in diameter), drilled a hole in the middle and stuck a sun umbrella there. In good weather this is where he held "Korzybski Court." Inviting friends, neighbors and business associates to his round table, he'd feed them—and while they chewed, he stuffed their ears with general semantics and expounded about the "five priesthoods."

"Tell me, is my patio still there?" Papa asks. I hear sadness return to his voice.

"It's still there, Papa," I answer him without further explanation. We are almost back to the building now. Before going inside, I try once more to get my question answered. "So what changed your mind about letting us play sports?"

"I wanted my patio!" He jokes. I laugh. He goes on more thoughtfully by saying, "I'm not sure. Maybe I felt you kids needed a distraction—something to keep you off the streets—close to home and out of trouble."

When we get back to Papa's room his dinner tray is on top of his dresser. It looks like a tuna sandwich with potato chips and carrot sticks on the side. No reheating necessary. Before helping him get settled in, I give him my magic marker and let him cross off today's date. "There you go, Papa. Only nine more days to your evaluation."

CHAPTER TWENTY-THREE

Dressing Up Papa's Brain

On the way to Littleton House, Eleanor and I listen to the news on the radio. We learn that actor James Coburn is to marry today. He is 65. His bride is 28 years younger. I comment to Eleanor, "I wonder if she has his power of attorney."

During the past nine days, I've visited Papa almost every day. I think I may have missed one. Mostly our time together has been pleasant. But sometimes I've found him sitting in the hallway among the bodies. And it seems as though he's been worn down, lost some of his fight. I worry that Donna's prediction of him getting used to being at Littleton House might be coming true.

Papa is in the lunchroom when we arrive. The plastic chairs and folding tables keep reminding me of a high school cafeteria. All around him, other residents pick at their food. My father's plate is empty.

"How was your lunch, Papa?" I ask, walking close to his chair.

"Well, look who's here!" My dad perks up. "Richard, my boy. How are you?"

I bend down and kiss him on the neck. "I'm fine, Papa."

Eleanor is beside me now. "Hello, Manny," she greets him.

"Oh, Eleanor. How are you, my darling?" He extends his hand in the direction of her voice.

Eleanor takes Papa's hand, then leans in to kiss him. He lets out a little squeal of delight. Then Eleanor asks, "How was lunch? It must have been good—I see you cleaned your plate."

"I couldn't tell you a thing about it!" Papa exclaims, then laughs. "Are you hungry? I could ask them to rustle you up something."

"No, it's okay, Richard, and I have already eaten."

We ask Papa if he's finished. He takes a last sip of coffee, gets up slowly and we all leave the dining room.

In the corridor on the way to his room, he asks, "So what brings you two here?"

"Don't you know what today is?" I ask.

"I have no idea!"

"It's 'E' day," I tell him. "Remember?" He looks puzzled. I go on, "Eleanor and I are taking you into Boston."

"Boston—sounds exciting. And what will we do there?"

Last night Papa and I crossed off the remaining day on his calendar. Last night he understood today would be his long-awaited evaluation day. He was a little nervous about it, but very much aware. Right now it is as if last night never happened. I wonder whether anything Eleanor or I said during the past ten days has stuck.

Undaunted, Eleanor picks up where I left off. "Manny, this afternoon you will get to tell your side of the story to a team of specialists in geriatric issues."

"Geriatric—sounds aged. Am I so old that I need this?"

I ask, "When were you born?"

"'05," he responds instantly.

"And it's '93 now, Papa. You do the math."

My father calculates aloud, but in German, then answers in

English, "88! No, impossible! You're saying I'm 88? No, don't tell me that!"

"It's true."

"But I don't feel 88." Papa dances the first few steps of a little jig he knows. His movements are familiar to us. Eleanor offers him her hand and the jig turns in to a waltz.

Watching them dance together makes me smile, as I'm reminded of an early attraction—her grace. Eleanor and Papa waltz down the hallway together with seemingly effortless ease. And they provide the entire musical accompaniment needed. "Da, da, da, da—dum—bump bump—bump bump," they sing together their own special interpretation of the *Blue Danube* waltz.

Both Eleanor and Papa have strong backgrounds in dance. For a time, he taught at Arthur Murry's' studios in New York. He and my mother participated in many ballroom dancing competitions.

Eleanor was taught Russian folk dancing at the age of four. As she got older she studied: ballet, jazz, ballroom, folkloric and international folk dancing. By 14, Eleanor was taking lessons six days a week and in her spare time, helping to teach dance to younger students. During summers off from college she worked as a camp counselor with dance as her specialty.

I'm feeling a little awkward now trying to keep up with them without getting in their way as they use the entire width of the corridor for their dance floor. But they know where they are in space. From watching them, you wouldn't suspect he was blind and she was born without a fully formed hip socket.

If it's true that opposites attract, then Eleanor and I have at least one area of extreme magnetism. Put me on a dance floor and more than one person's feet are sure to pay the price.

We reach my dad's room and they finish up with bows and curtsies. I feel compelled to clap. "Thank you for the dance, sir,"

Eleanor says in an overly formal manner. Then she adds, "You've still got it, Manny!"

"Well, with such a capable partner you make my job easy. Thank you, Madam." Papa bows one more time and nodding in my direction asks, "Doesn't he dance with you?"

"No, Papa. I stumble—move forward when I should go back, step right instead of left, and generally clobber all the toes I can find. It's something like the way I play basketball," I tell him. "You should see it—pure poetry in motion."

"He's not that bad," Eleanor reassures him.

Once we are inside Papa's room he plops himself down on his bed, then sits up again with a frown on his face. "Isn't that funny," he starts, and after a long pause, continues, "I thought all my sons would be dancers, artists and musicians—and now it seems I'll never see that. None of them show any interest."

"It's not lack of interest, Papa. It's lack of talent. I'd love to be a Mikhail Baryshnikov—I'd like to be a Michael Jordon too, but it's just not in the cards."

"Michael who?" he asks.

"Michael Jordan! Perhaps the world's greatest basketball player?" I question. I can't believe he's never even heard of him. I feel myself reacting to him, instead of acknowledging him. *This isn't good for either of us.*

Predictably he replies, "Well, if you say so. I suppose you should know. I don't really follow such things."

Eleanor comes over and whispers in my ear, "Look at him. We can't take him looking like that." I nod in agreement and she says, "I'll see what I can find."

I sit on the bed next to Papa and assess his outfit, *Vintage Dementia Style.* Mint green pants, worn at the knees. His fly is stuck at half-mast—permanently broken there. The orange shirt looks like it had been used as a table cloth at a three-year-old's birthday party—stains too numerous to count. The color combinations are expressly Manny, but the disheveled condition of his clothes is nothing like him. In fact, when I lived at home with my parents he often wore his business suit on the weekends if he wasn't working in the shop. I remember one of my friends thought we had a butler when my father answered the door in suit and tie on a Saturday, and said, "Ebner at your service. Whom should I say is calling?"

Papa hears Eleanor rummaging through his closet and asks, "What is she doing in there?"

"She's trying to find something presentable for you to wear to the evaluation."

He leans forward and surveys for himself. "I don't look presentable?"

"Let's just say I've seen you looking better."

Eleanor catches my attention. "What about this?" she asks, holding up a pair of gray dress pants in one hand and a pink button-down shirt in the other.

"Looks fine."

"There isn't that much to choose from. He needs some new clothes!"

"One thing at a time. How do you like what Eleanor has picked out for you, Papa?"

He turns. "I can't really see it from here." I get up and out of the way. "I suppose it's fine. I don't know what's wrong with what I've got on. Are we going someplace fancy?"

"Eleanor and I are taking you to Boston to the Deaconess hospital for your evaluation. Ever since Donna put you here, in Littleton House, you've been asking for your day in court. Well, this is the day. Only instead of appearing before a judge, you'll be talking to a doctor, a specialist in memory impairment.

"Oh God! There's no hope for me."

"You'll do fine, Papa."

"You really think so?"

"Yes. I know it. Eleanor and I will get you dressed up like the dapper dude you are. Then we will drive to Boston. She took the day off just to help us and she's letting us use her car. So I'll still owe you a train ride."

"Will Donna be there?"

"I'm not sure, probably, although we haven't talked about it. Does it matter?"

"I guess not. It's just—when I see her all I want to do is hug her and have her take me home."

Before I can come up with an answer, for after all, what possible answer is there, Eleanor deflects the situation by asking, "Manny, do you want me to leave the room while Richard helps you dress?"

"No, that won't be necessary. I have nothing to hide from you, darling." He gets up, unhooks his belt and pushes his pants to the floor. "Is my underwear okay?" he asks looking down. "If I'm going to see a doctor I think I should have clean underwear."

"I'll find you some," Eleanor offers. She picks up his pants and removes the belt.

I need to find a way to get the cobwebs out of Papa's brain if he is to have a chance at a good evaluation. Apparently dancing wasn't enough to stimulate him. I decide to try to get him to lecture me about something, have him play one of his "tapes," as my mother disparagingly called them.

Underpants go down and underpants go up, unabashed. Papa starts putting on the rest of the clothes Eleanor has laid out for him. While he starts dressing, I begin by asking, "Tell me about the, 'priesthoods' again, how many are there and what did you call them?"

"Five," Papa responds quickly. "But you should already know that if you've paid attention to my dissertations on the subject," he chastises me.

"Humor me, Papa. I'm not as smart as you. I need to hear something a few times before I get it. Remember, I nail boards together for a living. I haven't spent the time you have on intellectual pursuits."

"All right. I call out five priesthoods. The first is obvious, religious leaders and the other four are: politicians, lawyers, doctors and bankers. These groups use specialized vocabularies to cut us up in pieces, to treat as parts and not as wholes," he begins. I notice him having trouble with the t-shirt so I step in to help. With arms and hands free now, he powers up. "They give us no language for talking about our functioning or history, and derive an income from making decisions that should be the province of the individual. They operate from mostly theatrical skills."

I interrupt. "So why aren't actors part of the priesthoods?"

"Intent, my boy. The actor entertains and if the playwright has done his job we are perhaps provoked to learn and question. But we are always free to participate or not. If we go to a production, once the play is over it has no hold on us. It doesn't continue to affect our existence unless we choose to let it. With the priesthoods we have no free will."

"Okay, I think I sort of understand how some of them fit in, but why bankers?"

"Oh, bankers—now they're a sorry lot. They produce nothing, yet control everything."

I help steady Papa while he finds the leg openings to his pants. "How so?"

"Seed money, or so it's called. No enterprise gets started without it."

"And you think that's bad?"

"It's not a question of good or bad. It just isn't true capitalism; at least as I'd define it. You see, in an agrarian society one could only withhold seed for so long—then it rotted and one had no more market. Money, on the other hand, can be withheld indefinitely, so there is no such thing as non-agricultural capitalism—no free market."

Eleanor comes back with Papa's belt and helps him get it started. I'm not sure I get even half of what he's talking about. But it does sound lucid and better than always asking, "Where am I?" Since I've noticed that provocation seems to stimulate my father, I decide to provoke some more. "Sounds like you are a communist."

Papa stops fastening his belt buckle and glares at me. "Now I thought I taught you better than that! I'm not a communist—I'm a humanist and an existentialist!"

"I'm not so sure—you don't believe in capital investment and you don't believe in any form of a god—sounds pretty communistic to me."

"Oh, I see you're joking with me now."

"No, Papa, I'm serious. All you commies are atheists and all you atheists are commies. That's what I think."

He turns to Eleanor, "Listen to him."

"He's your son," she says while buttoning his shirt for him.

"That doesn't sound like any son of mine."

"Papa, finish buckling your belt. We need to leave soon. And yes, I was kidding—or rather playing devil's advocate—testing your reaction. Something I learned from you, by the way."

"No. I did that? No, never."

"Yes, you did and you know it too—so don't give me that innocent routine." Here, put this on. I hand him the tie Eleanor picked out.

188

"A tie. Do I really need this?"

"We want you looking sharp, Manny," Eleanor stresses. She goes back to the closet and returns with a brown corduroy sport coat. "This is the best I can find for a jacket. I'm telling you he really needs clothes!"

"I heard you the first time. Can we just get through today!" I snap back at her. Just as quickly I grab her hand and pull her close for a hug. "I'm sorry—kind of stressed out right now."

"Understandable."

"And thank you, really. I might not ever have been here if it wasn't for you." We separate and I start back in on my father. "Put your tie on!"

Papa pleads to Eleanor again, "You hear the way he talks to his father—how he bosses me around?"

"Manny, he's teasing you. And I think you love it too."

Papa smiles as he begins tying his tie. "Yes I suppose I do." He continues with the tying. His motions are efficient. The results are flawless.

"And another thing, this atheism stuff, you still believe that way?"

He looks surprised. "But of course!" he declares. "No rational thinking person could consider a god—outside himself."

"So now Manny Ebner is also a god."

"Hey, what are you saying to me? You haven't found Christ, have you?"

"Not exactly. But don't you ever feel a sense of spiritualism? I do. Here, put your jacket on."

He takes the coat from me, puts his arm in a sleeve and Eleanor helps him with the other. "What—you believe in ghosts?"

"No, not necessarily ghosts—I try not to put a label on it. It's just an underlying feeling that there's something more than what comes in through our senses. A sixth sense maybe—or maybe even more senses. Perhaps we have a whole host of receptors we are unaware of and just don't know how to use yet."

Eleanor stands in front of Papa now, working on fixing his collar, but he keeps moving side-to-side trying to establish a sight line to me. "Now you're just speculating—there's no scientific proof for what you're suggesting."

"I know that. But does everything we experience need proof to be relevant?"

"It does if you want Ebner to consider it!"

"Doesn't just the fact that so many people believe in some form of god—doesn't that alone make God significant?"

"Not to me. The world is full of foolish people. There are probably those who still believe the world is flat."

"In a way that demonstrates my point. Before anyone could prove the world was round, some people considered it possible. They didn't wait for proof before setting sail."

Eleanor breaks in, "Manny, do you have a hair brush?"

Dismissively he responds, "Yes, maybe—oh, I don't know. In the bathroom perhaps." Eleanor leaves to check for a brush. Papa can hardly contain himself as he comes back with, "You're confusing scientific hypothesis with daydreaming. By applying Newtonian physics, I can be assured the earth is a sphere. By knowing certain properties of the physical world around me, and applying those properties, I needn't try to step off the planet to know it's round."

Eleanor comes back. "All I could find is this comb. You really should have a brush, Manny."

"At my age I'm just glad to have hair."

"And you have a beautiful full head of hair," Eleanor tells him as she begins to comb it up and over.

"Okay, Papa, I'll give you that. But what if there are properties we don't know about yet? Things we haven't developed the scientific instruments to detect or measure. It wasn't that long ago when the existence of atoms was only a theory. Now physicists are talking about quirks or quarks or some damn thing like that. And black holes—maybe god exists in a black hole somewhere."

"Well, now you are back to fantasizing. If I want to I can make anything up to believe in. I can tell you I've been seeing visions—that doesn't make them real."

"So how long have you been having these hallucinations and what do they look like?"

"Always the kidder," Papa says. There is a trace of annoyance in his voice.

"I wonder where he got that from, Manny." Eleanor moves around to work on the back of his hair.

"I'm sorry, Papa. But since you brought it up, how do you explain people having visions?"

"I call them psychotic episodes!" he says with authority. "If I told you I saw a pink elephant in my room last night you'd have me locked up ..."

"Someone already did that," falls out of my mouth before I realize how tactless my joke is.

"Very funny," my father responds, and seemingly without indignation continues, "but if I say I saw the Virgin Mary in my room last night, people would call it a miracle. My room would become a holy shrine and millions would want to touch me."

"Now that's the best idea you've had in a long time, Manny," Eleanor says. She puts down the comb and begins to tickle him mercilessly.

Papa wiggles, giggles and screeches like a child. "Hey, you'll mess up my tie!"

"Actually I think we should ditch the tie. We don't want you better dressed than us," I suggest. "Shoes, though, and socks could be helpful."

"I know right where they are." Eleanor heads to the closet again.

I follow her and say quietly, "Thank you for all this. I'm getting off easy thanks to you."

"You're doing what you need to and it seems to be working. Your dad is much more alert than when we got here."

"Thanks, but I'm worried he'll fall asleep in the car and become fuzzy again. Would you mind driving us so I could keep him talking?"

"Of course not."

My dad's comment about pink elephants makes me think of the Groucho Marx two-liner, "One morning I shot an elephant in my pajamas. How he got in my pajamas, I don't know." I remember Papa liked the Marx Brothers movies and in particular Groucho himself. I think he used to listen to him on the radio and later watched his television show *You Bet Your Life.* Like Groucho, Papa ascribed to the principle that any club that would have him as a member was a club he wouldn't want to join, and his only exception to that principle was the Society for General Semantics. I wonder what Groucho would have thought about that club. Too stuffy and pretentious, I imagine.

"Shoes." Eleanor picks up a pair of brown, lace shoes. Moving to the dresser she calls out, "Socks—all set!" She walks to Manny. "Here you go, the finishing touch. Let me see those feet."

After helping him put on his socks, Papa notices the shoes she's picked out for him. "Oh, those things. They hurt my toes," he complains. "I'm not wearing them."

I offer a compromise. "How 'bout you just put them on when we get to the hospital?" They're going to have you take them off for your physical anyway. I doubt they'll be on long enough to kill your toes. You can wear your sneakers to the car." He accepts, puts his sneakers on and we leave the room.

As I sign Papa out I say, "I'm not sure when we will have him back. His appointment is at three and I don't know how long it will last. We'll probably take him out to dinner afterwards, so it's safe to say he won't need a tray tonight."

"Excellent! We're having supper out. So what are we waiting for? Let's get going, man!"

CHAPTER TWENTY-FOUR

Bumming A Ride

At the car, I get in the back seat with Papa. By his expression I can tell he finds this strange, but nothing is said. I help him with the seatbelt. Eleanor starts the engine. "How should I go?" she asks.

"I think 495 to Route 2 would be best."

At Foster Street, Eleanor questions again, "Left or right?"

"Left. There's no ramp from Foster. We have to go back through the center."

Soon we are on I-495 going south and two exits later onto Route 2 headed for Boston. Before the motion of the car causes Papa to drift off to sleep, as he wants to do from time to time, I strike up another conversation.

"Now, Papa, I'm still a little confused about these priesthoods of yours. Lawyers I get, especially considering our dealings with a particular one of late. Politicians seem to mostly be—or start out as lawyers before becoming lawmakers, so I understand them being on your list. But considering we are going to see doctors today, it might be helpful to know why you put them in the same category with the others."

"That's simple. Their mandate is to make me well and yet they only profit from my being ill. The incentives are backwards."

"You really think doctors want you to be sick?" What about the Hippocratic Oath?"

Papa smiles broadly as if he's already enjoying his next answer. "I call it the Hypocritical Oath."

"Nice word play, Papa. But please explain?"

"If I have no insurance and no money doctors won't see me, or if they do, I won't get the same level of care. How is this doing no harm? How does this treat all human life as having equal value? If I'm rich I may survive, but if I'm poor I'm much more likely to die."

"You might be better off not sharing that with today's doctors," Eleanor suggests.

"You should know Manny Ebner is a pragmatist above all else. I'm not going to let my philosophy interfere with my immediate needs. That is best left to the religious. They ..." Suddenly Papa gets drowned out by a string of motorcycles passing at a high rate of speed. "What's all that noise?" he asks, not being able to see out past my head.

"Bikers! A whole bunch of them on the left." More of them overtake us now on the other side. "And on the right, Papa. Look out your window!"

He turns himself and must catch a fleeting glimpse with his peripheral vision. "Wow! Where are they going in such a hurry?"

The ones on the right cross over in front of us and speed ahead to join the rest of the group. It gets quieter. I ask, "You used to ride didn't you, Papa?"

"Motorcycles—yes indeed! A Harley-Davidson! Seventy-five-cubic-inch—it was a big bike!"

Eleanor glances up at the rear view. "What color was it, Manny?"

"At that time there wasn't much of a choice—green, I think. Kind of a drab olive green—yes that's it—green like army vehicles. Harleys were green and Indians were red—you could always tell them apart, even from a distance."

While Eleanor wants to know about colors, I want the important stuff, so I ask, "Did you ride with a gang?"

"A gang?"

"Yah, a club. You know—like The Hells Angels. A motorcycle gang. Did you ride with the Angels? Did you, Papa?"

"Hell, no! I don't think they even existed when I rode. I don't remember ever seeing any of them. And even if they had—I wouldn't have joined. I've never been much of a joiner."

"So you rode alone?"

"No—well, sometimes, sure—but I had a buddy—Nelson Costello. He was a big man too—six-three and 240 punds or so I think—with a booming voice. What a figure he was on his Harley!"

I ask, "Where did you ride?"

Before he can speak, Eleanor asks, "Were you living in New York?"

He answers her first, "Yes, upstate New York. I hadn't moved to the city yet."

"And where did you go on your bikes?" I try again. "I mean, did you have a job—or were you just bumming around like *Easy Rider* or something?"

"Easy what?"

"It's a movie called *Easy Rider*. These two guys just take off on motorcycles to see the country—no cares—no responsibilities."

"No, no! I had a job and plenty of responsibilities. My family back in Austria was struggling and they depended on me sending them money. I wasn't a bum!"

Shame on me. I should know better than to make references to pop culture. My father kept himself insulated from all that. I can't remember ever going to a movie with him. I can't remember my parents going out to the movies either. Of course he could have already seen all the good ones by the time I came along. Or it might just be a generational thing, Rat Pack vs. Brat Pack. Whatever, now I've insulted him with my misinterpreted insinuation. *Best not to dwell on it.* "I said, 'bumming around,' Papa, not being a bum. So where did you work?"

"I worked for Nelson."

"Your motorcycle buddy was your boss?"

"That's right. He owned an electrical contracting business and I was his best electrician."

"A licensed electrician?"

"Of course! Well, not at first. You had to work as an apprentice for a time. So I was one of Nelson's helpers during the day and at night I went to school."

"When did you find time to ride, Manny?"

"On weekends. Nelson and I hit it off very quickly. He's the one who convinced me to buy my first motorcycle—I think he even loaned me some money to get it."

"How'd you meet?" Eleanor asks.

"Gee—I'm not sure. Let me think. Must have been at Ward Leonard."

"That was an electrical supply house where Papa worked," I add, just to fill in for Eleanor.

"Oh, you know of my exploits there?"

"Yes, Papa. You told me about that last week. It's on tape and it will be in our book too."

"How's the book coming?"

"Fine. I'll read some more to you over the weekend. But right now finish telling us about Nelson and your motorcycle conquests."

I'm hoping the third time will be a charm. "Where did you ride together?"

He starts, "We came up with this plan to go somewhere different every weekend," but says nothing else.

"Details, Papa! How did you decide where to go? What were the criteria?"

"All right, all right. We had this map—an atlas really—and we'd throw a dart at it, wherever it stuck—that's where we went. The only rule was that it couldn't be any place either of us had been before. I remember one time we rode to Norfolk, Virginia. God, it must have been four-hundred-miles each way!"

Eleanor keeps the conversation going and gives me a little break. "Did you stay over someplace?"

"Nope. I think we never rode any further than we could get back in the same day."

"How old were you then, Manny?"

"I must have been in my early 20s. Twenty-three, or -four, perhaps."

"So you had a young man's energy. Now that would have been just before the Great Depression."

"I suppose."

"When it hit, how did you fair? Did you lose your job?"

"No. I was very lucky, luckier than many people. At the worst of it, it was only Nelson and me, but he kept me on and he always seemed to be able to find work for us."

"You were never out of work?"

"Well, there may have been gaps between jobs—a week or two—never so long that I couldn't manage things."

"Pretty amazing, Manny. I've heard such awful stories about those times. Sounds like you did just fine."

"Not fine really. I got by better than others. It was still tough though. People were so sad. Many of them packed up and left the city to try and find work who knows where. There was a feeling of hopelessness on the streets that was palpable." Papa sounds and looks sad now himself.

Eleanor picks up on this and changes the subject. "Did you have a girlfriend at the time?"

"Oh, too many to mention!" Papa declares. "I was quite the catch. I had a job, a little bit of money—and—I was a gentleman. Women liked that back then."

"I think they still do, Papa."

We crest the hill in Arlington and start the long decent toward Cambridge. "There's Boston." Eleanor calls out. "Manny, can you see it? All the buildings are so clear today."

"I'm sorry my dear, I can barely see you. But I trust you're right. What road are we on?"

"Route 2."

"I always loved that approach to the city when I used to drive. If I close my eyes I can still see it." He closes his eyes for a second or two and after opening them again says, "Unfortunately with them open it's just a blur."

"Papa, I know, it is what you say it is, but I'm still glad we have a nice warm sunny day to be in Boston."

"Yes, yes—I am too. Will we be there soon? I have to make wee-wee."

"It's about ten or 15 minutes away depending on traffic. I can pull off somewhere sooner though if need be. Just tell me if you want to stop."

"No, it's all right, I think I can last that long."

We continue past Alewife station in Cambridge and eventually cross over the Charles River onto Storrow Drive. Deaconess Hospital is in the Longwood area of Boston and our route takes us very near Fenway Park. Fortunately for us the baseball season is over, for the Red Sox's at least, and traffic is light.

Eleanor drops my father and me at the door. She starts to pull away toward the garage, then stops abruptly and lowers the passenger side window. "Manny's shoes!" She calls out to me.

CHAPTER TWENTY-FIVE

What to Tell?

Before going upstairs for Papa's appointment, we find a place to make wee-wee and swap out his sneakers for the dress shoes I've been carrying. By the time we get to the office, Eleanor has already parked the car and is there waiting for us. We're late. Just a little, yet late. *Not a good way to begin.*

From an inner office, Donna's high-pitched voice spills out the open door and advances toward us as we make our way down the short hall. *Edith Bunker is here.* "Well, I don't know what's keeping them," I hear her say.

"Is that my Donna?" Papa asks, hearing her voice also, but hearing it very differently than I do. "Sounds like my Donna."

Despite all that has happened to him, I know my father still loves her. This is the hardest thing for me to reconcile and accept. However, accept I must if I am to really help him.

We step through the doorway, single file, me first and Papa sandwiched between us. "Oh, here they are!" Donna shouts out cheerfully, to the others assembled in the room.

It is a fairly small office, 10x12 at best. A woman sits at a table next to Donna. Another woman stands near a door at the back of the office. The woman standing introduces herself and her associate, listens to our introductions, and then says, "If you'll excuse me for just a moment, I'll let the doctor know you're here."

Donna gets up. She gives Manny a kiss. His lips don't move. When she backs off, he looks her up and down. Then Papa says, "So you think I'm crazy—well, I guess now we'll find out. The jig is up, baby!"

I'm somewhat surprised that he doesn't realize his last comment has racist overtones. For Papa, I know he means the dance is over and that Donna will be found out. But it is his physical reaction that surprises me most. I expected him to melt at Donna's touch.

Apparently it catches Donna off guard as well. "Oh, Manny. I never said you were crazy. Ha, ha, ha. You're so funny, Manny." Donna tries to make light of the situation, but it's obvious she is nervous now, and more than a little embarrassed. She turns, and aloud, but to no one in particular she says, "He's always joking, you know." None of us in the room respond in any manner. Donna sits back down.

The door at the rear of the room opens and Dr. Delfs enters. After greeting everyone, he explains his procedure. My father is to go with the doctor for a general physical exam, some blood work and some questioning. Donna, Eleanor, and I will, in turn, be interviewed separately by the two women. I choose to be last. The room empties out and I'm left alone with my thoughts.

What to leave out and what to leave in? Do I start back a year ago? Do I mention Bob Green and the mysterious Jeff? Should I talk about the bizzaro wedding when Manny didn't even realize he was getting married and fell asleep at his own reception? Would anyone believe even half of it? I'm not sure I do and I was there. And more importantly, if believed, would it help my father's cause? Probably not, for on the contrary, it likely demonstrates he is demented and belongs in Littleton House.

I'm worried about Papa being alone with yet another doctor analyzing him, making assumptions based on limited exposure and then judging him. I want to play some of our recordings for the doctor. I'd like him to read our book. And yet I know none of this can happen.

I don't care what Donna tells them, but part of me would like to be a fly on the wall just the same. Hearing her try to explain her actions to impartial professionals for a change might be interesting.

Eleanor I have no worries about. She is extremely articulate and gets Manny, always has.

I need to focus. My thoughts are too scattered. Must find an approach that makes sense out of the senseless.

Time passes. The back door opens again. I get up. "Joan Yesner," the woman entering reminds me while extending her hand. "I'm the social worker."

"Yes, I remember speaking with you on the phone—what—half a month ago now, when I was first trying to get this appointment. You were so kind."

"Well, thank you. I try. I'm sorry it took so long and I'm doubly sorry you had to wait in here alone, but staffing being what it is these days. Please, sit down."

I sit. Joan takes a seat two chairs away. She places a pad on the table in front of her and opens a file folder. "Give me a second." She skims the file. "I thought I remembered you had brothers, Peter and Carl. Have I got that right?"

"That's them."

"And will they be joining us?"

"Not today anyway. Peter was planning to come but when I spoke with him last night he sounded pretty bad—the flu."

"Yah, the seasons already started. That's part of why we are short staffed. And Carl?"

"I'm afraid not. He's at another hospital right now attending to his son."

"Oh, I'm sorry to hear that. Hope it's not serious."

I thank her for her concern, but don't add any details. My nephew's situation and reasons for hospitalization are too personal to be shared. *I'm feeling defensive.* Off to a bad start, first being late and now revealing I'm the only blood relative who will be attending today.

After answering what seem to be standard informational questions for the record, Joan turns me loose to give her my observations about my dad. I try to keep it focused on the differences I see between his reasoning abilities and his memory problems. I do my best not to make Donna out to be a horrible person and mostly don't mention her unless asked. Joan and I spend about 45 minutes in private together. When we are finished, I'm told she needs to leave and consult with the rest of her staff, but we will all reconvene back in this office in about 25 minutes.

Once everyone is gathered up and back at the table, Dr. Delfs goes over the results of Papa's physical. "Well, Mr. Ebner," he addresses my father directly while looking right at him, "I only hope I'm in as good physical shape as you are when I'm 88."

I'm guessing the doctor is in his early 50s. I look at my father and try to gauge his reaction. *Locked in to every word.*

The doctor goes on, "Your blood pressure is excellent—heart sounds good—lungs are clear—I see no reason why you won't be around with us for a good long time to come."

"That's good news—so what about the bad news?" Papa asks, suspiciously.

"Are you expecting bad news?" Dr. Delfs questions.

Papa comes back and answers with a question of his own, "Well, isn't that how people in your profession do it—tell somebody what they want to hear and then clobber them with the truth?"

"Everything I've told you is the truth. Physically you're a very healthy man. You do have a memory impairment ..."

"I do?" my father interrupts.

"Yes you have. And unfortunately because of your vision problem it's difficult to assess how extensive your memory loss is. This is why I'm recommending a complete neuropsychological examination with a specialist in the field. I have someone very good in mind." Dr. Delfs turns to Ms. Yesner. "Joan, will you please give the Ebners a referral for Dr. Weinstein before they leave."

On our way out I make sure I'm the one with the referral. I'm happy about the results of Papa's physical, but I never really expected anything less. And I suppose I should be glad that Dr. Delfs is being so thorough. Somehow though, waiting for yet another appointment to be scheduled and knowing how that wait will affect my Papa, leaves me worried. I guess I'm just disappointed there is no resolution today.

CHAPTER TWENTY-SIX

What's Her Name?

It's Saturday, October 23, 1993, the day after our first appointment at the Deaconess. I can hear Latino music coming from Papa's room as I approach. It has a nice cheery beat. Inside, Papa is still in bed with a pillow over his head. I don't think he appreciates the tune. For Papa, it's all classical all the time. The only exceptions are for dancing, and then a waltz or tangos are acceptable.

I walk over to the black boom box on Papa's dresser and shut it off. He stirs. Pulling the pillow away from his head he says, "Thank God! That was driving me crazy."

"Good morning, Papa," I greet him.

"Who's that? Is that my sonny boy?"

"Yes, Papa. It is I, your sonny boy."

"Well, gee—I didn't expect you. Or did I? I'm sorry to be in bed, but I couldn't get to sleep with that damn music blaring at me. What time is it anyway?"

"Almost ten."

"PM?"

"No, ten in the morning. But if you didn't like the music why didn't you shut it off or change the station? You don't have to suffocate yourself with a pillow."

"I didn't even know where it was coming from," Papa tells me.

"There's nothing wrong with your hearing, Papa," I remind him. "You should be able to find your radio with your ears. Look, it's right over there on top of your dresser," I direct.

"Where? On top of that big white thing?"

"Yes, the black box on top of the white dresser with the red, white and blue handles."

"That's not my dresser."

"Yes it is."

"Nope. Never built such a thing—never had such a thing," he insists.

He's partially right. This particular dresser is not homemade, like much of the furniture in Papa's house. "Peter and I got it for you. The one that was here was too small. Trust me, it's yours. Your clothes are in it."

"Well, if you say so. But I don't recognize it."

"Just remember red, white and blue handles. We chose them especially for you, Papa."

"You think I'm such a patriot?"

"Certainly not. We'd never accuse you of such a thing. When Peter bought your new dresser, it came knocked down in a box. As I helped him assemble it, we found three bags of drawer pulls— enough of each color for all the drawers. We knew how much you always liked bright contrasting colors, so we decided to mix all three together—sort of a tribute to those Mondrian cabinets you built."

"Petie bought that for me? And you helped him put it together. Now wasn't that nice of you boys." Papa sits up and stares over toward the dresser. "But I don't see anything, 'Mondrian' about it."

"I know, Papa. The drawer fronts should all be different colors and a black border around each of them would be helpful, but handles were all we had to work with."

"Well, it was still nice of you to think about me."

"Now, Papa, let me show you something." I go over and retrieve his boom box, then set it on his lap. "See these red arrows I pasted onto the dial?"

"Yes, yes. What do they mean?"

"They point to your favorite station, 102.5 WCRB. It's an all-classical station. And I posted a sign on the wall over there. It tells the staff to keep it tuned to the red arrows."

"Well, it's not working. Must be those Puerto Ricans? They're always flitting about in here while I'm trying to sleep."

"Papa! That's kind of a racist comment, don't you think?"

"No, not at all. Just a statement of facts."

"Well, it sounds prejudiced to me."

"Prejudiced, yes. I make no bones about being prejudiced. Everyone is prejudiced about something. I say beware of those who claim not to be! But I'm not a racist. I just don't like their music."

"Your tone sounds demeaning. When you say 'Puerto Ricans' the way you just did, that sounds offensive. It is as though you despise a whole people and not only their music. What was that GS phrase? 'The word is not the thing,' I think it went. Your tone is as important, perhaps even more important, than the words you chose."

"All right! I see your point." Papa seems embarrassed and annoyed at my using general semantics against him. "That's one point for you—10,000 for me. You've still got some catching up to do my boy." He laughs. "So what shall we do with our time together?"

"First you need to get dressed." I put his boom box back on top of the not so Mondrian dresser. "Then I thought I'd take you out

211

for breakfast, since they've stopped serving here."

"Excellent! I'm so hungry I could eat a horse—but I wouldn't want to."

"And after—if you're good—I thought I'd bring you to my house. We can hang out on the porch. Maybe we'll work on your book some. But you have to promise not to sneak away and confront Donna like the last time."

"I did that?"

"Yes, and it was an ugly scene. One minute you were on the porch with me—the phone rang—and when I finished the call, you were gone. You didn't even tell me what you were up to."

"Oh, that was rude of me."

"Worse than that, Papa. Naturally, I figured out where you went—but by the time I got to your house, you were right in Donna's face yelling at her. That's not helpful to your situation."

"I suppose you're right. I promise to be a good little boy," Papa tells me, with his now famous impish smile on his face.

I'm not sure he'll keep his promise, or even remember he made it. But I'm willing to risk it. "Also, if you are a 'good little boy', Eleanor said she'd like to cook supper for you tonight."

"Ah, Eleanor, the dancer! I haven't seen Eleanor in ages. How is Eleanor?"

"She's fine, Papa. It hasn't really been ages; you saw her yesterday."

"Oh, that's right, silly of me to forget. So you two are still together then?"

"Yes of course."

"How long now?"

"About 20 years." *As long you and Donna, why?*

"Twenty years! My, that's something!" Papa is up now. He puts on the pants I just brought him from his closet. "You know I was always curious about your relationship with Eleanor."

"Here's your belt. How so?"

"Well, I wondered what you were looking for—I mean in choosing an older woman. Eleanor is quite a bit older isn't she?"

"Seventeen years, yes. Your shirt, Papa." I help him find the sleeves. "So what are you getting at?"

"I don't know, I guess I wondered if you were looking for motherly love, or something?"

"And I suppose you were looking for daughterly love with Donna. You do remember she is almost 30 years younger than you, don't you?"

"Yes, yes, of course! But it's different for a man."

"Great, Papa! Now you're a sexist and a racist. Just kidding. Put your sneakers on and we can go."

He sits on the bed and starts to do as I ask but has trouble with the laces. They're all in knots. I kneel down to help him. As I work on the untangling, I feel his hand on my shoulder.

"I'm sorry if I offended you about Eleanor," he says.

This catches me off guard, both the touch and the apology. "I'm not offended, Papa. More disappointed, I think," I answer him without looking up.

"Disappointed with me, or Eleanor?" he asks.

"With you, obviously." Now I give him full eye contact. "Everything is fine between Eleanor and me. We love each other in every sense of the word. But I'm surprised that you could so misread the nature of our relationship. And my disappointment stems from your stereotyping. I thought that was another 'no no' for a good follower of GS."

"It's not that. I just—well, I remember how your mother always insisted you boys call her Judy and not Mother. I didn't know if that screwed you up somehow?"

This last question compels me to return his touch. I stop working on the laces for a moment and wrap both hands around his legs. Looking up I begin, "Papa, thanks for being concerned about me. But you needn't worry that I didn't get my share of mothering as a child. Judy didn't start that stuff until we were all in our teens. By then I'd already gotten all the motherly love I needed. It did seem strange to my friends that I called my mother by her first name; however, it had no traumatic effect on me. Remember, Judy was deeply involved in the women's movement and I think she just wanted to be free from labels."

"Yes, I remember that all right! I suppose that was it."

I start with the laces again, then stop and add, "You know, if anything, fatherly love is what I missed most as a child."

"I tried, kid. Early on I really did. But your mother always accused me of doing a lousy job with your older brothers. With you, she kept us separated. I think she wanted you all for herself. I guess eventually I gave up. I'm sorry."

"It's okay. We're working on it, Papa. Making up for lost time. Funny, but in a strange way, once again I think we have Donna to thank for that."

"Well, I'll tell her you said so, if I ever see her again."

"You saw her yesterday, as well. And she's here at least once a week," I reassure him. "Donna has not completely abandoned you. "Hey, your sneakers are good to go. Let's get out of here."

We walk down the corridor and Papa indicates he needs to use a bathroom. The public restrooms are closer now than going back to his room, so once there I point Papa to the right door. As I stand outside waiting, I see a nurse we've gotten friendly with coming down the hall toward me. She's not wearing her nametag. *Dammit! What's her name? I should know this.*

"Hi, Richard. How's the book coming?" she asks.

I'm taken by surprise. *Did I tell her about it? God, what is her name anyway?* Stalling, I say, "Pretty good I think. I'm taking my Dad out for the day and we'll probably work on it some more. He does seem to enjoy my reading his story to him and he certainly likes talking about himself."

"I'll bet he does," she says. "That's all he ever talks about these days—well, that and your dog of course. Where is she? What's her name? A funny name for a big dog if I'm remembering right."

"Baby," I tell her. "She's home. Waiting for Papa, I'm sure. I came in my truck today and there isn't room for the three of us."

"That's right, Baby, of course. Strange name for a Great Dane. She is a Dane, isn't she?"

This woman is doing much better than I am in the memory department. I nod yes. "Yeah, I suppose it seems odd. Are you a movie buff?"

"Somewhat."

"Older flicks? Carry Grant, Katherine Hepburn?"

She thinks for a few moments, then blurts out, "Oh! *Bringing up Baby.* I get it." She smiles. "Wasn't that a big cat, though?"

"A leopard, yes. But sometimes you have to work with what you've got. When we bought her she was already named. Nobody cared for Fergie, although we liked her namesake."

"The Duchess–the redhead?"

"That's right. It just seemed too British or Irish or whatever she is, for a German dog. And besides, we wanted our own name—you know?"

"Certainly, everyone wants to name their own pet."

"Right, and we needed something with the same number of syllables—to help her make the adjustment easily—and so we could remember it I suppose. While we were thinking of what to call her I noticed a TV listing for the movie. I tried Baby out on her and within a week she was responding. The name stuck."

"How long have you had her?"

"Five years. But it doesn't seem that long since Eleanor bought her for me."

"So is she exclusively your dog?"

"I guess you could say that, although my dad might disagree. When I was given Baby, Eleanor was going through some difficult health issues. She actually thought she might die and didn't want me to be alone if she did."

"Oh, I'm so sorry."

"That's okay. Eleanor survived and now I have both of them. I'm very lucky. And don't get me wrong, Eleanor and Baby love each other—it's just that my dog goes to work with me almost every day so we have become pretty bonded. Even when I go on vacation she comes with me. She's never even been inside a kennel. Or a nursing home, until recently of course."

"It's great that you can do that. You told me you are a carpenter—right?"

"Yeah, carpentry is my major skillset, but I run my own remodeling business and being self-employed I can make my own rules, mostly."

"And your customers don't mind having such a big dog around."

"You've met Baby," I answer, figuring that's all I need to say.

"Of course you're right! She's so wonderfully gentle and dare I say, polite. I just thought some people might be allergic or just scared of dogs in general."

"The frightened ones tend to come around once they meet her and if they are allergic, Baby doesn't go inside their homes."

"Nice. I guess you have it all figured out, but I'm a little confused. You said Great Danes are German. I would've thought they were Danish."

"That's all right, most people think that."

"So no wonder Manny likes Baby so much. She's from his homeland."

"Not quite—he's Austrian—but close enough. I think the dog and he speak the same language."

She touches my hand. "Gee, Richard; it seems I'm striking out all over the place."

You're doing better than me. What the hell is your name? "I wouldn't worry about it. You've got so many residents here to keep track of, and I've only got one Papa."

"And so how's it going? With Manny, I mean. Isn't his evaluation coming up soon?"

"We went to Boston yesterday. The Deaconess?"

"Oh, yes, they have a great reputation!"

"I was a little disappointed that it turned out to be mostly an informational intake session. My Dad had a physical and everything looked fine there, but now we have to go back for neuropsychological testing. I feel like we are in limbo again. It's hard for me to keep his spirits up. And my own I suppose." I get a sympathetic look and add, "Also, sometimes I wonder if I'm doing right by him."

"Why? What do you mean?"

"Well, stuff comes up that's hard for him to be reminded of. I don't want to make his situation any worse."

"You aren't," she reassures me and touches my hand again. "Trust me, the little things don't matter. What's important is the time you're spending with him. And what better way than to work on a book about his life? I think it's wonderful."

"Thanks."

"Is it hard to write? I mean it must be very different than carpentry."

"I wrote another book when I was 26, so writing isn't totally new to me. But of course, I probably wasn't that good at writing because that one never went anywhere and that's why I'm still doing carpentry."

"Well, I think your dad is fascinating and everyone will want to read his stories. You should hear how proud he is about what the two of you are doing. Sometimes, when he knows you're coming, he tells me he has to work on his book today. I think it's just great!"

"Thank you. That's good to know. Donna thinks I shouldn't keep reminding him about life before Littleton House. She thinks it hinders his adjustment."

"We all know Donna has her own reasons for wanting Manny to forget," she says as she gives me a wink. "Is he in the restroom?"

"Yeah, I should probably check on him."

"Okay, well, I won't keep you any longer. Good to see you again, Richard. And good luck with the psychological stuff. He'll do just fine. He definitely doesn't belong here."

"Thanks for the encouragement. Good to see you also," I say. *Whatever your name is.*

I tap on the restroom door. "Papa, are you still awake in there?"

"Just finishing up," I hear him call back to me.

He comes out. "Papa, your fly," I tell him. As I wait for him to zip up, it hits me. "Elaine!" I shout.

Papa startles. "What did you call me?"

"Oh, sorry, Papa—not you, I was talking to one of the nurses while you were in the bathroom and I couldn't remember her name. It just came to me now."

Papa says, "Careful, kid, you keep that up and they won't let you out of here."

CHAPTER TWENTY-SEVEN

Walking, Cooking, Listening, Reading, Living

After breakfast, Papa and I drop off my truck, pick up Baby in Eleanor's car, and go to a nearby park for a long walk. When Papa lived at home, he generally walked about five miles a day. Although he might be making the equivalent number of steps in the corridors of Littleton House, I doubt they are equally satisfying or as good for his health as a stroll in the woods with his favorite dog and me.

When we get back to Eleanor's house, our home, Papa and Baby spend some time in the backyard together before retreating to the screen porch. This porch is a ten-year-old addition I built onto the back of Eleanor's '60s-style ranch house. It has a cathedral ceiling with two large skylights and a paddle fan mounted in the center of the main support beam. There are self-made, wooden-framed, full, floor-to-ceiling screen panels on three sides. Facing the backyard, the view is of a 25-foot patch of grass bordered by three tiers of stonewalled flower gardens that form a line in front of a small area of woods. In the spring, then on through summer, there is a never-ending display of colors and textures. Bright blue snowdrops show up first, then the yellow daffodils, which in turn give way to the orange tiger lilies that last almost until fall. Now, in late October, only a few hardy mums remain holding on before winter comes to claim them as well.

Midday, temperatures got up into the 50s. Now, around 4:30 pm, it has cooled off some. Looking out the kitchen window, I check to see Papa still napping on the white, wicker chaise longue where I last saw him. My dog, his dog, lies on the wood floor next to him, his arm draped across her body. I go out and cover my father with a wool blanket. Whether by intention or not, Papa has kept his word today. There have been no escapes down the street to Donna's house.

When I first moved into Eleanor's three-bedroom house, she was in the process of a divorce. Back then her three children lived with us. Now they are all grown with homes of their own. Eleanor and I have talked about having Papa come here to live. Eleanor is a teacher and has the summers off. However, that is her time to be with her own aging parent, her mother. During the rest of the year we both work and my father would be alone all day. We haven't decided anything definitively, and yet neither of us can see how we would be able to take good care of him here.

As evening settles in over the backyard, Eleanor joins me in the kitchen and we begin to prepare dinner. Vivaldi plays on the stereo. Soon, Papa comes in from the porch. Baby is right behind him.

"Hi, Manny, have a good rest?" Eleanor asks.

"Wonderful! Ah, the *Four Seasons*," Papa notices the music. "This is so nice—what you've got here—that porch, this music and your home." Wistfully, Papa adds, "I used to have a home too, you know."

Eleanor dives in to change the subject, before I might respond otherwise, "Manny, we're making supper. Want to help?"

"Well, I don't know what I can do, but I'm willing. What are we cooking?"

"Wiener schnitzel, as you requested."

"Wiener schnitzel! Oh, my absolute favorite!"

Eleanor and I have given up eating veal for touchy-feely, left-wing liberal reasons. Tonight we are making an exception for Papa.

"With lemon wedges, caraway seeded noodles and asparagus," Eleanor completes the menu for him.

"Noodles and schnitzel. Now I've died and gone to heaven!"

"Are you sure they'll let you in, Papa? You're still an atheist, aren't you?" I tease him.

"Of course!" he retorts. "But that's okay; I think they've lowered the standards. Anyone can get in now. I suppose they were running out of qualified candidates."

I leave it there, put up a pot to boil the noodles, and a large cast iron frying pan for the veal. After pouring in a half-inch or so of olive oil, I light the stove, and then I'm off to my next task.

Eleanor sets out a cutting board for Papa. "Here, Manny," she says, while placing several pieces of the meat on the board and handing him a mallet.

Papa hesitates, and then asks, "You want me to tenderize?"

"Yes, Manny. Do you think they're small enough? Need a knife?"

"Well, they could be littler—it is schnitzel you know."

I snap off the dry ends of the asparagus, put them in the steamer and begin slicing lemons. Eleanor prepares three bowls: seasoned flour, milk with a beaten egg combined, and breadcrumbs with Hungarian paprika. Papa gets his knife and after cutting the veal into the proper schnitzel size pieces, he starts pounding them almost flat.

As the three of us work in the kitchen together, I'm feeling less and less unsure about my approach with Papa these past few weeks. And I think it was right to bring him here, despite his longing for his own house just up the street. At least tonight I can relax just a little, enjoy the conversation between Papa and Eleanor, and not always be the facilitator.

Eleanor is wonderful with him. I look over at her. Even with her apron on and flour in her curly hair, she still looks so beautiful to me.

She catches my gaze, turns up her batter covered hands and shrugs her shoulders, as if to say, "What?"

I place my hand over my heart and point across to her.

I'm rewarded with one of her Elizabeth Taylor smiles.

I have a photograph of Eleanor from before we knew each other. In it she looks just like Liz did in her 20s. When at first I saw it, for a second or two, I thought it was from one of the actress's movies.

Eleanor turns away from me and back toward Papa. "Manny, I've got everything ready. Can you hand me a slice of veal?"

"Here, my dear. They look so good. I can hardly wait to devour them."

Eleanor coats the first piece with flour, dips it into the egg mixture and finally covers it with breadcrumbs. "I'm not sure I do this like you, but it's the way I learned."

"You must have been taught by a master! Are you sure it wasn't me?" Papa laughs at his own joke, then adds, "Everything looks perfect, really."

"Thank you, Manny." Eleanor finishes breading. "We're ready to cook 'em up. Need to use the bathroom? These won't take long."

As the schnitzels begin to sizzle, and the air fills with flavor, we are all soon salivating.

After supper, after many of Manny's exclamatory accolades about the meal, we do a partial cleanup and move to the living room. Eleanor has offered to read to us from our book. She starts with Chapter 10, "Who's the lucky woman?"

I watch my father's expression as Eleanor reads. This is something I haven't been able to see so much of when I'm doing the reading. At times his eyes close and yet I can tell by his frowns, occasionally scrunched-up nose and little smiles, that he is paying attention and hasn't fallen asleep. Every now and then he laughs and both eyes open wide.

"Now, Manny," Eleanor interrupts herself at one point, "it seems odd you chose a church to be married in. Was that Donna's idea?"

"Well, I suppose so. She was a member there, but often I'd tag along with her. You need to know your enemies, I always say. A few times they even let me give a sermon."

"Really?"

"Oh, yes. Those Unitarians are quite progressive. I don't think they believe too strongly in anything. Or perhaps they believe everything?"

Eleanor asks, "What did you sermonize about? Do you remember?"

"No—well, most likely it had an atheistic message. Also, one time I think I gave an introduction to general semantics. GS pretty much became my religion, you know."

"Amen!" I say.

"My son the comedian," Papa looks to Eleanor.

"I was just agreeing with you, Papa," I tell him.

Eleanor finishes the chapter. "And that's the end of Chapter 10!" she announces.

Papa is silent. After a time, he says, "Was I really such a buffoon that I didn't know I was getting married?"

"Papa, you weren't a 'buffoon'; you've never been a buffoon. It was just that under the circumstances, I wasn't positive where your levity was coming from. I wasn't sure if you were joking when you said, 'Who's the lucky woman?' You had been very forgetful leading up to the wedding. It's one of the reasons I questioned the idea of your marrying Donna in the first place."

"I should have listened to you, my boy. Now look at the fix I'm in."

"And we are fixing the 'fix.' Remember we went to Boston yesterday—to the Deaconess Hospital?"

"Yes. It was a lovely day. Thank you both so much."

"You're welcome. More important, though, that was the first step in getting you sprung from Littleton House. You passed your physical exam with flying colors."

"And what's the second step?"

"Dr. Delfs, the lead physician on your team, has ordered a neuropsychological exam for you."

"I am so important as to have a team, or am I just so sick that I need one?"

"You're important to me!"

"Me as well, Manny!"

"As for needing a group of specialists, I absolutely think this is a good approach. Instead of one overworked doctor deciding you belong in Littleton House after only having a few minutes with you, your memory issues will be fully evaluated. Wouldn't you like to know why you feel so confused? And even better, perhaps there is something we can do about it!" I say, both empathetically and emphatically.

"Well, of course! It's just I'm getting impatient. I'm bored to tears in that place. I really don't know how long I can hold on. I'm afraid I'll become a zombie if I don't get out of there soon," Papa says, then gets up abruptly. "I really need to use a toilet. Where do I go?" he asks.

I show him the way, for what is the sixth or seventh time today, and then rejoin Eleanor in the kitchen.

"I thought I'd put on a pot of coffee," she says.

"Good idea. I'll load the dishwasher."

As Eleanor is measuring out the grounds, she asks, "When will his psych exam happen? I think it really needs to be soon!"

"I know and I agree! I'll call for an appointment Monday! There's nothing I can do about it tonight," I respond, defensively.

After a time, we hear Papa say, "Wow! A Knabe." He's back in the living room.

Eleanor and I hear the keyboard cover open on her baby grand. Papa does a few scales. "Ugh!—This piano is out of tune!" he shouts.

"I've got to get that taken care of. I'm embarrassed to have your father play it like this."

"Don't worry—once he's playing he'll be perfectly happy to ignore how bad it sounds."

Papa plays *A Bicycle Built for Two*. He stumbles a bit at first. Then, as he gets the melody down, he begins to sing, "Daisy, Daisy, give me your answer do! I'm half crazy, all for the love of you! It won't be a stylish marriage. I can't afford a carriage. But you'll look sweet upon the street. On a bicycle built for two. Whew-hew! That was awful." The keyboard cover closes with a bang!

Eleanor and I bring the pot, three cups, three saucers, three plates and a tray of strudel into the living room.

"I'm sorry my piano is so out of tune, Manny," Eleanor says.

"Oh, that's all right. I'm just a Klemperer anyway."

I put everything down on the coffee table. Eleanor sets out the strudel. Then she asks, "How did you learn to play? Did you have lessons?"

"No. I just picked it up. I've always been able to do that. I don't even know how I do it. Give me three notes—and if I've heard the tune before—I can pretty much reproduce it."

"You must have perfect pitch," Eleanor suggests.

"Well, I'm glad something is still working—the rest of me seems to be falling apart."

"Would you like some coffee, Manny?"

"Yes, that would be most agreeable. Where would you like me?"

"Come sit on the couch next to your sonny boy." Eleanor pours. "I didn't think to make decaf," she says. "I hope this won't keep you up? I could still make some if you'd prefer?"

"Oh, no, what would be the point in that! I never drink that stuff. Besides, I don't have any trouble getting to sleep. Why, I can fall asleep anywhere. As soon as my head hits the pillow I'm out— sometimes even before, but that can be dangerous." Papa laughs. "And what have you got there?" he asks, noticing the baked goods.

"Apple strudel, Manny. Have some."

"Oh *mein Gott! Apfelstrudel. Sie habe dies für mich?*"

"Yes, Manny. All for you."

"Well, I'll share some of course." He takes a piece, places it in his mouth and with full Manny dramatic effect exclaims, "*Trefflichsten!* Most excellent!" He smacks his lips. "And you made these just now?"

"No, Manny. I'm fast but not that fast. I did them up earlier today—when you were out for breakfast with Richard. Maybe the next time you come we can bake together," Eleanor offers.

"I don't know—I was really never much of a baker—but I'm happy to help with the eating." He takes another piece.

"Let me know when you're getting tired, Papa, and I'll bring you back."

Papa puts the strudel back on his plate and says, "I see—I've worn out my welcome—you wish to get rid of me."

"Not at all! I only thought you might be getting tired. Eleanor and I set aside the whole day for you. You can stay as long as you like," I invite him.

"I'm sorry. You know I never wanted to be a burden on you—on any of my children. I thought I had everything worked out—but I suppose I screwed that up too." Papa takes a sip of his coffee and continues, "I don't want to go back to my room just yet. There's nothing for me to do. Couldn't we read a little more?"

"I'd be happy to, Manny," Eleanor offers again. She goes to get the notebook.

While she's gone, I tell Papa, "Speaking of nothing to do in your room, I was talking to Peter and ..."

"Ah, Petie. How is my 'little professor'?"

"Wow, I haven't heard you call him that in forever. Where did that nickname come from anyway?"

"Oh, I don't know. He was always thinking. I remember as a child he asked me a million questions about everything, 'What's that, Daddy?—How does it work?—Show me.' He was always looking for the answers—many times he'd have things figured out before I could tell him."

"And Carl wasn't like that?" I ask.

"Carl—well, you know, I never knew with him. I couldn't tell what was on his mind. He didn't talk very much."

Papa doesn't offer any more, so I go back to my brother Peter. "As I was starting to say, Peter and I talked recently and he'd like to get you a keyboard. If you think you'd use it? It might help with the boredom."

"A keyboard? And what does one do with such a thing?"

I wonder what he thinks it is. "An electric piano, Papa. You play it just like a real piano—but instead of it having strings, it produces the sound electronically."

"And this is better?"

"It's much smaller and it's portable so you could take it with you when you move."

"I guess I could try it."

"Okay. I'll call the 'little professor' back and tell him he's solved another problem."

Eleanor returns. "Ready, Manny? Chapter 11—Remodeling."

In some ways, this chapter seems even harder for Papa. Perhaps because it tells about when the life he thought he had ended so abruptly.

He connects with my metaphor when he says, "She just threw me away like an old stick of furniture."

Eleanor finishes reading. Nothing more is said. I take Papa back to Littleton House.

CHAPTER TWENTY-EIGHT

The Klystron

Around ten, Baby and I are in Papa's room. The room is empty. Baby sniffs around the beds and over to the base of the bathroom door. There she begins to whimper quietly. "Is Papa in there?" I ask her. Baby's tail wags and I have my answer. I knock on the door. No response. "Are you all right in there, Papa?" Nothing. "Papa!"

"Who's that?"

"It's your son Richard," I answer him. "And your favorite doggie."

"Oh, Richard, my boy! And my doggie, doggie come to visit me. I'll be right out."

Baby and I wait patiently and then not so patiently. *He must have fallen asleep on the toilet again.* "Papa!"

The toilet flushes. The door opens. "Ah, there's my sonny boy. Been here long?"

"About ten minutes," I say.

"Ten minutes! Was I in there that long? Well, I guess I really had to go. Ha, ha, ha. So, what's new with you?" he asks, and then without waiting for me to answer, Papa and Baby take up their long-lost reunion.

I'm getting used to being ignored. Actually, I've started enjoying it. When Papa's mood declines or conversation lags I can always rely on my canine pal to get things back on track. The task I have taken on, while rewarding in unmeasurable ways, is at times daunting. I don't know how those working in nursing homes maintain their spirit. And I don't understand why they are paid so little. *Strange that we will, collectively, give grown men millions of dollars to continue to play children's games, and yet subject those who feed, dress and clean our loved ones, to pay that is less than a living wage?*

Speaking of dressing, I need to get Papa dressed and out of this room. He is sitting on the edge of his bed now, still petting his doggie. "Papa, let's go to the family room. I have some really good news to tell you and something to show you."

Papa pops off the bed spryly and says, "Ready when you are, my boy!"

"You might want to put some clothes on first." He is wearing white boxer shorts and nothing else.

"I'm not okay like this?"

"It depends. If you want to stay cooped up in here it's fine with me, but I thought you'd like to get out of this room for a while."

"And there's something wrong with my ensemble?"

"If you go out into the public spaces as you are, other people might be offended," I tell him.

Papa takes an Olympian pose, then says, "How could they be offended by this?"

"All right, depressed then, nobody can compete with that!" I say. And I'm not just patronizing him. His body really does look great for a man nearly 90. All that early gymnastics training has served him well. At home, since retiring, Papa was used to walking around naked in his house, that is, when not wearing a three-piece suit. It was all or nothing for Dad. Having to be appropriately dressed in here is another difficult adjustment for him.

Reluctantly, Papa puts some clothes on and the three of us move to the family room. I give Papa the news that he needs to wait only three more days for his evaluation. He is glad about the shorter than expected wait, but now seems nervous about being prepared.

"So what must I do?" Papa asks me.

"Stay sharp!" I tell him.

"And how might I accomplish this?"

"I've never had a neuropsychological exam myself, so I'm not sure what they will ask of you. I imagine they will test your memory. And I think they will try to establish how well you can reason."

"My memory is not so good, you know."

"I know, Papa, but your reasoning is just fine! That is the more important thing, I think."

"You do?"

"Yes! Also, some of your memory skills are still intact. When we work on our book together, you are able to dig stuff out from long ago. I've done some research on some of the things you've told me about and you have been spot on. For example, you said that during the '20s, Harley motorcycles were green and Indian bikes were red. When I looked it up, you were right!"

"Good for me. Maybe I should get a motorcycle and just ride out of this place."

"If only you could, Papa, I'd ride out right next to you." I'm feeling Papa's sense of helplessness. I need to distract him from that feeling and focus him on his memory skills. I take out the recorder. "Papa." His eyes are closed. "Papa!"

He startles, opens his eyes and says, "Yes, my son?"

"Where did you go? You're not falling asleep on me, are you?" We've got work to do."

"Oh, no, I was just resting my eyes. What can I tell you?"

This phrase triggers another childhood memory for me. Our father disapproved of his children sleeping late, or taking naps during the day. If I slept in on a Saturday, when I got up I could count on hearing that the best part of the day was already gone. It always made me feel like there was no point in staying up then, and I might as well go back to bed. Father always stressed the importance of reading instead of sleeping. Sometimes, however, when he wanted to nap, he pretended to be reading. More than once during daylight hours, I caught him sitting in his chair, book in hand, head down and eyes closed. When confronted about what I felt was a double standard, he'd respond by telling me he was only resting his eyes and thinking about the passage he'd just read. That answer never explained the snoring.

"I'm glad you asked me that. The recorder is on and I'd like to pick up your story after the Depression."

Papa thinks for a moment, then says, "I'm not so much depressed, more frustrated and angry than anything else."

"Not your depression, Papa, the Depression. You told me how lucky you were to have had work all during those years. What came after that? Did you keep working as an electrician for Nelson? When and how did you meet Judy?"

"Your mother?"

"Is there any other Judy?"

Papa laughs. "I suppose not," he agrees. "Well, let me think. It might have been through dancing. Judy was quite a dancer in those days. Kid, I tell you she was like no other partner I ever had." There is a broad smile on Papa's face.

"So, did you meet at a dance? Did someone introduce you, or did you just walk up to her and ask her for a dance? Details, Papa, details!"

Papa takes his time answering me. "No, you know, I think I placed an ad for her. I didn't even know she could dance when we first met. That came later, as I remember now."

"An ad? You mean like a personal ad for a date?"

"Oh, no, no, no. I needed a secretary. I had started this business with a partner and neither of us was too good with the office stuff. Your mother was an excellent organizer and she was great with people on the phone."

"So what was the business?"

"Exhibitions Inc."

"Ah, so you were an exhibitionist."

Papa chuckles. "Funny guy," he says. "No, my partner and I—oh—what the hell was his name—gee, isn't that funny—I'm drawing a blank. Well, anyway we started this enterprise designing, building, and setting up displays."

"Like for museums?"

"Museums, yes—all kinds really. But things truly got going in 1938. The World's Fair was being built. Our timing was perfect. Gosh, I remember we had more work than we could handle. Those were exciting times, my boy!"

"Where were you living then? Were you still in Mount Vernon?"

"No, I don't think so. In Queens maybe? That's where the fair was, at least. And that's why I hired your mother—she kept everything in order for us. She even handled the books. We were making a ton of money!"

"So you were Judy's boss. Did you chase her around the desk?"

"Hey! What are you suggesting? Ebner is always a gentleman—I let her chase me. Ha, ha, ha."

"Seriously, Papa. When did the romance start?"

"Soon, I think. She was funny and smart." A sweet smile comes over Papa's face. "Beautiful too—I made up my mind pretty quickly.

I think dancing just sealed the deal. We won contests, you know?"

"So I've heard."

"With my moves and her ability to follow, we were something. Oh, it was fantastic!" Papa sways back and forth rhythmically in his chair.

"I thought Mother told me that you two used to teach ballroom."

"That's right—Arthur Murray Studios, in New York—we were instructors for a time. Nights—it was just a part-time thing. We did it mostly for fun—they didn't pay much. And we really didn't need the money anyway. We were doing all right!"

"So when did you marry and start making babies?"

"Carl wasn't born until '45. I'm not sure when we married. The war broke out and kind of disrupted everything."

"How so, Papa?"

"Well, the display business tanked. But my partner had some connections. He came to me one day and showed me a huge order he had signed to make coffins. But I just couldn't do it. I couldn't bring myself to profit from man's ultimate act of stupidity!"

"What did you do?"

"I sold the business to my partner and found a job."

"Was it hard to find work?"

"Not then. Anyone who wanted to work, could. Everyone was needed for the war effort. I was hired by Sperry Corporation."

"And that must be where you earned this." I pull Papa's Klystron tube plaque from the paper bag next to me and hand it to him.

"Oh my gosh! A Klystron. Where did you get this?" Papa asks, while grasping his prize.

Mounted on a round black base, approximately 5 inches in diameter, the tube itself is split down the middle exposing the insides. The entire tube with its base stands about 8 inches tall. At the top is what looks like a spark plug surrounded by some metal fins. Engraved in the base are the words; SPERRY KLYSTRON.

"Peter and I found it while looking for more clothes at your house. He said you told him it was your reward for helping on the project during the war."

"Frequency modulation, that was what it did. Amazing really. Hitler didn't see the value in it. Fortunately for us, Britain and the US did. It was the key to radar you know. Really helped us win the war."

"What was your part in it?"

"See these fins?" Papa puts his fingers on them. "I suggested that."

"What are they for?"

"Cooling, my boy! The tubes themselves were overheating so they didn't last very long. These fins dissipated the heat."

"Pretty cool, Papa. Now, when they hired you, weren't they worried about your connections to Austria?"

"Oh sure! I had to go through clearances. I think they even read my mail to and from my family. But I was always adamant about my opinion of Hitler. He was insane—had to be stopped. I told my family that often."

"How long did you work at Sperry?"

"At least through the end of the war. Sometime after that I got a job with Gottlieb."

"Gottlieb?"

"The clock company. You never heard of them?"

"Sorry, no, Papa."

"That's okay, I forgive you my son. They were very prominent in NY back then. I was hired to design and install clocks all around the city."

"You know I remember a clock in our apartment that was digital, but mechanically, I think. If I'm correct there was a box made of wood and through an opening, I could see these numbers that represented the time. Was that one of yours?"

"Probably. Sounds like something I might have made."

"How did it work?"

"Most likely there was an electric motor with a shaft connected to a gear box of some sort. The numbers, 0 through 9, were engraved on a series of 4 wheels with flats on them. Each wheel turned at a different rate. One moved at 1 minute intervals, the next at 10 minute intervals and so on. This allowed for the numeric representation of time. Quite ingenious really. I only wish I had invented it in the first place, but I can't take credit for that. I just assembled the thing."

"Funny—you know I remember when I started going to school, I had trouble reading an analog clock. And I think my teachers thought it odd that I always told the time as a number and never said half past or quarter of."

"I'm sorry. I hope you blamed it on me."

"It's okay, I adjusted, and anyway most everything is digital now so I have no problems anymore."

"What can I tell you. I guess we were just ahead of our time my boy."

"Nice pun, Papa. And to return your question about, 'What can I tell you' that wasn't really a question at all, when did we move to Massachusetts?"

"Oh, let me think." Papa pauses.

I'm enjoying this. He's so present. I only hope this Papa will show up for his evaluation on Thursday.

"You were little—hadn't started school yet—maybe you were four or five."

"But why did we move? Did you lose your clock job?"

"Oh, gosh no! I was already on to something else by then.

Manny Ebner never lost a job! It was always my choice to move on if I thought there was something better for me."

"And so, what was better in Mass?"

"I traveled up there for an interview at Sylvania. I didn't get the job I applied for, but I talked them into a position they didn't have yet."

"Really?" *Actually I'm not surprised by this revelation.*

"Yes. They gave me a job as a Value Engineer."

Papa, I want to hear more about this, but I need to call a customer to say I won't be showing up at all today. Are you okay to stay here with Baby while I find a phone?"

"I don't see why not."

CHAPTER TWENTY-NINE

Passions

As I get back to the family room, I expect to see Papa once again resting his eyes. Instead he is standing by the window. When he sees me he says, "Oh, there you are. I was wondering how my doggie got here without you."

"So sorry it took that long," I apologize, but don't clarify.

Papa needs to use a bathroom again. Once this is accomplished, we settle back in and resume where we had left off.

"You told me that you created your own job position as a Value Engineer. What did you do?"

"I looked for ways that Sylvania could be more efficient. That was an amazing job really. They sent me all over the country to different plants—some that we owned and others that were vendors. It was the last time I ever worked for someone else."

"That's when we lived in Waltham, right?"

"Waltham, yes, but you're leaving out Sudbury and of course Chelmsford. I had my job at Sylvania for 22 years or so. What do you remember about Waltham?"

There's a switch. "You want to test my memory now?"

"Turnabout is fair play, my boy."

"You're right. Isn't it funny that when we are children we need our parents to keep reminding us about simple things, and when we get older it reverses?" Papa doesn't agree or disagree, so I go on. "Waltham? I was so little then—I'm not sure what I remember. I think we had a dog."

Upon hearing the word *dog*, Baby applauds with a single thump of her tail on the floor and goes back to sleep.

"Yes, yes, Daisy. A sweet sheepdog, mutt," Papa fills in her name for me.

Hesitantly, I say, "You know, I never thought you liked dogs all that much. In fact, it seemed to me that you barely tolerated us having pets."

Papa looks puzzled. "No, not so. I always supported your having animals to take care of. It encourages responsibility."

Better leave it there. "I remember you teaching me to ride my bike without the training wheels. You ran along beside me with one hand on the back of my seat to help stabilize me. At a certain point, I must have gotten cocky, and thinking I didn't need you, I started peddling really fast. You couldn't keep up. There was a curve in the road. I couldn't turn, and bam! I crashed into a tree. I think I had to go to the hospital."

"Oh, yes! Your mother was furious with me for that one."

"Oh, and do you remember when I got the tick in my ear? It swelled up, but you couldn't see it inside my ear and I couldn't hear anything on that side. We all thought I was going deaf."

Papa smiles. "I remember when the doctor discovered the tick and he said he was going to use ether to get it out. You became very scared and started crying. When we asked you what was wrong, you said you didn't want to be put to sleep. Then the doctor told you he was putting the tick to sleep and not you." Papa laughs, then asks, "Are hospitals and doctors all you can think of? Don't you have any good memories?"

"Thought-provoking question, Papa. I might need a while to come up with something."

"Take your time, kid. I have nowhere to go," Papa says, and adds, "Unfortunately."

"I do remember your having an Arlo Guthrie moment in Waltham."

"Arlo? You mean Woody."

"No. Arlo, Woody's son."

"I didn't know he had a son."

"Well, he did, and like his dad he was a singer/songwriter. And one of his songs was the basis for a movie called *Alice's Restaurant*."

"A movie about a restaurant, you say?"

"Partially about that, but also a commentary on moral dilemmas and trash. That's where you come in, your Arlo Guthrie moment."

"I have no idea what you're talking about."

"Let me explain."

"Please do."

"It all started when you had us kids help you get rid of some household junk. We loaded everything into our trailer and went off to the dump. I'm not sure if it was on a Sunday or it was a holiday or what, but when we got there the dump was closed. So you told us there was a spot you knew about where we could unload the trailer. We drove for a while, I don't know where, and we stopped by some woods. Some ways back in the woods, there was a big pile of junk, like old couches, broken chairs, lamps, scrap wood and such. You started pulling our stuff out of the trailer, and you had us drag it to the pile."

"I did?"

"Yep."

"That doesn't sound so good. And this is a happy memory?"

"Wait, it gets worse, but it also gets funny at the same time."

"I certainly hope so."

"So, we were almost done, when a police car pulled up behind the trailer. The cop got out and began reading you the riot act. He was very agitated while telling you that it was illegal to dump there and you would be fined for doing so. In a New York minute, like Don Henley wrote about, ..." I get a look, "Sorry, another singer that made an impression on me. Anyway, you responded by saying we weren't dumping, but rather we were taking things that you thought we could use and putting them in the trailer. Thus, we were not adding to the junk pile, but rather reducing it. Then you called to us, saying to put everything in the trailer back on the pile.

Papa chuckles. "And the cop bought it?"

"I don't think he believed you, so much as he appreciated your quick-thinking sense of humor. Anyway, he let us go."

"Well, I don't recall any of this. Perhaps I've blocked it out. Not a very good example to set for your children."

"It's one of my happy moments. You asked for it."

"Whatever pleases you my son."

This trash story is one of my best memories of being with my father when I was a little boy. Whenever I think of it I smile. He was so quick and cleaver. He had nerve, but it was tempered by his humor and thus not threatening to the police officer. The cop even said it was the best damn excuse he'd ever heard while on the force.

That day in the woods, I appreciated my dad. I felt safe with him. I thought he was cool and every kid wants a cool dad. And yet, I'm not sure I was even there that day. My older brothers may have told me the story. Or I might have overheard my father retelling it to friends, before he blocked it out of his memory. Considering I was so young and that I was my Mommy's boy, either of those scenarios are more likely. Probably, I was at home with my mother when Papa had his Arlo moment.

Still, it feels very real for me. I can picture the surroundings, see the woods and the discarded belongings. I can hear my dad's voice and the cop's voice.

The more time Papa and I spend working on his memory and trying to prepare him for the upcoming evaluation, the more I realize that memory skills are a poor way to judge a person's value. Everyone's memory is fluid and unreliable. Memories are not facts. Perhaps the word memory should be forgotten and supplanted by the word perception. I hope there will be more to his assessment than asking him what day it is, or who's the President.

"We didn't live in Waltham very long, did we?"

"No. A year or so."

"How come so short?"

"I'm not sure. The place was somewhat small for the five of us. And I needed room for my workshop. I always had one you know. Even at the apartment in the city. I remember talking to the landlord in Flushing and convincing him to let me have some space in the basement for my Shopsmith. I bought one of the first ones ever made. Oh, I loved that machine. With that one tool I could cut, sand, and drill. It even had a lathe. Four functions all together I think. Do you remember it?"

"I remember the Shopsmith, but not in NY. I was very little then and I think I was scared of the basement. In Sudbury I remember you using it though."

"31 Greenwood Rd. I liked that house right away. The big double lot, my garage and even a breezeway for you kids to play in. I built my first dome there," Papa says proudly.

"Now you're talking, Pop! I liked it there too. And I remember the dome. I remember the day it blew away."

"Oh gosh! That was something." Papa is chuckling.

"How do you do that?"

"What? What am I doing?"

"How do you laugh about something that must have been so painful?"

"Well—in the moment when it happened—it was just amazing. Not painful—really. The sight of the thing rolling across the grass like a giant tumble weed. There was nothing I could do about it. I was just glad it came to rest against that big oak tree and didn't blow into the neighbor's yard."

"But you had put so much time into building it, I would think that was a terrible loss."

"The time was already gone when the thing blew away. I just started over with the next one. And I learned to stake it down."

I was there that day when the wind took our screened-in-dome away, or at least I perceive I was. The day after, when nature calmed down, my father was calm as well. He slowly began picking through the ruble to see what he could save and reuse. Snapped wooden 2x4s, twisted metal plates, torn insect screening and four canvas hammocks had wrapped themselves around the old oak tree at the edge of our property. The tables and chairs remained almost in the same spot where the dome used to sit, just outside the back door of our ranch style house.

The 2x4s, in groups of three, had formed the triangles which in turn were attached to each other until pentagons were created. At the nodes, metal discs were set into the wood at angles that allowed the structure to become a half sphere. Bolts held everything together and once tightened, insect screening was attached to the edges of the wood from outside. A separate, single triangle, was hinged to act as a door.

The hammocks were hung all around the inside of the dome, which was about 25 feet in diameter. Papa's homemade kidney-shaped tables had adjustable legs to accommodate multiple uses and seating arrangements. One height for serving food, another when seated in one of the different brightly colored, folding butterfly chairs. The chairs were store bought. Everything else, including a fire pit in the center, was built by Papa. It was a very cozy summertime space.

At night I would I would lie down in my favorite hammock, the one which had no tree branches overhead to obstruct my view of the stars. As the adults sat around the tables and talked about matters of consequence, I just contemplated the constellations above me and imagined I could float up into the universe. It felt very safe in that world. The world before my parents went to war with each other and ultimately brought us children into the battle.

"Papa, I was just thinking about the kidney-shaped tables you made. You called them butterfly tables, and I can see either name working. But I always wondered why you put those three holes in the surface at one end. They were only about ¾ of an inch in diameter, not big enough for an umbrella pole. What were they for?"

"In design school we were taught how to create visual interest. One way to achieve this is to break the plane. My three little holes did just that."

"Eureka, Papa!"

"And you waited all these years to ask me?"

"I suppose I did. Anyway, the tables were great. And the domes were even greater. I remember having sleepovers in them. All my friends thought they were the coolest things. They were amazed that I had a dad who invented stuff and who could also build anything you thought of."

"So your friends liked me?"

"Well, I wouldn't go that far. They liked the domes." I get a dejected look, so I quickly add, "Yes, Papa, everyone likes you. As you have often postulated, what's not to like?"

There was another dome failure in my father's dome building career. And it was a big one, both the dome and the failure. He had gotten the idea that a screened enclosure over a swimming pool would enhance the experience of owning a pool, especially in New England. First of all, his proposition was that swimming in the evening after work, which for many would be the only time available during weekdays, would be more enjoyable without those evening mosquitoes. Secondly, much of the work in maintaining a pool involves cleaning debris. A screened dome over a pool would address both issues.

My dad started designing a larger version of our backyard dome. After he finished the drawings, he went to a pool company in Framingham that had an in-ground pool on site. Manny sold them on the idea of putting his dome over it and offering packaged deals to customers wanting to have pools installed along with his screened enclosures.

Then he got to work building the display dome. I think my brothers helped out and he may have also hired a carpenter. By the summer of 1961, my dad's screened dome sat proudly over the pool at the Framingham store. The response from customers was very positive. Orders were taken for the following year's installations. My father got busy locating sub-contractors to build and install them.

Winter came. Snow began collecting on the screening. After a particularly large snow storm, the dome began twisting under the weight. It collapsed. And his new business venture collapsed with it. The pool company wanted nothing more to do with my father and his domes. Manny tried to convince them he could fix the problem, but the owners of the pool company had lost their trust in him. They were just relieved that no one was hurt when the dome came down. All they wanted was for the wreckage to be removed from their pool. My father complied with their request and went back to concentrating on the smaller, screen houses.

Papa's ability to deal with adversity and maintain a positive attitude is a quality I have only recently begun to appreciate. He has a strength of character that is remarkable. I only wish he had been better at knowing his own limitations and wasn't always trying to do it all. Had he hired a structural engineer to review his plans, the domes would have been designed to withstand the snow loads and his business might have taken off.

"So, Papa, as I recall we only lived in Sudbury for about three years. We moved to Chelmsford when I was in the middle of fourth grade. Why another move so soon?"

"I always wanted to own a house. A co-worker of mine lived in Chelmsford and he told me about a new development that was being built. Your mother and I went and took a look. They had seven or eight model homes to choose from and the best part was that you could customize—to a degree anyway."

"Did you get to pick the site?"

"Oh, yes! Right after the curve at the top of the hill. That was the best location in the whole neighborhood, 24. (*He does have that address down cold*). Although I think the lot number was different during construction. They hadn't even finished the road when we bought. I got to watch the whole house be built. I'd often stop by on my way home from work to see the process. It was amazing!"

"When we moved, you and Judy had separate bedrooms. How come?"

"I guess your mother and I needed our own space," Papa reasons, and adds, "Your mother did anyway. Judy needed lots of space."

"But I also remember Mother worked with you on some of your

inventions."

"Reluctantly, yes. We were always at odds about how much time to put into my product ideas. Wistfully Papa says, "Maybe I didn't spend enough energy on our romance.""

"I remember her spending lots of time on the Cube-Art project. She even had me help her cut those small fine art prints out of the books and glue them onto the blocks you made," I tell him.

In the garage in Chelmsford, my father had built a woodworking shop, a spray paint booth and a separated art and photo mounting space. He cut his blocks on the Shop Smith, painted them black and hung them on drying racks. Once dry, they were transported to the next room where the art was mounted. These block were approximately 3 and ½ inches tall, 3 inches wide and 1inch thick. They had beveled edges on three sides to simulate the look of a picture frame. The front, back and bottoms were flat. In the back near the top, a small hole was drilled to accommodate hanging. Cubed-Art blocks could sit on a desk or be grouped en masse on a wall. We had a whole wall filled with them at 24, perhaps 75 pictures; some were fine-art prints and others just random interesting photographs. The wall they were mounted on was painted black. It was way cool!

"She tried, but she never seemed satisfied about anything," Papa laments.

"I also remember her selling a large order to Macy's. Something like 500 of them I think. She took me with her to New York on the sales trip and again when we delivered them." I can see that Papa is concentrating on what I'm saying, but he says nothing in response. "You know, exposing me to all those artists' works, really helped me in my high school art classes. Intellectually anyway. I knew of more artists and could identify more works of art than any of my classmates. It didn't really improve my drawing or painting capabilities though."

"But I remember you always loved to draw," Papa speaks up.

"I did—still do, but I'm not talented enough to make a living at it."

"Don't ever sell yourself short, kid. Follow your passions and at least you'll enjoy life. Too many people never do."

"Good advice for both of us, Papa. You might not realize this, but writing has always been an unfulfilled passion of mine. My first attempt at writing a book never got published. So maybe our writing your story together is meant to be."

"Never is a longtime that hasn't happened yet," Papa points out the semantic implications of my chosen word. "I don't know how much help I am, but it is good to have the time together."

"You can help by telling me when, why and how you started Foto-Cube Inc."

"Oh, I don't know—in the late 1960s, I suppose. I couldn't keep making all those blocks myself by hand. Plastic injection molding was what I needed for large scale production. But the setup for the dyes was expensive. I didn't have any seed money—so I formed a corporation and talked a bunch of people into investing. Friends and co-workers mostly and also some of my cohorts at the G.S. Society."

"And when did you hook up with Polaroid?"

"Sometime later. I was intrigued by their instant camera—so I designed the Insta-Frame to fit the size of those snapshots. I pitched the idea to Edwin Land himself. Polaroid was just down Route 128 from Sylvania. I remember getting an appointment and taking the afternoon off from work. By the time I left his office that day we had a deal."

"Very Manny of you, Papa. And I remember when you told us about the order Polaroid later placed and the projected sales potential. We thought we'd be on easy street then. You started looking at Porsches to replace your VW bug. What happened? I want to know why we didn't get rich."

"Yes, those were wild times! The idea was to give coupons for the frames to anyone who bought film for the Land Camera. Polaroid was giving the frame free as a value-added incentive. This meant there was no markup, which also meant all the profits went to me—or well—to me and the stockholders. The original order was in the thousands."

"So what happened?"

"Unfortunately the damn things arrived to the customers broken. The mailers didn't protect them well enough. Polaroid completed their contract obligation and bought all the frames on order. Then I believe they just melted them down. It was a shame really. There was nothing wrong with the frames—only the mailers were the problem."

And who designed the mailers? That would be Manny. I decide to change the subject again. "You know my favorite of your frame inventions were those magnetic frames. The big ones where you could change the art or photos quickly and store more prints inside the frame. Very clever, Papa."

"Thank you. I should have patented those too. I suppose by now someone else has also thought of the idea."

I can tell Papa is getting hungry and it is only about ten minutes until lunch at Littleton House. We decide to go back to his room and I keep him company while he washes up. One last time, I remind him, "Remember your psych evaluation is this Thursday coming up. The appointment is at ten a.m., so I'll pick you up no later than eight."

CHAPTER THIRTY

"On with the inquisition!"

Three days later, at 7:30 in the morning, I find my father occupying a chair across from the nurses' station. A place where I had hoped I'd never see him settled. He is asleep, sitting up with his head tilted and leaning against the wall. Unshaven and unkempt looking, he appears like a homeless person you might encounter on a park bench. All the other residents must still be in their rooms, as the rest of the chairs are empty.

I'm feeling frustrated. Our appointment is at ten. We need to get on the road and soon. It takes nearly an hour to get to Boston from here and that is without rush hour traffic. My frustration overspills as I step over to the counter and accost the nurse on duty. "What the hell are you trying to do to us? You were supposed to have him ready. I can't take him for his psych exam like that." I point to Papa, "Now he even looks crazy!"

Defensively, she answers, "We fed him and tried to find something nice for him to wear, but when we asked to shave him, he wouldn't have any part of it. After that he didn't even let us dress him. Your father is very strong you know—I wasn't going to fight with him."

"I'm sorry. It's not your fault. I know you can't force him to do anything he doesn't want to do. I'll wake him and see if he'll shave for me."

Papa wakes up grumpy. But after some cajoling, that includes pointing out how pretty the nurse is, he agrees to let her shave him. The clothing situation I prepared for in advance. I brought one of my sport jackets and an extra tie.

A little after eight, we are in my truck and on the road to Boston. It seems like everyone else in Massachusetts is headed there as well. On Route 2 in Cambridge, at the bottom of the long hill that eventually leads to the Fresh Pond Parkway, traffic is backed up as far as I can see. I make an executive decision—slip into Alewife station and take the "T."

We find a parking space on the top floor of the garage. Once parked, Papa asks, "Are we there?"

"Not quite. Traffic looks bad, so I thought we'd ride the train the rest of the way. Is that okay?"

"Well, of course! The train—you know I love trains."

"I thought so, Papa. And I think I owe you a ride—you got cheated the last time we went to Boston."

At Alewife station there is an escalator, the longest one I've ever seen, two and a half stories without a landing. My dad and I step on. Fortunately, his muscles and his muscle memory are still very much functional. As we descend, two men in three piece suits quickly slide by us, bumping into Papa as they push past.

"What's their hurry?" Papa asks.

"Oh, they are very important men—men of consequence, Papa. You can tell by how they're dressed," I say, in a voice loud enough for them to hear.

One of the men turns and catches my eye. Within his gestures, I see my misjudgment. He mimes, "I'm sorry" and turns back, continuing on his way. I can't know what his hurry is, but I do know I've accused him falsely. Perhaps he too has an elderly parent consuming all his thoughts. There isn't time nor the opportunity to undo the damage, but I will remember this moment, and hopefully in the future not make such hasty judgments. *Note to self; try to stay humble and kind.*

Once off the escalator, I buy two tokens. We go through the turnstile and step onto the Red Line train that is already there waiting for us. Papa becomes very excited as the doors close and the train begins moving. "All-a-board!" he calls out, "tickets please."

Some of the other passengers give us a quick look and then disengage. Most don't even pay any attention to Papa or me. The car is crowded so my father and I stand holding on to the same pole. I notice a little girl, about five or six I'm guessing. Her eyes remain fixated on my father. She sits on the bench across from us, feet folded under herself. A woman sitting next to her, puts her arm around the girl and keeps an eye on Papa.

As the train gets up to speed and rounds a corner, Papa leans into the turn and imitates the sound of metal wheels scraping against steel rails. The little girl laughs, and I say to the woman, "He loves trains—what can I tell you?" She manages a smile but says nothing.

At Park St. station, we walk up and down several flights of stairs, making our switch over to the Green Line track. Now we are on our way to the Longwood stop. While riding there, I think about my father having just climbed stairs, gotten on and off trains and negotiated an escalator. And it reminds me about Donna's claim that Manny can't get around very well anymore. She even bought him a blind man's white cane. I have since made sure the cane got lost.

From Longwood station we walk several city blocks, turn right at Brookline Ave. and pass by the Deaconess. We are in "hospital alley." Pale green lab coats dominate the sidewalk fashion. Ambulances are as numerous as taxicabs.

Finally, we find the right building, take the elevator up, and enter the outer office of Dr. Weinstein. A receptionist hands me some forms to fill out. My dad and I sit and go over the papers together.

I read aloud to him from a list of: afflictions, ailments, conditions, debilities, diseases, disorders, ills, infirmities, infections, maladies, sicknesses and syndromes. And I ask, "Ever had any of those?"

"No, I can't say I have," he answers.

I remind him about not seeing so well, and he agrees we should probably mention this on the form. But when I bring up his overnight stay in the hospital a few years ago, he has no recollection of that. "You were admitted because your heart was racing much too fast," I tell him.

"Was there a woman involved?" he wisecracks.

"I don't know, Papa. Was there?"

"Well—I can't imagine what else would get my heart beating so fast."

I tell him that whatever caused it, his medication seems to be keeping things under control. We finish filling out all the forms. I return them to the receptionist and sit back down next to Papa. We wait.

After a time, a woman in her late 40s or early 50s, with dark hair, a warm smile and an even warmer voice, comes over to speak with us. "Hello. I'm Doctor Weinstein," she introduces herself, then she looks down at some papers in her hand. "And you must be the Ebners."

Papa pops up to his feet and stands very straight and tall. Doctor Weinstein offers her hand. He takes her hand in his, bows, and just as he's about to kiss her hand, he turns his and kisses the top of his own hand instead. "Ebner! At your disposal." I see a puzzled look come to the doctor's face. Then my father explains his behavior by saying, "Strictly for sanitary reasons, Madam."

She turns to me. "Richard," I say and we exchange a more conventional handshake.

"Why don't you two sit here a moment. I have one short phone call to make and I'll be back in a second to get you."

"One-thousand-one," Papa counts aloud, "times up!" he says.

"Oh, you're quick! I can see we are going to have fun this morning," she says with a big bright smile on her face. "Let me rephrase that. I'll be back in a minute—well, maybe a couple of minutes, but I won't be long. I promise."

I am encouraged that Dr. Weinstein seems to find my father amusing, instead of "crazy as a loon." His pointing out the literal meaning of what's just been said, while annoying at times, is not done because he suffers from dyslexia or because he's a lunatic. Rather, as a General Semanticist, he often demands that people's statements match their intentions. This, he would contend, is to avoid misperceptions and provide clarity.

Five minutes pass and Doctor Weinstein, my dad, and I settle ourselves into the doctor's office. She asks my father how he'd like to be addressed, and she tells us, we can call her Cheryl. Papa goes for Manny. I tell her I will respond to any form of Richard, with any of its multitude of nicknames.

As hospital offices go, the space is homey. There is art on the walls, family photos on the desk, table lamps instead of overhead lighting. Our chairs look comfortable. The seating is arranged living room style and the doctor's desk is unobtrusively off to one side. A large window lets in whatever sunlight manages to filter in past the shade of the surrounding buildings. We are on the fifth floor. Looking out the one window, I can see construction going on down in the street. Still, the room is fairly quiet and the steady rapping sounds of jackhammers are mostly in the background, easily ignored.

Cheryl has placed herself in a chair directly in front of Papa. No desk between them. I seat myself to my father's left, just a foot or two away. Dr. Weinstein begins, "I'd like both of you to tell me why you think you're here today, and why don't we start with you, Richard."

I tell the new abridged, Reader's Digest version of *Saving Papa's Tales*. Cheryl listens patiently and only interrupts when needing clarification. Having told the story so many times now, to so many different people, I've come to recognize some of the places were newbies get confused. I try not to lose her in the sequence of events.

When I finish, Cheryl turns to my dad, "Mr. Ebner ..."

"Manny, please. Let's not be so formal," Papa interrupts her.

"I'm sorry. You did say to call you Manny—my fault, I forgot. Now, Manny, were you able to follow what Richard just told me?"

"Yes, yes."

"And would you agree that it's an accurate presentation of the circumstances that bring you to see me today?"

"Yes, I suppose so." My dad nods in short movements, some up and down, but some side to side as well. He pushes his chin and bottom lip forward while nodding, then adds, "I guess he has caught the flavor of the situation."

Dr. Weinstein urges more, by asking, "Is there something you'd like to add, or change—something you take issue with?"

"Well ..." Papa hesitates.

"It's okay. We are here to help you, and to listen," she encourages him. "Go ahead."

"He said I have a memory problem. This I don't understand."

"You think your memory is okay?"

"Yes I do. I mean sure—I forget some things—but everyone does that. Don't they?"

"Of course they do! We all forget things," Cheryl reassures. "But you feel you don't have a particular problem remembering?"

"No I don't. If it is important to me, I'll remember."

Okay, good! That's one of the things we're going to check out this morning." The doctor reaches to the desk next to her, removes an alarm clock from among some papers and turns back to face my dad. "Now, Manny, I'm going to set this clock for ten minutes. When it goes off you will hear a bell like this." She demonstrates, then continues, "When you hear that alarm I want you to ask: When will I see you again for another evaluation? Okay—will you do that for me?" Cheryl asks as she takes Papa's hand in hers.

"Yes, of course! Your wish is my command."

"Good! What a dear sweet man. Now I want to borrow your shoe."

"My shoe?"

"Yep. Come on—give it to me."

Papa is laughing now as he looks over to me. I say nothing and just nod yes. He bends over and removes one shoe. "Here it is—but I don't think it'll fit you," he adds while passing it to the doctor.

"That's all right. I'm not going to wear it. Now I need your tie."

Papa shakes his head while unbuttoning his collar. "What are you trying to do—undress me?" he asks.

"Just a little bit," Cheryl responds. "I need something else—let me see." She looks up and down at my father's outfit. He is wearing the gray sport coat I loaned him. "Anything in the pockets?" Cheryl asks. My father pulls out a black comb.

That's a surprise. I know the pockets were empty when I gave him the jacket. How'd he slip a comb in without me noticing?

"That will do fine. Give it here."

Papa does as she asks.

"I am going to ask Richard to put your comb in his pocket." Cheryl hands the comb to me.

I catch a look from my dad. "Don't worry, you'll get it back. I use a brush."

"Manny, I want you to watch where Richard puts your comb, because I'm going to ask you where it is later. Okay?"

"Okay, but you know I don't see too well?"

"Here, Papa," I take my father's hand. "Here—feel this. Your comb is right here in my breast pocket."

"Good," The doctor says, then gives me an approving wink. "Now, Manny, pay attention because I'm going to hide your shoe and your tie somewhere in the room—and I want you to remember where I put them. Can you do that for me sweet man?"

"Well, I don't know why not."

Doctor Weinstein places my father's shoe on the window sill behind a potted plant. As she does, she tells Papa what she's doing and reminds him to remember once again.

I watch my father. He follows her every move, all the while shaking his head and quietly chuckling to himself.

Repeating the process with his tie, she puts that in the top drawer of her desk. While there, she picks up a stack of glossy photographs and reseats herself across from my dad. She begins shuffling through the stack of five-by-eight photos in her hand. I can't see what they are about. Papa and I turn to each other and shrug our shoulders almost simultaneously.

We turn our eyes back to the doctor as she begins, "All right, good. Now let's move on." She turns one of the pictures toward my dad. "Can you see this photograph, Manny?"

He leans in closer and studies it for several seconds. "It appears to be a portrait of a woman. I don't recognize the face. Should I know this woman?"

"No. But we are going to call her Cathy Taylor. I want you to remember that name. When I show you this picture again later, I want you to tell me her name—Cathy Taylor," she repeats. "Got it?"

"Yes, yes, Cathy Taylor," my father answers her in a slightly tetchy tone.

"Good." Dr. Weinstein puts the photo face down on her desk. "Now I'm going to ask you a few questions about yourself and I want you to answer as best you can. Okay sweet man? She takes Papa's hand in hers again. "How old are you?"

"How old am I?" my father repeats the question instead of answering it. "You must have this information. You have my records, no?"

"Yes, but I need you to tell me."

Papa goes through his age calculating routine, complete with the exaggerated display of shock and denial as he announces the answer. "No, I don't want to be 88!" he protests.

"Why don't you like your age?" Cheryl asks.

"Oh, I don't mind my age. I just don't like hearing about it—it sounds so old."

"I understand," she sympathizes. "But look at all you've accomplished in that time—your children and grandchildren. How many grandchildren do you have, Manny?"

"Grandchildren? I have grandchildren? Papa looks to me. I say nothing. "He's not answering—I guess he doesn't remember either."

"I think Richard knows, Manny. He's not answering you because we both want you to tell us."

"Well, I don't know. I suppose I must." Again my father turns toward me. "You don't have any kids, do you?" he asks me, then quickly follows with, "Oh, that's right, you're not supposed to tell me."

"Go ahead, tell him," Dr. Weinstein directs me.

I refresh my father's memory. Papa's lack of connection to his offspring doesn't surprise me. When I was growing up, he could never keep track of which month I was born in, let alone the actual date. Children were never of interest to my dad, except for lecturing other parents on how to raise them. *What must the doctor be thinking?* I see her writing notes on a pad.

Suddenly, the alarm clock goes off. "What's that?" Papa asks.

Cheryl shuts it off and says, "Your signal, Manny."

"My signal?"

"Yes. What were you supposed to ask me when you hear that bell?"

"I'm supposed to ask you something? Let me see," my dad pauses, then comes up with, "Is breakfast ready yet?"

"That's funny, but it's not correct." Dr. Weinstein waits a few more moments until it is clear Papa cannot remember, then she reminds him and resets the clock. "The next time you hear this clock ring, I want you to try and remember what to ask me," she says while putting the clock back on her desk. She repeats the question one more time. Now she picks up the photograph and shows it to him. "What's this woman's name?"

"I know her name?"

"Yes. I told it to you a few minutes ago."

"Well, I don't seem to remember."

"It's Cathy Taylor."

"Oh, yes, yes—Elizabeth Taylor."

"No. Cathy Taylor," she corrects him. "Now look at the picture and say her name for me."

"Cathy Taylor, Cathy Taylor, Cathy Taylor! But I tell you I don't know this person."

"That's all right. I understand you don't know her. I just need you to connect her face with the name. Now where is your comb?"

Papa points to me. "In his pocket. If he's still got it."

"Good! And your shoe?"

"Over by the window some place."

"Good, very good! What about your tie?"

"What about it?"

"Where did I put your tie?"

"In your desk, I think."

"Excellent! I'm impressed. You did very well with that, Manny."

My dad straightens up a bit, then says, "Well, these are pretty simple things you ask of me. Haven't you got something more challenging?"

Easy, Papa, I think to myself. *This is no time to get cocky—don't forget about Elizabeth Taylor, and the breakfast clock that isn't.*

"Indeed I do," Cheryl responds to my dad's question. "Now, Richard, ordinarily I would ask you to leave me alone with your father so that I might assess his cognitive capacity without inference—however, you have been so good at not prompting him—I would be comfortable with letting you sit in, if you'd like. But I need to warn you that some of this may get painful for you."

"I'd like to stay. And I'm a realist—I know Papa's limitations and I've come to accept them for what they are."

"Okay, fine." Doctor Weinstein reaches into her desk and pulls out what I assume are more questions to ask my father. After reading to herself for a few moments, she looks up and says, "Will you please excuse me for a minute? I'm not going to use these—I think they are too simplistic for your dad. I don't want to insult your intelligence, Manny."

"No, please don't do that," Papa responds.

Cheryl gets up. "I am just going to go to another office and get

261

some more appropriate questions to ask. Can I get you anything else while I'm gone—water—coffee?"

"Water would be good," I say.

"Manny?"

"I wouldn't mind coffee."

"How do you take it?"

"Cream or milk or whatever you've got. But no sugar!"

"Fine. I'll be right back."

A little while after she is gone, Papa asks, "What's she up to now?"

"It's all your fault—you complained her questions were too easy so she's gone to find harder ones."

"Oh, stupid me!" Papa scolds himself.

While we wait, I ask him how he feels and what his impressions are of Dr. Weinstein. He answers that he feels fine and that she seems nice. The alarm goes off. I'm tempted to ask him what he's supposed to say—show him the photo—and see if he remembers where all his stuff is. I don't, instead I shut the alarm off and reset it. The doctor returns. Papa gets his coffee and I get my water.

"I'm sorry it took so long but I had to make the coffee. At least it should be fresh." Cheryl arranges the papers in her hands and begins, "Now, Manny, I'm going to ask you some general questions and I want you to answer them as best you can. No pressure. Ready?"

"Yes, of course—Ebner is always at the ready!"

"Good."

I listen and follow along as she asks some geography questions. Papa flies through the first five answers. In my head I've only managed to answer two. I'm glad I'm not the one being tested. A few questions later and we are on to world history.

Cheryl asks, "In WWI, who was the enemy?"

Papa thinks for a second, then answers, "The Russians, I suppose. It seems the Russians were always our enemies."

"In WWI, I said," the doctor clarifies.

"Yes, yes, WWI. I heard you."

"The Russians were our allies in the first world war," Dr. Weinstein corrects him, then she begins writing something on the questionnaire.

I assume she has marked his answer as wrong. I raise my hand and wait. In time, she acknowledges me. "I hate to interrupt, but I think my dad is right—I mean from his perspective."

"Please—explain," she offers.

"Well, you asked him who the enemy was. During WWI my father was living in Hungary and his father was an Austrian colonel stationed there. As asked, my father's answer was correct. Russia and Austria were indeed enemies."

"I see your point," the doctor says. "I'll throw that question out."

I am in shock. My faith in the medical establishment is momentarily restored. The doctor goes on with more questions. Papa continues to answer better than I could have. The alarm sounds again. Cheryl shuts it off and waits.

My father senses a response is expected from him. "Am I supposed to say something? You're waiting for me to ask you something? What's on the stove?"

"No. You are supposed to ask me—when will I see you again for another evaluation?"

"When will I see you again for another evaluation?" Papa repeats her words precisely and emulates her every tone.

"Where's your comb?"

"In Richard's pocket."

"Your shoe?"

"By the window."

"The tie?"

"In your desk."

"What's this woman's name?" Cheryl holds the picture up again.

"Elizabeth Taylor."

"Ah ha—that's interesting," she says. "Manny, we agreed to call her Cathy Taylor, not Elizabeth."

"Cathy, Cathy, Cathy," Papa repeats. "But I tell you I don't know this Cathy!"

"It's okay, sweet man, you're doing fine," she tells him. "Let's just continue. Pretend you are standing in front of Mount Rushmore, from left to right who is the second president?"

"Jefferson," he answers without hesitation.

The doctor looks down at her papers and then up at me and says, "He's right. Even I wasn't sure of that one. Maybe this won't be as painful as I thought."

Not a very professional medical comment perhaps, but refreshing for its humanism. I look over to my father. He remains undaunted by all of this. I don't know where he gets his strength, and I'm feeling a tremendous sense of respect for him.

Our doctor resumes. "If I were fielding a football team how many players would I need?"

"I have no idea and I couldn't care less," Papa says defiantly.

I raise my hand again. I'm recognized and say, "You know my dad never took any interest in sports—so do you think we could toss that one out too?"

"Let's just see how Manny does with them. There are only a few sports questions." She continues. He can't answer any of them.

In my head, I do considerably better than Papa on this section.

Cheryl moves on to numbers, asking my father to repeat a serious of digits forward and back. Up to seven digits, he is flawless.

Beyond seven we both start to lose it.

The alarm goes off several more times. Each time Papa has no trouble remembering where his possessions are. However, he still can't remember the questions he's supposed to ask, and Cathy Taylor becomes Elizabeth, permanently.

Cheryl explains that the next group of questions relate to road signs. "Normally, at this point I'd show you this series of pictures." She turns the booklet in her hand so that we can see it. "But I think these may be too small for you, Manny—so I'll describe them instead, and you tell me what they represent. Okay?"

"Well, sure, I'm willing if I still know them. I don't drive anymore, you know."

"Just see what you can do. A triangle?"

"That would mean give way—yield."

"Good. A rectangle with a number in it?"

"Speed limit sign."

"A red sign with six sides?"

"Step on the gas and go like hell!" Papa catches a look from the doctor. "Sorry, just kidding. That would be a stop sign."

I think Papa is getting a little bored.

"Now, I'm not sure how to describe this next one." She shows it to me. "What would you call that?"

"A shield, I guess," I answer.

"Yes, of course. Manny, this one is shaped like a shield, or a badge, and it has three numbers inside. What would that mean?"

"A highway marker—route number."

"Very good. Very good indeed! Okay, last one. I'm looking at a rectangular sign with a circle painted on it. Inside the circle there is the letter "P" and across the letter there is a diagonal line."

"I have no idea."

"Any guesses?"

"A "P" you say—with a line through it—Piss Stop!" Papa bursts out laughing.

Cheryl and I laugh as well, albeit somewhat more subdued than him. When we all settle down, I feel compelled to come to his defense again. "That's an international symbol. My father stopped driving before they were in vogue. I doubt he's ever even seen one—so how could he remember what it is?"

"Point taken. That answer is gone," she says, and crosses it off her questionnaire.

With Papa's road test over, Cheryl makes some notes and then takes another stack of questions from off her desk. Looking over at Papa, I can see he's nodding off.

"Manny, are you with us?" Dr. Weinstein asks kindly. My dad startles, slightly. "Getting tired, sweet man?"

"Oh, no—not really, just resting my eyes."

Code name: napping.

"Well, it won't be too much longer now—another 30 minutes maybe. Can you hang in that long?"

"Yes. I think I can manage that. I'm getting kind of hungry, though."

"As soon as we're done I'll take you out for lunch, Papa."

"Ah! Now you're talking, kid. On with the Inquisition!"

Cheryl smiles, then says, "I'm going to read you a story and when I'm finished reading I will ask you some questions about it. So listen carefully."

She reads a short, one-page story. There are only two characters—a hotel clerk and a man wanting to rent a room. The man checking in has one small suitcase. He goes upstairs to his room and falls asleep. In the morning he opens the suitcase to reveal a rope and nothing else inside.

After asking my dad to retell the story, which he does, leaving out only minor details, Dr. Weinstein asks, "Now, what do you think the man intended to do with the rope?"

Forever the general semanticist, my father responds by telling her, "Now, my dear woman, you've not given me sufficient information to make such assumptions. He might want to hang himself. I don't know."

"Interesting—what makes you say he wants to commit suicide?"

"Could be he's depressed. Why else would he rent a room alone and bring nothing but a piece of rope?" Papa questions. "Certainly not to make love." Then he adds, "Suicide has always been a philosophical problem really."

I feel he is being coy with her—holding out from giving her the answer he knows she wants. When I was around eight, my father sat me down and made me take tests that he called "Uncritical Inference Tests." They were developed by a college professor and distributed by the General Semantics Society. The tests consisted of short stories with a list of statements about each story. Those statements could be answered as true, false or questionable. Answering questionable meant the statement could be true or false, but based on the information given in the story you could not be definitively certain.

I remember scoring pretty well on those tests. And now I think I know what's up with Papa. He is trying to teach a Ph.D. in psychology to think more critically. From the facts in the story Dr. Weinstein read to him, he cannot be definitively certain what the man intends to do with the rope. She's not letting him use the questionable answer, and I'm sure this annoys him.

"Can you think of any other reason the man brought a rope with him?" she asks.

"If I put my mind to it I could probably give you a hundred possibilities. Maybe he's a rope salesman and this is his sample rope.

Or perhaps he is a magician and it's a trick rope. But I suppose I should just tell you the answer you want to hear and be done with it. Using his rope, he intends to slip out the window and climb down to avoid paying his bill," Papa gives in finally. I breathe a sigh of relief.

"Good, very good!"

Sarcastically, Papa says, "If that answer pleases you, then I'm happy for you."

Dr. Weinstein reads three more stories. Fortunately, my father is less feisty in his answers and things move along more smoothly.

When all the stories are over, Cheryl tells Papa, "I want you to imagine you're in a supermarket."

"A supermarket," he repeats.

I feel a sense of, "What now?" Papa's tone and expression tells me he's getting tired of being on the hot seat. And he probably is hungry. I know I am.

"Yes, a supermarket—and I want you to tell me all the different kinds of food you might see there. I'm going to look at my watch—and when I tell you to start, you name all the foods you can in thirty seconds. Understand?"

"What's not to understand? Potatoes, car …"

"Not yet!" Cheryl interrupts.

"Oh, sorry."

She looks at her watch and says, "Go!"

"Potatoes, carrots, zucchini, oranges, pineapple, spinach, avocado—a," he hesitates, and tries to continue, "potatoes—no I said that already. A supermarket—well, what else is in a supermarket?" Papa falters. He can't come up with anything else.

We sit and wait for another ten seconds or so. It seems like forever. And in those seconds, I feel the pain Dr. Weinstein warned me about.

Time's up—okay," Cheryl interrupts herself with a sigh, then goes on, "I only have one more item on the agenda for today. However, I'm not sure—with your vision impairment, Manny—I don't know if you can do this next task for me. But let's see how it goes." She gets up, goes to her desk and comes back with a marker and a blank sheet of paper on a clipboard. "I'd like you to draw a few shapes for me. Can you draw me a circle?" Papa does as she asks. "A triangle?" He completes it quickly. "And how about a box or a square?"

To this request Papa asks, "Which is it?" and without waiting for an answer he draws both.

"Nice," Cheryl says. "Okay, last one. Let's get you a clean sheet." Now do you think you can see well enough to draw me a clock?"

"Well, I should. I used to design them, you know?"

"No. When was this?"

"Oh, a long time ago. In New York." Papa reaches out and touches my shoulder. "Before Richie was born, I think."

Richie?

"What sort of clocks were they?"

"Oh, all types."

"Papa designed and built clocks for displays in signs—on stores and other commercial buildings," I add.

"Really?"

"Yes. If you go to the city you can still see some of them," Papa says, then wonders aloud, "that is if any of them are still up."

"Well then, why don't you design one for me?" Doctor Weinstein scooches her chair closer to Papa. Then she places the clipboard on her lap and hands Manny the marker.

He leans over, bringing his face to within a few inches of the paper and presses the marker down. "Am I in the middle?" he asks.

"You're just fine."

Slowly, my dad draws. His hand goes around and connects his line back to the starting point, creating an even, full circle. "There," he says.

Cheryl asks, "Can you number it for me?"

Papa places the numerals around his circle at all the appropriate locations. This takes a little while. Then he says, "I suppose now you'll want hands. What good is a clock without hands?"

"Yes. Could you set them at ten minutes after ten?"

"If that pleases you," he responds.

I watch Cheryl's face light up, as Papa draws one long arrow and one short one in the precise locations she called for.

"There, done! Your clock is set, Madam," he says, while handing the marker back to her.

Dr. Weinstein turns the drawing around to face her, then comments, "I couldn't have done that well with a compass! I guess you really did design clocks. And you haven't forgotten how to do it either!"

With Papa's neuropsychological examination over now, I give him back his comb. Cheryl collects his shoe and tie. He sticks his tie in a pocket and begins putting his shoe back on.

We all stand up and Cheryl says, "It was so nice to meet you today. You and your son obviously have a very special relationship. Manny, you must have given Richard lots of love as a child."

"Yes, well, he was always a good kid—never gave me anything to worry about."

I no longer feel the need to set the record straight. And now, in this moment, I know Papa and I do have a very special relationship, no matter what happened in the past.

Before we leave, I ask the doctor how long it will take her to write her report, stressing my concerns about Papa staying at Littleton House for much longer.

"Today is Thursday. I'll finish it over the weekend and it will be ready the first of next week," she promises.

"And will you be at the final meeting—when we get all the results? I'd like you there, and I think Papa would as well. He doesn't have too many friends in the medical establishment, and I can tell he feels comfortable with you."

"I'm not sure. I act as a consultant for the Deaconess. Generally, I just conduct the consultation and then turn in a written evaluation." My eyes beckon her for something more, and Cheryl adds, "But call my office when you get a date and I'll see what I can do."

CHAPTER THIRTY-ONE

"Leave it to me, kid!"

Back out on the street the day is improving. Morning clouds are giving deference to the sun. The air has heated up into the 50s. Instead of going back to the Longwood stop, Papa and I are walking hand in hand, along the Muddy River section of the Emerald Necklace, toward Brookline Village and the Green Line station there.

I feel relieved and at peace. Although I cannot know what Dr. Weinstein will write in her report, I think Papa proved to her he is not demented. And I got the sense she liked the sweet man.

It's not time to totally let my guard down; however, I need to give myself permission to enjoy this day. The sun feels good on my skin. Trees, with some of their leaves still hanging on, the colors muted now and mostly in the browns, show themselves to me as they stand scattered about the walkways of this inner-city oasis.

Olmstead, the designer of the Emerald Necklace, was another of Papa's heroes. Had Papa been in Boston when he first came to this country, instead of New York, I could imagine him riding in a horse drawn carriage under one of these still beautifully magnificent stone bridges.

Papa and I don't say much as we walk. I think he is all talked out. I don't need words either right now. It is enough to know he loves me. And this I can feel in the way he holds my hand, not to steady himself, but just because he's enjoying the contact.

Once in Brookline Village we find the MBTA stop, sit down on a bench, and wait for the train. After a time, Papa asks, "When are we going to lunch? I thought you said something about taking me for lunch."

"As soon as the train comes, Papa."

"Oh, we have to take the train first? There's nothing around here?"

"I don't know what's around here, but I want to take you for a nice sit-down lunch in Boston. Remember that Thai restaurant Eleanor and I took you to, right after your first evaluation?"

"Oh, yes! That was lovely," he says, enthusiastically.

"Well, if we take the "T" to North Station, we can walk to the restaurant on Charles Street. If you are up for a little more walking." I'm not sure if he really remembers, or if he's just trying to please, or if he's covering up again, and whichever is the case, none of it matters to me. I just want to reward him for all his effort today. I want him to have some small measure of pleasure.

The "T" arrives. Papa and I get up and attempt to board. I hand the operator a 20. "What's that," he says without touching my money. With a look of repugnance, he tells us, "Tokens or exact change only!"

We get off and walk to a nearby store. There is a large sign on the door. "CHANGE FOR OUR CUSTOMERS ONLY!" I read it to Papa and ask him what he thinks we should do.

"We could buy something," he suggests.

"I know, but I only have two 20 dollar bills. We need money for the train and for parking. I'm afraid if we spend anything here we won't have enough for lunch and to get home."

"Well, you needn't buy me such a fancy meal. I'd be happy with a sandwich."

"No, Papa! I want to take you someplace special." *What's wrong with me?*

A few moments pass, then suddenly, Papa grabs me by the arm. "Leave it to me, kid," he says and he drags me into the store.

A balding, middle-aged man behind the counter is reaching up to fill an overhead cigarette rack. "Excuse me, fine Sir," Papa starts in to catch the man's attention.

"Help yah?" he asks, placing the half empty carton down on the counter in front of him.

"Yes my good Sir! We are a couple of poor ignorant suburbanites here in your fair city, and we have recently been informed that we cannot access your fine subway system using paper currencies. We have heard the story of a fellow who could not extricate himself from the train; however, our predicament is the opposite. Could you possibly make change for us?"

"Your name ain't Charlie, is it?" Replaced by a smile, the disinterested expression on the clerk's face dissipates.

"Oh, most certainly not—Manny Ebner, at your service!" Papa declares, followed of course by a bow.

"Well, Mr. Manny, didn't you read the sign out front?"

"Actually, I am legally blind and no longer possess such skills."

"He blind too?" the clerk asks, pointing to me.

"No, he is my son. Isn't he a fine looking boy?" Papa puts his arm back around me, pulling me in close. "And he is so nice to me—he escorted me to the hospital today for my checkup—I'm ninety you know. And he's taking me out for lunch too. That is, if we can ever get back on that infernal train," Papa presses on. Today he is not to be denied anything.

Now the clerk is chuckling. "All right, let's see whatcha got?" He takes the bill from me. "A 20! Man oh man! Now see, that's why we got the sign—people come in here all the time asking for change for the train. We ain't a bank you know." He starts shaking his head and I think we're doomed.

Undaunted, Papa chimes in again. "Kind Sir, we will gladly purchase something inexpensive if this would help. You see in your hand all the money we have. If you could find it possible in your heart to make an exception for us, we would be eternally grateful, and we will promise to never darken your door in the future."

The clerk gives in and opens the register. "Ah right, ah right— I've heard enough of this sob story. Here's change." He starts to hand me the money, then pulls his hand back for a second and says, "I'm only doing this cause of your Fadda—I think he's a scream— never heard nobody talk like that. Made my day!" He gives me our train fare.

"Thank you Sir. You are a gentleman and a scholar!" Papa says. He bows one final time and we leave.

CHAPTER THIRTY-TWO

"What's the verdict?"

On November 5th, at yet another conference table, Papa, Eleanor and I sit together as others continue to arrive. Today is the day our whole family will learn the diagnosis. Eleanor is on my left and next to her my brother Peter seats himself. Beside me on my right, Papa is cracking his knuckles. I think he's nervous, anxious.

I know I am.

Across from us, Donna and members of her family are getting settled. I see her son, daughter, and her daughter-in-law. And of course, Donna's lawyer. Once they are all seated, our side of the table exchange civil hellos with their side.

It feels somewhat surreal.

Standing and milling about, I recognize some of the Deaconess staff from Papa's first appointment here. Dr. Weinstein enters the room.

I am surprised and pleased at the same time.

When I called her office last week to tell her the date of this meeting, I was told it fell on her day off. Her staff wasn't sure if she could make it today.

Cheryl Weinstein walks around the table and reintroduces herself to Papa. "How are you doing today, Mr. Ebner—I mean, Manny?"

Hesitantly, he replies, "I'm not sure yet. Ask me when it's over."

Cheryl reaches out and places a hand on my dad's shoulder. "You're going to be just fine, sweet man," she reassures him. "You have so many people here to help you!"

"I do?"

"Yes. Just look around the room," she instructs.

Papa scans the office the best he can, then looks back at Cheryl. "I see. And you think they are all here on my behalf?"

"Yes! All these people are here because they care about you," she assures him.

I say hello to Dr. Weinstein and introduce her to Eleanor and Peter. Then she leaves us to take a seat a few chairs away.

Papa taps my shoulder and quietly asks, "Do I know that woman?"

"That's the woman who gave you your neuropsychology exam," I tell him. From his expression I can see he still can't place her. "Remember the day you and I went to Boston and rode the trains?"

"Oh, yes! Now that was a wonderful day."

"Remember we saw a doctor that day who kept asking you questions—and hid your shoe," I remind him.

Papa smiles and shakes his head, almost exactly the same way he did when Cheryl first asked him to give up his shoe. Then, "Oh," is all he says.

"Well, that's the doctor, Papa. Her name is Cheryl Weinstein, and she came here today, on her day off, just for you. She likes you."

"I suppose she must," Papa agrees.

As those still standing begin to find their places and we all wait for Dr. Delfs to start the meeting, I continue to contemplate my father's situation. I'm trying to think only positive thoughts about today's outcome. It feels like it has taken several years to get here and not several weeks.

Basically I am a pragmatist, another trait I most likely acquired from my dad, and I realize he cannot manage on his own anymore. There is the reality of his condition; he forgets. And even though the things he forgets are simple things, they are not, contrary to his opinion, unimportant. Clearly, Papa could be a danger to himself. In this Donna and I are in agreement.

Agreement, even if on only one issue, could be a starting point for better understanding. But I'm not sure Donna wants to understand my concerns for Papa, or whether she even possesses the capacity. She seems to find nothing wrong with tricking him to do what she wants as long as she feels it is best for him. Or best for herself.

I think Donna sees my dad as a senile old man. She acts as though he is someone who needs to be stored away with other poor demented creatures, and then when convenient, to be visited, talked pleasantries to, and taken out for an occasional airing. Donna treats Papa like there is no point in involving him in the decisions of life, of his life.

I see a man with severe vision and memory impairments, and yet someone still capable of understanding complex ideas. I see my father, scared, in denial, and needing to know what is happening to him. I want to know also. However, whatever the causes are, the more important consideration for me is how to help Papa have the best quality of life possible for him despite his limitations. He needs to live somewhere that supports his passions of good food, classical music and conversation. Littleton House provides none of those for him.

Dr. Delfs arrives, sits directly to the left of Papa, and calls the meeting to order. "Good morning everyone. I'm Dr. Delfs and I head the evaluation team for Mr. Ebner. First off, I'd like to thank all of you for attending today. Here at the Deaconess we believe very strongly in family involvement, so it pleases us to see so many of Mr. Ebner's loved ones here." He pauses, looks down at his notes for a moment, and continues, "Perhaps we should start by going around the table and introducing ourselves." The doctor looks to his right and says, "Joan, why don't you start."

"Joan Yesner. I'm a social worker here at the Deaconess."

"Hello, everyone. I am Cheryl Weinstein and I am a consulting psychologist for the Deaconess."

"Laura Stanley, staff nurse."

"Attorney Rafanelli, I'm Mr. and Mrs. Ebner's attorney."

"Donna Ebner. I'm Manny's wife."

"Robert Peterson. Donna's son."

"Dena Peterson, Robbie's wife—Donna's daughter-in-law."

"Donna's daughter, Dawn."

"Peter Ebner, Manny's son."

"Eleanor Royte. I've known Manny for over 30 years, and during that time I've grown to love him deeply."

"Richard Ebner, Papa's youngest." I turn to my dad. He doesn't speak up, so I add, "And you are?"

"Oh—you want me to speak? I thought everyone already knew me," Papa says. A short burst of laughter breaks out around the table. When it stops, he says, "Emanuel Carl Maria Ebner von Eschenbach, at your disposal." From under the table I hear him click his heels.

More laughter ensues. Dr. Delfs speaks. "That's quite a title, Mr. Ebner. I don't believe I have ever heard your full name before."

"Yes, well—I suppose since you are the Big Cheese, you can call me Manny."

"All right, Manny. How are you feeling today?"

"You're the doctor. You tell me."

"A little nervous perhaps?"

"Perhaps? It's not that often that one draws such a crowd. What's the verdict? Am I on my way out, or just crazy?"

"No, no, Mr. Ebner. You're not on your way out," Dr. Delfs tells him. "And no one here thinks you are crazy either!"

"You're saying I'm not crazy?"

"That's right. You're as sane as anyone in this room."

"Well, I suppose that could be an encouraging thought," Papa responds.

"You do have some memory impairment, however, and we will address that in a moment." Dr. Delfs turns and directs himself to the table in general. "First of all, since I know Mr. Ebner must be anxious—you're all probably a little anxious—let me begin by stating that it is the assessment of the ElderCare team that Mr. Ebner is competent—both from a medical ..." he glances at the lawyer, interrupting himself for a half second, then continues, "and a legal point of view."

Now I look over at the lawyer. Attorney Rafanelli's face is already showing signs of redness. She's stopped writing on the pad in front of her. Instead she just clutches a number two pencil with both hands. Her knuckles appear whiter than normal.

Time to let go and untie your hands, lawyer.

Next to her, Donna remains silent, but her mouth hangs open. I turn to Papa. He is concentrating on Dr. Delfs. I see no indication of celebration or even relief in his expression. Eleanor touches my shoulder and we exchange long awaited smiles. Just below the tabletop, Peter gives me a very discreet thumbs-up.

As I've been people watching, the doctor has continued

speaking. "… Mr. Ebner has the capacity to make decisions, with appropriate presentation of the information as well as reinforcement of the data," I hear him saying. "Mr. Ebner does have a severe, but relatively focal memory impairment. Other cognitive functioning appears relatively preserved. Additionally, recent historical data suggests a mild disinhibition that we cannot explain by his memory dysfunction."

Always has and always will, I think to myself, and I'm not sure I agree with it being mild.

Dr. Delfs reaches for a glass of water. "Excuse me." He takes a sip and goes on, "This profile of dysfunction versus preservation was confirmed by neuropsychological testing given by Dr. Weinstein. At this point I'd like to turn things over to Dr. Weinstein, as she is better able to speak to this issue. Cheryl."

"Hello again, everyone. First of all, I'd like to thank you for letting me evaluate Mr. Ebner. Manny is a very delightful, engaging man, and it was a pleasure working with him." Cheryl stops for a moment and opens a folder in front of her. "Mr. Ebner and his son Richard came to my office on October 28th, 1993, at 10 a.m. During our visit, I administered selective subtests from the following: the Mattis Dementia Rating Evaluation, the Boston Aphasia Examination, the Denman Memory Scale, and from the River Meade Memory Tests." Cheryl pauses.

I look across at Donna's lawyer again. Her pencil, held in one hand now, races across the top of her yellow legal pad.

Dr. Weinstein continues, "I also had Mr. Ebner draw me a clock, which he did, placing the numerals in the correct locations and he was even able to set the hands at ten past ten, as asked." Cheryl looks up from her notes to face the room. "By the way, Manny also draws an excellent three-dimensional cube," she adlibs, smiling directly at my father.

Realizing Papa can't see that far, I whisper to him, "I guess she really liked your drawing—you've got her smiling at you." My father doesn't react, but rather remains fixated on Cheryl.

Dr. Weinstein returns to the papers in front of her. "These are some of my behavioral observations and a partial summary of the test data," she introduces. Then she begins reading from the report, "Mr. Ebner presents as a delightful, gregarious gentleman. He is somewhat disinhibited, although he was appropriate at all times. Language was well organized and coherent. There were no signs of verbal paraphasia. Auditory comprehension was intact for extended language. In addition, there were no signs of delusions, hallucinations, or psychotic thought processes. Mr. Ebner was not oriented to time, date, or place. However, he did sustain his attention for a 90 minute period. He worked on very demanding tasks and easily followed the conversation between the examiner and his son. Moreover, he asked very appropriate questions." Dr. Weinstein stops to scan a few more pages.

I reach under the table, placing my hand on Eleanor's knee. She turns her head and leans into me. "Exactly as I remember it," I say quietly. Eleanor gives me a kiss on the cheek, and then, recognizing Cheryl is about to speak again, we disengage.

"Overall, Mr. Ebner presents as an intelligent gentleman and it is estimated that premorbidly his intellectual functions were in the above average range. Attention functions for straightforward tasks are intact. He repeats up to seven digits forward, and as noted above, he sustains attention and effort over a 90-minute period. Visual constructions are excellent for a man with decreased vision. Abstraction skills are preserved and Mr. Ebner has an intact vocabulary. Comprehension of simple and complex questions is flawless. When the examiner reads Mr. Ebner simple and complex passages, he can answer questions about the passage, and can even perceive the humor of the passage. He has good recall of remote nonverbal information and can answer questions such as, 'What position is Thomas Jefferson in on Mount Rushmore?'" Cheryl looks up from her notes. "Even I had trouble with that one," she admits.

I wonder what Papa is thinking about all of this. And I can't imagine what it would feel like to have a room full of people hearing an assessment of my capabilities. I hope I never have to be in Papa's place.

"In contrast to the strengths described above, Mr. Ebner has very focal dysfunction in new learning and complex language skills. Word generation skills are compromised, and his recall of remote verbal information is poorer than would be expected given his intelligence. Even with repeated drilling, Mr. Ebner was unable to remember this requested task, 'When the alarm clock goes off, ask me: When will I see you again for another evaluation?' Remarkably, however, he did recall where three personal objects were hidden in the examination room. There seems to be a discrepancy between learning information that is personal versus learning new information that has no value to Mr. Ebner."

He'd say he doesn't want to run out of room in his memory bank.

"Nevertheless, his insight into the nature of his disability is diminished. While he acknowledges that he has memory problems in the office today, he expresses no concern about these memory problems. They were not important to him. In contrast, when he is in the nursing home and is made aware of the immediate situation, his son states that he becomes distressed and very agitated." Dr. Weinstein closes her folder. "My full report, along with my recommendations, will be included in the Deaconess Evaluation Report. But in closing, I just want to add that because of Manny's cognitive strengths, his obvious high level of intelligence, and his ambulatory physical functioning, placement in a low-level nursing home would naturally be very distressing for him. As to the possible causes of Mr. Ebner's memory dysfunction, I'll let Dr. Delfs address that diagnosis. Any questions?"

I wait. No one speaks up, so I raise my hand. Dr. Weinstein acknowledges me, and I ask, "When should we see you again for another evaluation?"

Cheryl smiles. "Good question, Richard," she says. "In order to help determine if Mr. Ebner's memory dysfunction is progressive, or relatively stable, I'd like to reevaluate him in nine months. And now, if there are no further questions, I'll excuse myself and turn the meeting back over to Dr. Delfs." She collects her things, gets up, but before leaving comes over and says goodbye to Papa.

Dr. Delfs takes over again. "Making a diagnosis in a case like this is a somewhat difficult task. The diagnostic issues center around whether Mr. Ebner's memory dysfunction is from strokes—from another focal structural process—or caused by an early and unusual presentation of a more global neurodegenerative process."

And the diagnosis is?

"Given Mr. Ebner's history of atrial arrhythmias and the focality of his cognitive loss, we must consider the possibility of multiple, bilateral strokes—particularly in the medial temporal areas." The doctor turns to my dad. "Did you understand what I just said, Mr. Ebner?"

"I'm having strokes?"

"Had—or I should say, may have had strokes. You're not having them now."

"And when did I have these strokes?"

"Probably three or four years ago."

"You say they've stopped—so do you know why they started in the first place? And why did I stop having them?"

Good questions, Papa!

"Yes, Mr. Ebner. We think the strokes may have occurred when your heart started beating too rapidly. From your medical records we know you were admitted to Lowell General Hospital three years ago for atrial fibrillation. It is our conjecture that this might have led to the rupturing of a blood vessel, and a subsequent blood clot—or clots—in a portion of your brain known as the hippocampus."

"Sounds serious," Papa says. "And what are the ramifications?"

"Well, it is serious," Dr. Delfs reinforces. He speaks directly with my father, as if he were sitting alone next to him, and none of the rest of us were even in the room.

This pleases me greatly.

"Serious, but we believe the initial problem that caused the strokes was dealt with effectively—you're being given medication to control your heartbeat and you've not had any reoccurrences of fibrillation since starting the medication. However, the damage left behind causes you considerable problems."

"It does—and what problems are these?"

"Your memory, Manny. It's not so good anymore."

"You think it's not good?"

"I'm sorry to say, I do."

"Isn't that strange, but I don't notice such problems."

I want to cry.

"I know you don't, and that is part of your difficulty. But you need to trust that the people in this room are here for you. And our ElderCare team has come with some recommendations that may help things be a little less confusing." Dr. Delfs reaches over and places his hand on Papa's arm. "I'm just going to finish telling you and your family my diagnosis, and then Joan will speak to some of the other issues that must be concerning you. Is that okay with you?"

"Yes, of course! You have my undivided attention—if I can remember what you just said."

Once again, laughter breaks the tension in the room.

That's my Papa. Playing for the crowd as usual.

"All right then, as I've already stated, our diagnostic considerations center around definition of whether there is evidence for focal structural disease, or if the evidence points to a more generalized neurodegenerative process, with apparently focal cognitive loss related to the fact that Mr. Ebner—Manny—was extremely intellectually gifted at a baseline. Given his history of atrial arrhythmias, other structural processes are less likely. However, discerning this information is particularly important in the case of strokes, as he is at risk for having had multiple embolic events. This is an important issue because of the therapeutic considerations of the need for anticoagulation if strokes were the case. I am further recommending that an MRI of the brain be done to delineate this possibility. —Joan?"

"Hi, everyone, Joan Yesner here. I'm the social worker, just to jog your collective memories. Well, I want to tell you, Manny, all of us on the ElderCare team have really enjoyed our time with you. We understand how unique your situation is, and how difficult it must be for you. And we also know how difficult this can be for the whole family. But Manny is certainly worth the effort. I'm sure you all agree."

I'm not sure all agree, but it's the right thing to say.

"One of the major problems with memory loss is that the person with the loss is most likely unaware of the problem. Because we have all experienced forgetting something, it doesn't seem that unusual to the one with a memory impairment. And many times it can be subtle at first. The important thing for family is to be patient with Manny. Always remember, he is not forgetting things deliberately to annoy you."

Although he might enjoy that capability.

"As Dr. Delfs has told you, we at the Deaconess have assessed that Mr. Ebner is fully capable of making decisions about his life and care. For example, where he wants to live and with whom. However, he will need to have information presented to him clearly, reinforced, and carefully spelled out so that such issues as safety and the need for twenty-four hour supervised settings are figured into the decision-making process, regarding his place of residence."

All I ever wanted from the start. Finally, true professionals have listened and spoken.

"We further recommend a process of facilitated conflict resolution for the family. This could be accomplished with a mediator from the Deaconess, or if preferred we can provide a referral. The goal would be to establish a process to promote good decision-making by Manny and to mentor appropriate interactions between all concerned. Thank you for attending today," Joan finishes.

Dr. Delfs closes the meeting. Some discussions happen about a time and location for a family meeting. It's agreed that Joan and her assistant will serve as mediators, at least initially. In groups of two and three the staff is thanked. The room empties.

Downstairs in the hallway, I overhear my brother. He has the attorney cornered and asks her, "How soon can you make the arraignments to have my father transferred to Sutton Hill?"

"I'm not sure my firm can involve itself in such matters," she responds. She looks nervous—very nervous.

"Are you thinking that now there is a conflict of interest?" Peter follows up.

"No, I'm not saying that. I just don't know if we are best equipped to handle this. You know, Donna has also engaged another attorney—a specialist in elder affairs—the best in the state,

I believe. I'll check with my boss first, but perhaps her other firm could better take care of this—as things are, I mean. I'm sorry but I must get back to the office. I have client meetings this afternoon."

Peter backs off, and as she ducks away, he says, "Well, thanks for coming."

I figure this is the last time I'll see Attorney Rafanelli, but I don't feel compelled to say goodbye.

Eleanor goes with Papa to help him find a bathroom. Dena, Donna's daughter-in-law, leaves the area where her family is still milling about and comes over to me. After saying hello, we are joined by my brother. Dena greets Peter, then says, "I just want to tell you that we are all in shock. From everything we've be hearing from Donna lately, Robbie and I assumed your dad was completely out of his mind. We thought today would be the day the Ebner boys would have to face facts. I guess the surprise is on us. If there is anything I can do to help, please call me. We're just down the street, and I want you to consider us as family. I always thought Manny was kind of neat."

Peter and I thank her. Eleanor returns with Papa. On our way out of the building we encounter Donna.

My father goes up to her and asks, "So I'm going home with you now?"

"Oh, Manny," is her response.

Eleanor chimes in, "Donna, just be honest with him. That's all anyone wants of you."

Donna directs her next question to me. "Will you take him back?"

"Yes, Donna."

"Manny, you're going with Richard," Donna tells him.

CHAPTER THIRTY-THREE

Blue Skies

On a cooler than normal July day in 1994, Papa and I sit at a table, under an umbrella, on the white concrete patio at Sutton Hill. The assisted living center where he now resides is across the street from a horse farm. From where we are seated, I can see several horses milling about the paddock.

Inside the recently built facility, there is a real, restaurant style dining room, and Papa has not complained about the food during the few months since moving here. He has made friends to talk with, or lecture. Several women seem interested in him, as women tend to be. Donna continues to visit and Manny continues to ask her when he can go home, but less often it seems. My brother Peter bought him that electric keyboard, which we set up in his room. I'm told he plays it every day.

Behind us, the Harold Parker State Forest borders the back edge of the Sutton Hill property. There are miles of logging roads and trails in the 3,000-acre reservation. Plenty of space for Papa to move around. And dogs are welcome. Later, the three of us will go for a walk. Right now, Baby is curled up in a tight ball on her beanbag bed. She looks cold. Our writing project is on the table, but we haven't worked on it as of yet today. No one else is in sight.

"Good to get outside for a while, hey, Papa?"

"Glorious! Look at that sky, nothing but blue." Papa gestures, pointing to all he sees above him. Then he holds his hand out beyond the shade of the umbrella. "Imagine, the sun is some ninety-three-million miles away and yet in an instant it warms me. This is living, I tell you. Of course it isn't really an instant. At the speed of light, it takes seven or eight minutes to reach us. But for all intents and purposes, that's instantaneous."

"So what would you do if you only had seven or eight minutes to live?"

"Do you know something about the sun?"

"No, Papa. As far as I know the sun is fine. I'm just musing. What if you only had a few minutes to live—what would you want to do?"

"What a thought. Do you know something about me—am I sick?"

"No, Papa, you're fine—I mean, other than your macular degeneration, arthritic knees, occasionally erratic heart and short-term-memory loss, you're just perfect. Good to go another ten years easy."

"You think so?"

"I know so, Papa. In the last six months we've seen more doctors and specialists than most people see in a lifetime. Trust me, you're in great shape. So—how about it? If circumstances were different and you were about to check out, what would you want to do?"

"I guess I'll have to trust you."

"And trust me, you can. But indulge me as well. What would you do with your last eight minutes?"

He considers. "Well—I suppose I'd want a last meal."

There's a surprise.

"Knackwurst would do. Did I ever tell you why it's called knackwurst?"

Only 50 times or so. "No, why?"

"Well, if it is cooked just right it crackles, and when you stick your fork in, it goes *k-nack*. Oh, that is a wonderful sound. Why, I could eat one right now!"

"Papa, you just had breakfast. What else?"

"I'd probably like a good beer to go with my meal. Something with a nice head on it."

"Okay, we've got the food and the booze covered. What's next?"

I get Papa's infamous raised-eyebrow look. "Listen to you, 'booze.'"

"A Heineken then?"

"That would do nicely. And I'd like to hear Beethoven one last time."

"His Ninth?"

"Sure, but it really wouldn't matter. You can't go wrong with anything Beethoven."

I remember a little anecdote my brother Peter told me about not long ago. Apparently, the last time Manny and Donna were at Peter's house, my brother played a recording of Beethoven's Ninth for Papa. Peter had just gotten a new surround sound system and he knew our dad would appreciate listening to his favorite music on something better than his old record player. As told to me, father and son were hunkered down in chairs that had been moved to the middle of the room for full stereo effect. Manny, eyes closed, swayed to the music and conducted from his seat, at times even standing up. At one point Donna, who had been in the kitchen, came into the room and started talking about getting the oil changed in her car. Apparently, Manny yelled at her, screaming,

"Good God, woman! Do you know what you've just done? That's Beethoven, for Christ's sake!"

"So far, Papa, we have Knackwurst, Heineken and Beethoven. Care to add anything else?"

Papa takes a few moments, gives me his impish look, then says, "A beautiful woman to sit on my lap—without a stitch on! Ha, ha, ha, ha." Papa's laughter is somewhat maniacal at first, but soon changes and becomes more like that of a five-year-old that's just said *underpants* aloud, in front his parents.

I can't help laughing as well. *I guess some things are worthy of interrupting Master Beethoven.* "You sure make the apocalypse sound like fun."

"We all have to die sometime."

"I know, but isn't the thought of all humanity being wiped out at the same time just a little more unsettling? I mean, isn't there some comfort in knowing that your offspring will live on after you're gone?"

"Perhaps, but that's a luxury of thinking that you can only partake in while you are alive. Once I'm dead—I'm sorry, kid, but Manny won't give you a thought. I won't hear anything, I won't feel anything, and I won't see anything."

"But, Papa, even Jesus had his moment of doubt. You really don't think there's anything more to life than this?"

"First of all, Jesus was just a man—nothing more—and all men have doubts—except for me of course. Just look around. Breathe in and out—touch, smell, taste—listen—talk to me. Life is exquisite! I just don't understand why everyone is so dissatisfied. It's all pretty damn marvelous, if you ask me." Papa pauses. "What, you want it to last forever? Sorry—that's not going to happen." And he adds his all too familiar mantra, "Kid, you've got to go with what you are given. The past you can't change—the future you can't know—

always live for the moment."

"True enough, Papa. I'm glad you are living for the moment. And I try to do the same, but sometimes I wonder if there isn't something more—some state of being after we die—physically, that is."

"Life after death? A pipe dream, my boy. That is the nonsense of religion. People have been deluding themselves with that kind of thinking, or I should say non-thinking, for many centuries. Understandable for the caveman to construct fantasy gods to help mitigate the scary unknown. But in this day and age we have science."

My father's tone feels demeaning to me. Filled with arrogance. "Science doesn't explain everything. What about intuition?"

"Examples, my boy!"

"Okay, when I was nine, I remember being home with Mom when the phone rang. Before she answered, I said aloud that it was Carl and that he had been hurt. It turned out the call was from the hospital. Carl had cut himself badly at work. How do you explain my knowing that?"

"Happenchance." Papa responds in less than a second.

"How so?"

"You may have been worried about Carl for any number of reasons. The phone ringing simply triggered your subconscious to express itself. The scientific approach would be to establish how many times in your life the phone rang and you had no clue. I'd venture to guess that, statically, your one experience has no validity in confirming the existence of intuition."

There've been others. Part of me knows I'll never change my father's views about anything. And yet I keep trying. I'm not really sure why. "Since you are an atheist, Papa, I know any form of a god is out of the question for you, but I can't be so sure. That's why I'll

295

remain an agnostic."

"And I thought I had raised you to be a good little atheist," Papa says.

"God knows you tried! I guess it just didn't stick. But more important, you raised me to think critically and always question authority. And it seems a bit pompous to say you know for certain that there is no such thing as god, or some form of existence after the one we are experiencing right now. Just as it seems presumptuous for any one religion to claim to have the true answer. Call me a fence sitter if you like, but I'll remain an agnostic and just let the mystery be."

His demeanor softens, becomes less high and mighty, as he jests, "Well, I only hope it isn't a picket fence you are sitting on." He leaves it there.

I leave religion there as well and neither of us brings up politics. Although, politically we most likely agree. But what does any of that really matter?

Noticing some activity at the front of the building, Baby uncurls herself, gets up from her bed and concentrates in that direction. A car has just pulled up and a man with a white cane is being guided into the lobby.

"What's up with her?" Papa asks, not being able to see what the dog sees.

"A man with a white cane is being helped into the building. He must be blind."

"I see—said the blind man."

"Papa, you're too funny. And speaking of being blind, how is it that most people don't have any idea you are legally blind?"

"Well, that is between me and my lawyer."

"Seriously! Even Dr. Schreiber … *reinforcement* … your new primary care physician here at Sutton Hill, even Dr. Schreiber didn't realize you had vision problems until he read it in your records. And Dr. Schreiber is a specialist in geriatrics, so he must know what to look for. How do you seem to fool everyone?"

"You want to know my secret. Okay, I suppose since you are my sonny boy I can tell you. My peripheral vision is still pretty good—especially on a bright day like this. If it's cloudy or in the evening when things are mostly grayed out I don't do as well." Papa turns his head slightly to the right. "See those orange marigolds in the pot next to me—they are marigolds, aren't they?"

"Yes, Papa, marigolds they are, and orange too."

"Well, by turning at just the right angle I can distinguish things just fine. Early on when my central vision started to go, I noticed that people seemed uncomfortable with me for some reason. I soon figured out that it was because I wasn't making eye contact anymore. People don't like it when you aren't looking them in the eye. Makes one appear shifty, I suppose." Papa turns his head back to the left. "By maintaining a 15-degree angle or so, I can see you out of the corners of my eyes, and yet to you it seems as though I'm looking straight at you."

"Amazing, you're right! I can't tell." He looks proud and happy. *I'm proud to be his son.*

Baby gets back into her bed and goes to sleep, while Papa and I just sit quietly for a while and stare into the clear blue sky together.

CHAPTER THIRTY-FOUR

Richard-24—Papa-seven

If this story that Papa and I wrote together were a novel we might have ended it with that blue-sky day back in 1994; the Hollywood *happy ending* version. Technically our story is considered a memoir, and since that genre is based on real events, we didn't have the ability for total control over our outcome. But if you, as the reader, wish to end Papa's tale there, you can stop reading now. Papa was always a big supporter of individual choice.

So, what is the story and how does it end?

Is it "… a story of human redemption told with dignity and compassion," as my editor Teresa Franklin Foden wrote for the back cover? I hope all who have read thus far agree with those kind words of praise. Personally, I do not feel redeemed as of yet.

Aside from having Teresa scrutinize my words, I invited 13 avid readers I know to read all the chapters except this last one, which isn't even finished yet, but is in part inspired by their reactions. Some of the feedback I received asked for more backstory and for me to tell what happened after chapter 33. I was asked, "Why did it take you so long to write when the story being told took place in a time span of only two years?" Fair question. My best attempt to answer will follow.

I think I now understand the feedback that confused me the most. Several of my prepublication readers wanted to know more about the Judy that was my mom. At first I thought—what is ambiguous about the title? It is not called *Saving Ma and Pa's Tales*. Then I considered the fact that all my readers were women and mothers themselves. Give 'em what they want.

Behind the scenes

Some of the backstory asked for by my minyan of readers, ten of which were Jewish women, is material contained in the original 600-page manuscript that was rejected by publishers from 1994 to 1996. Throughout the first 33 chapters I feel I have followed at least one publisher's advice and limited the scope by keeping the storyline mostly about Papa. This last chapter is mine alone, so— like Sinatra—I am going to do it my way!

The early years of Sutton Hill

There were many more walks in the woods, afternoons on Eleanor's porch and evenings in her kitchen. We all cooked, talked, listened, read, and tried to always live in the moment. But Papa continued to ask when our book would be ready for others to read.

Year one

I met a customer who was a published author and a writing coach. I told her about our story. She was intrigued and offered to have a look. Soon we started bartering my carpentry skills for her literary knowledge, and I enrolled in some of her writing workshops. Eventually she connected me with her agent.

The agent, after reading the first half of our story, favorably compared the writing style to that of Albert Camus. *Albert who?* I thought at the time. Being more cultured than I, Papa knew of Camus. He even corrected me when I spoke the silent letter at the end of Albert's last name. I decided to read the *Plague*. It depressed me. However, I have come to realize that if I live long enough I will face the plague that is being old, and as of yet there is no vaccine for aging.

Despite my ignorance of Camus, we had an agent willing to sign and she advised Papa and me to have professional publicity photos taken of us. Papa's tales were on their way—or so we thought. After completing the second half of our story, which was filled with every awful experience of my childhood, the agent dropped us.

Undaunted, and consumed with arrogant ignorance, I sent my own query letters to the major publishers of the time. All turned us down, or to be more precise—turned me down. Most of the rejections were polite single-paragraph, snail-mailed letters. Only one publisher agreed to review the entire manuscript. That publisher liked Papa's character, but felt, "… the story is not told in a manner that we feel would captivate our readers." Too much son and not enough Papa. I tossed out 300 pages of me. However, a complete rewrite became necessary. Our project stalled. To paraphrase John Lennon, life happened while we were busy making other plans.

Lawyers

Contrary to my assumptions about never meeting attorney Toni Raffanelli again, she and I did have further business together. Along with a lawyer my brothers and I hired, Toni was instrumental at helping draft a new power of attorney for Papa. As a result, Donna maintained control over Manny's finances. My brothers and I agreed not to challenge her right of ownership to our father's house. I was officially, in writing, given the power to make medical decisions on Papa's behalf.

Without Donna's established trust in her own lawyer, I doubt she would have agreed so easily to such an arrangement. Once again, I was forced to adjust my judgmental attitudes about lawyers in general, and this one in particular.

Manny's Donna

Good to her word, Donna visited Manny almost weekly. Our visits overlapped at times, like birthdays and holidays. Those are the busiest days at senior citizen institutions. I wouldn't say Donna and I ever became good friends but we found a way to be civil with each other. And I did come to understand and accept that Donna truly loved my father. I think he made her feel that she was intelligent. I don't know that anyone else in her life ever allowed her to feel that way about herself. After all, the mere fact that he married her proved she was smart—Manny didn't hang with dummies. But more important to me was my sense that Papa never stopped loving her.

Year two

During that second year at Sutton Hill, there were more blue-sky days and gray rainy ones as well. Papa and I had the opportunity to ride on the escalator and take trains to and from Boston again. The "sweet man" was reevaluated by Dr. Cheryl Weinstein to measure the progression of his cognitive loss. Everything remained stable for a time.

Year three

In year three, Papa had a brush with a complete recovery from his memory dysfunction. Not only could he remember what he had for breakfast, but he also remembered supper from the night before.

He could tell me all who had sat at the table and remembered the conversations shared over the meal. Papa had three such lucid episodes like this, each lasting about three days.

I remember the first episode most vividly. In the car on the way to visit Papa, Eleanor and I had been arguing over money, or rather my lack of it. On the elevator we managed to drop the argument for the moment. When we entered Papa's room, he was standing beside his bed, staring at one corner of the ceiling.

"Are you all right, Papa?" I asked.

Without changing his gaze, Papa answered, "Oh hello. I didn't know anyone else was here." Then he said, "You should have told me we have company." His words seemed directed at that same spot he was fixated on.

"Papa!" At that he turned toward us. "What are you doing?"

"Sorry—I was just conversing with my angel up there," he said, while turning away again and pointing to the ceiling. "Too bad—she's gone now." Then Papa looked back at Eleanor and me. "How are you two doing?"

I walked over and gave him a hug. When we separated I said, "So you are seeing angels now. Who would have thought that could happen? You do realize there is no one else in this room but the three of us, don't you?"

"But of course! Manny Ebner is nobody's fool! She wasn't a real angel—whatever that means—she was just a hallucination of what I'd like an angel to be—if there were such a thing. She looked like Elizabeth Taylor too—and—she was naked!"

"I suppose I should be happy for you," I said. "But I hope this doesn't mean there is something wrong with the sun and we only have eight minutes to live. Seriously, though, I wonder why you are having hallucinations. Tomorrow I'll ask the doctor if they changed any of your meds."

The conversation shifted as Papa asked, "How's work going?"

At that, Eleanor spoke before I could. "Work—what's work?" she questioned sarcastically.

I became enraged, left the room and walked the 18 miles from North Andover to Ruthellen Road in Chelmsford. The next morning, after my temper tantrum had subsided, Eleanor told me about the rest of her visit with Papa. Apparently there was no sign of any memory loss. I needed to witness that for myself.

Driving this time, I went back to see Papa. He was just finishing breakfast when I arrived. When he was done, we went out to the patio and I asked my typical question, "How was breakfast?"

"Scrambled eggs with sausage—quite good actually! The cooking isn't too bad around here," was Papa's response. I was surprised by this, but what he said next amazed me even more. "Eleanor told me you filed for bankruptcy. I didn't know that you were doing so poorly financially. I wish you had told me. I might have been able to help."

"I'm sorry. I guess I didn't want to worry you, Papa."

"Don't worry about me. I'm fine. If you need to visit less so you can concentrate on work, I'll miss you—but I won't have any trouble finding someone to talk with. Shy, I'm not!"

"It's not that. Visiting you isn't keeping me from working. I just don't find being a contractor fulfilling. I mean—I like the interactions with my subcontractors and my customers—well, most of them. And I do like being able to see what I've created by the end of the day. I suppose carpentry might beat being a lawyer for endorphin production, even if the pay isn't much of a match. But my brain is starving for more sustenance."

"You need to decide what you want to do. Life goes past pretty fast, sonny boy. If you want to be a writer—then just be one. Figure it out and do it! And if you also need to be a carpenter until you can support yourself with your writing—just do that too. Don't like what you've become or where you are at? Reinvent yourself!"

Over the next two days we talked about ways he could help with my business, not the book. When Manny used to work for Sylvania he was nicknamed the Silver Fox, partly for his hair color but mostly for his silver tongue, metaphorically speaking. Manny could convince anyone to do just about anything Manny wanted.

Papa's eyesight was too poor to assist me with office work or carpentry. However, his tongue seemed to be working better every minute. He offered to call all of my past customers to see if he could drum up some work. We even talked about him moving in with Eleanor and me.

Suddenly, I not only had my Papa, but I also had the father I always wanted as well. The father who would counsel me and help me figure out how the world works and what I really wanted to do in that world.

Then just as suddenly, by day four, that father was gone and Papa's ever-shortening short-term memory reappeared. I have no explanation for what happened inside Papa's brain. His medications had not been altered. All the medical professionals were intrigued but as baffled as I was.

We were invited to participate in a study. The Simulated Presence Theory study (SPT) was being offered by the Veterans Administration in cooperation with Harvard Medical School. It consisted of my making recordings of myself, and then someone on staff would play them back for Papa between my visits. This fit in well with the process of recording *Saving Papa's Tales* that we had already been using. The goal was to see if there might be improvements in memory, mood or behavior. During the course of the study, which lasted about three months, I could not perceive of any clear changes in Papa. And Papa's three, three-day periods of total clarity did not overlap the study period. I was never informed whether the efficacy of SPT had been established or even analyzed.

Papa's other two episodes of clarity are not as clear to me. I think I anticipated they wouldn't last, so I didn't invest as much in them. Strange, though—how they came in threes. Of course, Papa would say that was happenchance.

Back to work

Like my father before me, I had already reinvented myself many times: born again agnostic, babysitter, dishwasher, drug store clerk, soda jerk, high school dropout, office worker, commercial popcorn popper, vacuum cleaner salesperson, encyclopedia salesman, warehouse foreman, motorcyclist, school bus driver/carpenter, lumber truck driver/carpenter, carpenter/snowplow operator, drug user, writer, drinker, carpenter/contractor, home inspector, radio talk-show host, newspaper columnist, caregiver, gambler. What next?

I called past customers myself. Slowly, I grew my carpentry business. I hired an assistant, who despite having no carpentry skills became my best employee. I continued to take writing workshops. In secret, I gambled. In private, I drank too much. I was paying my bills on time once again. I rebuilt my credit and bought two trucks. Eleanor and I reestablished our relationship. From the outside, I looked successful. Inside I still felt unfulfilled.

Papa and I kept talking about our book project for another three years. He started to struggle more with remembering. I continued to struggle with the structure of the story. When I read my unfinished writings to others, often they were confused about where the story was chronologically. Sometimes I was confused as well—and I wrote it. Only a special few authors can take their readers forward and back without losing anyone. This is an incredible skill that I confess I do not have. My lazy solution for this last chapter is the bold subject headings centered on some of these pages. Hopefully they will help you stay located in time. You might also want to use them as an arbitrary place to take a break.

Y2K

While much of the world was concerned with electronic devices losing their minds and not being able to distinguish the current century from the next or the last, and thus we all might not know what day it was and whether our paychecks would arrive on time, my concerns were focused on Papa's state of mind. He didn't seem to care about most anything anymore, least of all the date.

Food and our shared dog still provided a reason to keep living, but even those interests were waning. Papa had been diagnosed with age-onset diabetes during those early years at Sutton Hill. He was put on a restricted diet. When out with me, the restrictions were gone. His having made it to 95, I felt, gave him permission to eat whatever he wanted.

In 2000, he started wearing diapers. And strangely enough, he seemed to be trying to send a message to the staff, fellow residents, and perhaps me. I remember sharing a meal with him and his compadres upstairs on his living floor, for he no longer attended the formal dining room downstairs (ties not required—but loaded diapers frowned upon). One of his buddies was furiously waving his hands as an indication that he was about to soil himself. Papa said to him, "Just let it go, man! What are they going to do—throw you out of here?"

Papa had a few falls in the new millennium. Or was it? There seems to be some controversy over that. Are you of the Gregorian mindset or another? Anyway, my father didn't give a shit about what century we were in and neither did I.

What I did care about was keeping Papa safe. And after one occasion of his having fallen, I followed the ambulance from Sutton Hill in North Andover to Holy Family hospital up on the hill in Methuen, Mass. Within a mile of arriving I could already see the lighted cross on top of the hospital building. I wasn't terribly worried, however, as I knew Papa's poor eyesight and his position in the back of the ambulance saved him from seeing what I saw. But I did perceive some irony. Manny the atheist being delivered to a Christian hospital for salvation.

The x-rays proved negative. No broken bones. Why is it in the health field a negative, often means the desired positive outcome?

Back at Sutton Hill life went on. I started being coerced to sign a DNR (do not resuscitate) order for my father. Administrative staff gave me pamphlets to read about how awful it would be if and when Papa might have his ribs broken just to save his life for a few more moments. I read that most never survived the intervention and those that did were worse off than being dead. Their lives would be miserable thereafter. The lucky ones spent their remaining days in a coma.

During one meeting, it felt like I was also being pressured to feel guilty about what the nurses, doctors and EMT's might have to go through during the process. *If I had some strong religious conviction that made me believe all life must be prolonged and preserved at any cost, would they be hounding me so?* I wondered to myself. *Or, because my dad was an atheist and I was an agnostic, should I just be submissive to their rather aggressive requests that bordered on demands?* I chose not to acquiesce.

My refusal to sign had nothing to do with my being in denial about the facts, although it may have been perceived that way. Observationally, I felt I noticed a higher level of attentiveness for residents that did not have a signed DNR. Legally, some old lives seemed to matter just a little more than others. I could have been wrong.

As for the frontline troops in eldercare, they have my gratitude and my sympathy. A for profit approach to taking care of the elderly must be a difficult business model to construct fairly. It seems most people I've met in this field are overworked, underpaid and severely stressed. I wonder if some of them might want to reinvent themselves and their jobs.

The year 2000 was extremely stressful for me as well. Papa was no longer interested in Papa's own stories. Our conversations lacked focus. If not for Baby we wouldn't have had anything to talk about.

2001

Early in January, Papa took control of his life with the only powers he had remaining to him. He stopped eating, refused to get up, and made no efforts to use his bedpan, although for the first couple of weeks he did allow me and one of his favorite aides to spoon-feed him supper. But it was obvious he was just humoring us.

So began my early training in the techniques used to change diapers, change sheets and generally maintain a bedridden adult life form. Initially my offers to help were refused by the nurses and aides, as they asked me to leave the room whenever they needed to clean up my dad. Aside from fearing I'd be in their way, I think they were embarrassed for me.

On one short-staffed day, that all changed. I learned how to remove a soiled diaper from a person unable to help, and too heavy to carry to a changing table. Papa's favorite aide taught me her procedure to move Papa safely to one side of the bed so dirty sheets could be extracted and fresh ones could replace them. Working in unison we became comfortable with each other and within a couple of days we made for a pretty good team. And even though this aide was from Puerto Rico, she never changed the station on Papa's boom box. All classical—to the end of time!

By midmonth we moved Papa to a private room right next to the nurses' station. I called the local chapter of Hospice. And I signed Papa's DNR.

January 21, 2001

Baby and I entered Papa's room a little before dawn that day. "Baby, come wake Papa," I asked her, and then as I lowered the bedrail I added, "Go easy." Papa was curled up in a semi fetal position with his torso and legs under the blankets. His head and arms were exposed. Our dog licked his face—just once. One sweet gentle lick. He did not wake. "Good girl, you tried," I told her and patted her head.

I found one of Papa's hands and sandwiched it between my two hands. His hand was still warm and soft. "Papa, it's Richard and your doggie," I whispered. There was no answer. I felt his pulse. It was not strong, just strong enough. I squeezed his hand and the hand responded in kind. He said nothing.

Nearby there was a blue, hard plastic chair. I grabbed it, then slid it close to his bed and sat. With the rails of the bed down I could lean in. "Papa, I love you," I told him. His eyes remained closed. It was not the first time I said I loved him, but I feared I had not told him that often enough. I felt I had failed him. Papa's tales were almost over and still no book.

There was one large window in the room, almost as wide as the room itself. Outside a windy mix of snow and rain had taken control over the local environment and obstructed any view of sunrise. I watched fat fluffy snowflakes twirl in the air and collide against the window. There they would stick for a moment, before slowly sliding down the glass as they melted.

Other than occasional voices from the corridor all I could hear was Papa's breathing. It was quiet, shallow breathing, but seemingly unlabored. Hospice had referred me to a pharmacy that made a morphine rub for him. It did its job nicely. Papa had no iv's attached and no machines that go beep. The only tube touching him was the mask-less cannula for oxygen. He didn't appear bothered by that and it certainly made breathing easier.

I wanted to call Eleanor so I looked in my jacket for my cellphone. It was not there or in my pants pockets. I put the bedrail up and told Baby to stay with Papa. Then I went down and out to my truck. No cellphone.

Back at the nurses' station I called Eleanor from the desk phone. "Hi, sweetie," she answered. "How's he doing?"

"He was okay when I left him."

"Where are you? I can barely hear you."

"Sorry—I'm on the station phone. Kind of noisy—shift change!"

Nurses and aides were busy passing on information about the overnight. Some of the conversations were about Sutton Hill residents and their needs. Others talked of husbands, children, boyfriends and pets. No one was trying to be loud and distracting. In that moment, no one other than me had a father who was about to die.

"Where's your cellphone?" Eleanor asked.

"I was hoping it was home with you."

"Oh. Wait a minute—I think I see it—yep, got it. Do you want me to bring it when I come?"

"If you come. The weather kind of sucks—and Papa is pretty stable so far. The last thing I need right now is to worry about you getting into an accident."

"Okay. But let me know if anything changes. Oh, did you call Donna?"

"No. I think one of the nurses did. I kind of hope she doesn't come. I know she has a right to be here, but I really want him to myself just now."

"I understand. Call me later—bye. I love you!"

"I love you too, bye."

I put the receiver down and slipped back into Papa's room unnoticed. Baby greeted me with a few thumps of her tail as it hit the hard tile floor. Her bed was with us in one corner but she had chosen to be closer to Papa. I got down on the floor with her. "You're such a good doggie, doggie." Baby leaned into me and wagged her tail more enthusiastically. "Yes you are—oh I know— yes the best dog ever." I began rubbing her tall straight ears.

Great Danes are not born with their ears standing up. At birth their ears are similar to a Hound dog's floppy ears. A procedure called cropping forces them to look like those erect ears I painted for the cover of this book. The surgery involved in cropping is elective and some feel it is very unnecessary and maybe even cruel. Baby was already 11 months old when Eleanor bought her for me, so the deed had been done. I'm not sure what I think or feel about cropping.

"Maybe if you had been my dog back then instead of Sargent things would have turned out differently," I told Baby. Although, if she had been that dog, Baby would also be dead now, just not murdered. I switched from rubbing her ears and began messaging her belly. She sighed a relaxing sigh.

During the rest of the morning nothing much happened. The nurse checked in on us several times. Papa got his morphine chest rub. I moistened his lips from time to time using a straw. Dried lips were the only discomfort I was able to perceive. He'd purse them ever so slightly, indicating to me he was thirsty. After dipping the straw into a cup of water, I'd cap the top with my finger. Holding it closely over, but not touching Papa's lips, I'd release some water one drop at a time. As soon as I saw that Papa had swallowed I would stop.

By afternoon, it was snowing less, but still snowing. As of then, Donna had not arrived. Eleanor and I spoke on the phone a few more times. At some point the room felt cold so I turned on the room heater that was located under that large window. I had shut it off earlier so that I could monitor Papa's breathing audibly as well as visually. After the room was warm enough again, I opened the control cover and shut down the unit. Once the momentum of the fan dissipated the room became quiet and still.

Too still. Too quiet. I put my ear to Papa's chest. There were faint sounds of life. Some air and fluids continued moving inside Papa's body, but when I squeezed his hand that last time, the hand did not say, "hello" back to mine.

I called Eleanor, who offered to call Donna and the family to let them know Manny would be leaving us very soon. None of them arrived in time to watch Papa take his last breath. I got my selfish moment.

"Papa," I began, after I was sure he was no longer alive—physically, "you did that well. No drama. You just slowly let the air out of your tires. I am happy for you and I am thankful to you for teaching me much about life and death." Out of respect for Manny—that was the closest I could come to saying a prayer for Papa.

Another ending

If *Saving Papa's Tales* were a tragic opera, this might be another good place to stop. After escaping the nursing home and embarking on telling his life story, he dies before publication, and much to his son's chagrin, Papa never has the chance to be the star at any of his own book signings.

At home when I was a child, on most Saturdays, Papa would listen to the live radio broadcast of opera from the Met. That was before the Toll brothers paid the bills and Texaco was still the major sponsor. "You can trust your car to the man who wears the star, the Big Bright Texaco Star!" Wasn't exactly opera, but a catchy jingle nonetheless. Sometimes I stayed long enough to hear my dad start singing along in his native tongue to the German operas like Wagner's or Mozart's. Usually, though, I tried to leave the house when I heard the Texaco ad begin and thereby manage to skip the opera altogether. Well, are Papa's tales over? No. They are not over until *the skinny sonny boy sings*.

Funeral for an atheist

How do you burry a nonbeliever? I started by bringing Donna a dozen red roses and letting her know they were from Manny. This gesture was genuinely appreciated by her and she agreed to having us plan the service together.

Back beneath the white steeple of the Unitarian Church in Chelmsford Center, where Donna and Manny had wed nine years earlier, many of the same cast of characters gathered to say goodbye. I gave a eulogy. Actually, it was the first public reading from the annals of *Saving Papa's Tales*. I chose Chapter 30, "On with the Inquisition!" In case you need a reminder, in that chapter Dr. Weinstein recognized the sweetness in my father, and Papa was—well—so Manny.

My encomium went on too long, I'm sure—still I figured no one would leave while praise was being delivered for the dead, and I saw nothing wrong with taking advantage of my captivated audience. Papa missed the opportunity to sign off on his life's story but Manny had a moment to shine, even if it was posthumously.

Being better at long-range planning than I, Donna had already handled the gravesite and marker thing many years before. Cremation had been Papa's expressed choice, but he never said anything to me about where he wanted his ashes to settle. Section one, lot number 66, grave one, in Chelmsford's Pine Ridge Cemetery would have to do. Donna had obtained a three-for-one deal. Eventually, the two-time widow would rest with both deceased husbands. As of then, though, only Ken and Manny shared a plot in eternity.

My obsessions

Papa's passing was both a relief and a letdown for me. I no longer had to witness his struggle to remember. He had prided himself on an ability for total recall, even if at times it was for obscure facts—especially for obscure facts—if anything really is a fact.

My disappointment was that he had not fulfilled his promise to stay alive until this book was published, thus I could no longer give him equal billing. The truth is I was disappointed in myself. I wasn't a good enough writer yet and Papa couldn't wait long enough for me to gain the necessary skills.

After about a year's hiatus to grieve, I began working on our story again. Eleanor was supportive to a point. However, Eleanor's mother, Hilda, was by then in her mid 90s and could no longer live on her own in Florida. Eleanor moved Hilda up north. I helped.

Every two weeks, Eleanor and I would count out Hilda's pills. She had more than 20 different medications that needed to be put in the proper compartments of the two, morning and night, times two, seven-day pill dispensers. At Hilda's assisted living center she had paid privately for aides 24/7, but they weren't allowed to dispense medicine. Twice a month, Eleanor or I, or both of us, would drive the 12 miles each way to drop off the meds for her mom. As long as Hilda removed the pills from the containers herself, everyone was covered legally.

Nearly every Saturday night we would take Hilda out for dinner and a movie. All three of us were movie enthusiasts so it was a comfortable way to spend time together. But supper out was not always that pleasant for me. Still, I felt I owed some payback to Eleanor. And after all—I was the one with the most experience in the process of managing an elderly parent's last years.

Back at 4 Ruthellen Road, in Chelmsford, household carpentry projects were in disarray. Many were started and most not finished. Customer's projects were also always getting behind. My obsession with *Saving Papa's Tales* was again impacting my life in mostly, but not all, negative ways. And I worried that my other obsession of trying to be a people-pleasing caregiver would win out over my writing. In an attempt to silence my idées fixes, I continued to drink too much alcohol.

Between my being the health-care proxy designate for Eleanor, Papa and my brother Carl, and also riding shotgun for Eleanor with her mom, I could have written a travel guide, instead of this book, to many of the area hospitals in Eastern Massachusetts and Southern New Hampshire. I sampled food from the cafeterias of all of them, and sometimes stayed overnight with my patients.

Friends, family and my brother Peter in particular got sick of hearing about a potential book. In Peter's case I think I asked to borrow money from him too often. He counseled me to just get a *real job* and get over this writing thing. If you are still reading now, then you already know I did not heed his advice.

Goodbye, Baby

The year after Papa's passing I had to say goodbye to Baby. She had grown old with Papa. It was a good life, but too short for my liking.

Great Danes' average life span is from about eight to ten years. Baby made it to almost 11, or in people years about 72. I still miss the times the three of us had together.

Eleanor and me

Eleanor was my parents' friend before she was my friend and lover. We met when I was just 15. It was a one-time babysitting gig for her three children that brought me into her life momentarily. At first, I didn't like her. But back then I was angry most of the time and aside from my mother, I didn't really like any adults.

At 20 we met again. It was 1973 and my mother had organized a women's consciousness-raising group. The seven women in the group met at my parents' house once each week. My dad made plans to be out of the house on those nights, or if not, he knew best to stay in his room.

I was back under my parents' roof having moved home again when the war in Vietnam and the draft seemed to be ending. No longer burdened by my low lottery draft number of four, I changed my plans to attend college and instead found work in the textile industry as a warehouseman and truck driver.

Those condos located in the five-story brick mill buildings at 200 Market St., in Lowell, were at that time the home of Pandel Bradford. The company manufactured synthetic suede used in the footwear industry. Pandel gained notoriety with the white Go-Go boot material that Goldie Hawn wore on the television show *Rowan and Martin's Laugh-In,* the TV show I consider to be the forerunner of *Saturday Night Live.*

When the employees began trying to unionize, the big bosses promoted me to foreman and I became part of the lower-tier management. There were 15 workers I was in charge of and most were much older than I. It was my first and only experience working for cooperate America. I worked second shift.

Often when I got home around 11:30, most of the women in my mother's group were still hanging around talking about their troubled relationships. All of them, except my mother, were in their mid- to late 30s. Eleanor was one of those women. She was 37 and in the process of a divorce. Over time, as their collective consciousness was raised, three others including my mother followed Eleanor's lead and divorced their husbands.

In high school, I did have a girlfriend close to my own age, but that ended not long after my delayed graduation. She was a Catholic. My atheist parents were always challenging her about religion, and I had not become an agnostic yet so I wasn't very supportive of her.

From then on, my interest in girls my own age waned. They didn't seem to have anything to attract me, or perhaps I wasn't attractive to them. Older women, however, were fascinating. They had lived, given birth to children and wanted to share their perspectives and feelings with those who'd listen. Apparently, I listened well.

Usually I was hungry when I got home from work, and all of my mother's *sisters* seemed to want to feed me. While I ate whatever was left over from their potluck supper, I was bombarded with questions about what men thought and why they behaved so poorly. What did I know? I was still really just a boy. I offered no opinions. As it turned out, that was a good strategy, although there was nothing deliberately planned on my part.

Even though the peace movement was winding down as the war ended, some of the concepts spawned by that era were still in force for many of us hippie types. *Love the One You're With*, a Stephen Stills' song, was still being played fairly often on my stereo. I interpreted the lyrics to mean that it was okay to sleep with someone other than your chosen partner, if that partner was far away in Vietnam. None of the women in my mom's group had husbands overseas. Their feelings of distance and separation occurred while living under the same roof with their partners. I had romantic encounters with two of the women, but I was most intrigued by Eleanor.

When Eleanor spoke, we were simpatico on almost every topic. Over time, and because we lived just 20 houses away on the same street, we began walking each other home after the meetings. I'd walk her to number four. She'd check on her children and then walk me back to 24. Sometimes we'd repeat this process several times on the same night.

Eventually I got the nerve to invite her into my room to listen to music. Every artist I liked, she liked. We listened to the Moody Blues, Bob Dylan, Cat Stevens—or Yusuf Islam as he wishes to be called now, and Joni Mitchell—especially Joni Mitchell. Eleanor even managed to change my opinion about opera by introducing me to the Italian ones, like La bohème. I became moonstruck with Eleanor.

Tensions at home continued to increase as my parent's marriage disintegrated. I moved back to Lowell. At 115 Nesmith St., in the Belvidere section, I found the perfect first floor apartment. Situated in a two-story wood framed building, with only three other one bedroom units inside, there was a little side yard and I was given permission to plant a vegetable garden. A small covered porch, just big enough for two, faced west. Often Eleanor and I would sit there watching the setting sun turn the brick buildings in the city below into a fiery reddish orange, and the windows of those buildings into thousands of sun-filled mirrors.

In April of 1980, I officially moved into Eleanor's house for the long haul. In the beginning none of my family or Eleanor's family understood us. No one expected us to last one year—let alone 31. I remember an interesting phone call that demonstrated the prevailing sentiments of the time.

When I answered Eleanor's landline, the voice on the other end said, "Who is this!" There was no question in her tone, only annoyance.

Although caller id was not available yet, I knew who was on the other end. "Hi, Hilda," I answered.

"Oh, never mind! Get me Eleanor," she demanded.

When her mother questioned why I was answering Eleanor's phone, Eleanor responded to her by simply saying, "Well, he does live here. Remember?"

In Hilda's way of viewing my being her daughter's partner, I already had three strikes against me; I was too young, didn't have a college education, and I wasn't Jewish.

2004-2011

Skipping forward in our relationship past 25 or so Passovers, Eleanor and I started going for couples' counselling. She needed to hear, in front of a witness, that I was done having affairs with other women. To break the silence on the first day, I came prepared with a poem that I read aloud.

"I call this *A Conversation with Myself*," I began.

I'm talking to you, Mr. Intellect, speaking now about cause and effect.
I cannot let you rule any longer, I am Heart and I am stronger.

Be careful what you choose to do, I am Brain and I think things through.
Without me you're at a loss, remember now who is your boss.

Your time is over, foolish mind, you have been reassigned.
You've led me down a crooked past, but I am here, here at last!

You cannot be serious, emotions have made you all too delirious.
I've been here since the start, let me go now and you'll fall apart.

That's a chance I'm ready to take, listening to you has been my biggest mistake.
Keep your thoughts inside, now is my time to decide.

I don't know how it has come to this, living large I thought was our bliss.
Many a woman is still out there, experimentations are everywhere.

Robert Rimmer has left me slowly, and in this regard so have you.
Eleanor is my one and only, and from this day on I'll stay true.

After a few moments to let my words dissipate into the walls and the furniture in the office, our therapist asked Eleanor how she felt about what I had just read. "I always liked his poetry. It was one of the things that made me fall in love with him in the first place," Eleanor responded. Then she looked at me and smiled. It was a short, quickly fleeting smile.

"Good—good, but how does this particular poem make you feel?" The counselor asked. "Had you ever seen or heard this one before Richard read it to us?"

"No. Not the poem itself. But he has promised not to cheat on me before and he never keeps his promises." Eleanor spoke as if I had left the room and didn't even glance in my direction. "I'm worn out. I don't know if I can invest in trusting him again. Things can seem okay for a couple of years—and then—just as I'm beginning to trust that our relationship is real—well—he confesses that he's slept with someone else."

At that point I needed to speak up. "Sleeping with other women doesn't mean you and I aren't in a real relationship. After all—you are the one who asked me to read *The Harrad Experiment* in the first place." I heard my head respond—instead of my heart.

At first Eleanor denied she was the one who gave me Rimmer's book. Then she disremembered, and finally acknowledged what I said was accurate. But she dismissed it by saying, "That was too long ago to even talk about. He should have been done by now."

What could I have said to that? My heart knew she was right and my head knows it now. Ironically, my heart had already assumed command a few years earlier. Prior to counseling, I had remained monogamous for about four years, or almost twice my usual cycle of infidelity. Too little, too late.

But I still feel the elephant in the room that day wasn't about my sleeping around, and it wasn't in my pajamas. During almost two years of couples' therapy, I cannot recall one mention of my drinking too much alcohol. We talked intensively about my poor work ethic and my lack of financial responsibility. Eleanor finally expressed her displeasure with what she herself had started calling my "obsession with *Papa's Tales*."

"Papa is gone. Time for Richard to move on," she told the therapist.

I know my drinking bothered Eleanor, but I think she felt that if we spoke about that, I'd get too angry and she'd pay the price when we got home. Please understand, I never hit Eleanor or any other woman. I can't say I always practiced the same restraint with men, but we men can be a different breed, as some of us only respond to anger with more anger, leading to physical contests and too often to actual attempts at bodily contact, clumsy as that most often is, and usually for all the wrong reasons.

For me, when it came to alcohol and anger, I behaved much

like my mother did, but stopped short of the spitting, hitting and tendencies to throw objects at my father, which I had witnessed so many times in my childhood. Instead I got loud, swore and slammed a few doors on my way out. Then I'd go for a long walk to calm myself down. Although I never verbally threatened Eleanor or gestured any intent of physical harm, my yelling and slamming were threatening enough.

In 2011, a few days past Thanksgiving, and shortly after Hilda's Hospice nurse had been assigned, I slammed Eleanor's doors for the last time. She locked the front door behind me, and we never shared another night under the same roof again.

Hilda and me

I know that some peoples' impressions about who I am have not changed over time. They probably think I am still a selfish bastard. I've felt that way about myself for a long time. However, Hilda's opinion of me did change for the better. In her 96th year of life, she said to me, "Don't ever leave me. I feel so safe when you are around." From then on I got a genuine hug and a kiss on the cheek whenever we said goodbye. The hugs and kisses lasted almost six years, two months shy of her death at 102.

My separation from Eleanor

The first year of our final breakup was extremely contentious. My office, my workshop, my supplies and all the tools that didn't fit in my truck were on Eleanor's property. I had to prearrange every visit to 4 Ruthellen Road in order to access my computer and workshop. Understandably, since she wanted me gone, she wanted my stuff gone as well. For various reasons, some hers and some mine, this took another five years.

During that half decade, I was bombarded with texts and emails from Eleanor in which she pointed out many of my failings as a human being, and as a carpenter. Her written words were often fully capitalized and peppered with multiple exclamation marks. It felt like she was yelling at me—something she had never been able to do in person.

The carpentry issues pertained to various projects at her house that were still unfinished when we were finished. I did my best to connect her with some of the several tradespeople I still had good working relationships with, and I explained to all of them what remained to be done to reach completion. My other shortcomings remain my own problems to adjudicate.

Gone

I received only one handwritten letter from Eleanor during our dissolution. It came addressed to me at one of my many temporary locations of those years. A couple a little older than I had given me the opportunity to babysit their home while they spent the colder months in Florida. I used my contractor skills to maintain their property and in return they allowed me to stay there rent free. I am extremely grateful to them and so many others that had my back in those difficult days.

Set down low from the road and within 65 feet of active railroad tracks, the house I watched over and lived in had a back yard that consisted of extensive wetlands. This property seemed like the outcast of the suburban Billerica neighborhood where it existed. Built in 1874, it had been there long before most of the other houses on the street and was once an official railroad master's house. Rumor had it that some of the Hells Angels also lived there for a time. A perfect setting for a castaway like me.

The day Eleanor's letter arrived, I remember walking up the steep driveway to the mailbox that was across the street and two houses away. It was early evening and the MBTA commuter trains to and from Boston and Lowell were running every 25 minutes. When I pulled the day's mail from the box, I instantly recognized Eleanor's handwriting on one of the envelopes.

Back at the kitchen table, which always shook noticeably as the trains passed, I studied the envelope before opening it. The lettering was playful and multicolored—much like letters and notes we wrote to each other when we were one. I was hopeful that the message inside would match the impression I got from its container. I opened it slowly.

"You don't know what you've got till it's gone," Eleanor started by quoting from a Joni Mitchell song. The song is about not valuing our environment—but I knew what she meant from the get-go. Then she reminisced about all the ways I had listened and seemed to understand her better than anyone else in her life ever had. On November 30th, 2016, almost a year to the day after my receiving that letter, Eleanor died. Simpatico once more—I didn't know what I had until she was gone.

Me in my 20s

A few months after moving into my apartment on Nesmith St., Pandel started laying off nonunion employees and generally downsizing. The oil shortage created by OPEC drove petroleum prices up and caused sales for Pandel's products to drop. The company's production process relied almost totally on oil based chemicals.

Also, President Nixon, a Republican, had created the Environmental Protection Agency in 1970, and the EPA may have been looking into some of the colorful things going in the canal at the back of the mill. Periodically the waste chemicals emitted into the canal would be ignited by carelessly discarded cigarettes. I witnessed displays of blue flames traveling atop of the water along the length of the canal. Below the surface bright orange carp could be seen swimming, seemingly unaffected by the conflagration above them. The image was eerie and had a dreamlike quality. But that was back when America was great and we could take pride in our productive pollution.

Because I was the least senior foreman with no dependents, I was the first to be laid off. The company gave me six weeks' severance pay and my unused vacation days. The timing was perfect. It was late spring. I had just purchased, in cash, a brand-new motorcycle and a four-year-old, really hot Mustang convertible with a 351-cubic inch engine. Hello summer!

I know it wasn't that smart to buy a gas guzzling car during a gasoline shortage. There were very long lines at the stations. You could wait in line for over an hour and finally pull up to the pump, only to discover the underground tanks below were empty. However, because I wasn't working I could choose times to fill up when others could not. The Mustang had a large gas tank and my little Honda motorcycle could go 80 miles on one gallon of gasoline. I became quite skilled at syphoning fuel from the car to my bike.

While the economy was in stagnation I was thriving—or so was my perception of myself. Unemployment benefits were extended, allowing me to collect $90 a week for nine months. My one-bedroom apartment cost $125 a month, with all utilities included. I was required to look for work, but I couldn't be forced to take a job that paid less than my last one. There were few employment opportunities available, and even fewer at my former rate of pay, which back then was almost five times the minimum wage of $1.60 per hour. And no potential employers were going to hire me in particular once they heard my story. To be in my early 20s, with only a high school education, and to have had the level of pay and responsibilities I'd been given, didn't add up. During job interviews I got the sense that no one believed me.

The best part of being unemployed was the freedom it provided. I had plenty of time to explore and experience life. I painted, wrote poems, created a multimedia art viewing box that I showed at open exhibitions—and I joined a saloon members softball team. My explorations also included sex, drugs and rock-and-roll. Alcohol wasn't experimental anymore as it was when I had started drinking at the age of 11. By the time I reached 20 drinking was, to me, just a known staple that it seemed everyone took part in—and it was actually mandatory to drink in the bar-softball-league.

As you know, I read at least one book about alternative lifestyles. The permission it gave me to have multiple simultaneous relationships fit in perfectly with the situation I had stumbled upon. Over time, as Eleanor and I grew closer, she wanted me all for herself. Unfortunately, I kept the experiment going far too long.

When my unemployment benefits finally ran out I took the training to become a school bus driver, and after passing my road test, I began driving students to Lowell High, and the Greater Lowell Technical High School where Eleanor taught. To supplement that income, I started what was initially a handyman business that I registered in 1977 as *the Village House Surgeon*.

I find it interesting the assumptions derived from a name. Some years later when web sites came along and I built one for my own little enterprise, I began receiving complimentary magazines for my nonexistent waiting room. According to a few software/marketing gurus, I'd become a doctor without ever going to medical school.

If you look up the business name on Angies List today it appears as though I'm still running a construction company even though I closed that chapter of my life in 2015 when one of my knees wore out. Misperceptions and disinformation created on the internet seem to remain there indefinitely. I suppose it is just part of the *fake news* phenomenon I've been hearing so much about lately.

At first my little side business did pretty well. I was making more money doing carpentry than I was driving a bus. I sold the Mustang, bought a Dodge Power Wagon with a Fisher plow and I quit the school bus gig. My plan was to plow snow during the winter when outdoor carpentry work would be less reliable.

This might be a good time to reassure you that I am not going to embark on telling you about every line of work I have ever tried or every experience I've had. I already skipped over: dishwasher, drug store clerk, soda jerk, office worker, commercial popcorn popper, vacuum cleaner salesperson, and encyclopedia salesman. I assure you, none of those particular categories will be revisited. I'm not making any such promises about the others on my list. Anyway, aren't you a little curious about my claims of being a radio talk-show host?

I started plowing in the winter of 1978. Anyone that experienced the blizzard of 78' in Massachusetts might agree that it had a surreal effect on them. In Boston and surrounding towns most roads were closed to commuter traffic for more than a week. Much of Route 128 was a parking lot of abandoned cars. When Governor Michael Dukakis declared a state of emergency banning all nonessential driving—cross country skis and snowshoes became common means of transportation—and fun too I suppose for anyone able to participate in the aftermath of the storm in that manner.

For those of us engaged in snow removal the storm also had a captivating effect. At one stretch I spent over 35 hours in my truck without any sleep. From February 5th until the 12th all I did was drink coffee and move snow. I refer to the experience as snow removal rather than plowing, because with the drifts and the sheer quantity of snow, there was no place to plow it to. Shovels, snow blowers, frontend loaders and dump trucks were also needed. A shovel I had. The others had to either be bought, rented or hired. In all cases the necessary equipment was in short supply.

My route consisted of 27 private driveways, three retail stores and two apartment complex parking lots. This was a big work load for one piece of equipment and one operator. Even though there was no place to drive to, everyone wanted to know when their driveways or parking lots would be cleared.

During the last storm of that season, at two in the morning, while plowing the parking lot of what was then an auto parts store located just outside of Chelmsford's center, the universal joint at the back of the front driveshaft failed. As a result I had to crawl under the truck in about six inches of salty slush and remove the shaft altogether. The right replacement part was inside that store, but of course the store was closed. I finished plowing in two-wheel-drive.

Plowing was supposed to be my perfect solution to carpentry's slow season. That plan was done and so was I. The following winter I wouldn't be plowing for hire, but rather just for survival.

Even though I never drank or used drugs while operating the plow or other potentially dangerous equipment, at most other times I did. This became a problem. On Christmas day in 1979 I packed up the essentials: my hand-held tape recorder, stereo receiver, amplifier, turntable, vinyl records, reel-to-reel and eight track tape decks. Then with the plow attached, I prepared myself for the drive to the White Mountains of New Hampshire for a three-month sabbatical from everything except writing/recording and listening to music. Before I left my father predicted I wouldn't last a week. His prediction alone, was motivation enough for me to tough it out.

Staying Stoned

The title of my first book *Staying Stoned* is somewhat misleading. In isolation—at what was a summertime only, campground and youth hostel, called Lime Kiln Camps—during an exceptionally cold winter, I reflected on my past drug uses. While there I remained straight and shared what was happening all around me by talking into my tape recorder. The cabin I stayed in was uninsulated as summer cabins usually are. There were two woodstoves for heating, but I hadn't stocked in any firewood prior to my arrival. I never claimed to be very good at advanced planning.

During those three months, with my first Great Dane named Misty, we witnessed nature's complete disregard for our wellbeing. Some nights the temperatures outside went down double digits below zero. Inside the cabin I often woke in the morning and discovered that the water in the dog's bowl had turned to ice. Out on the Chippewa Trail, Misty and I encountered coy dogs and the bloody aftermath of the deer they had attacked in order to survive themselves. The trail was closed to tourists in the winter, so Misty and I had the place to ourselves, but we shared it with the native wildlife of course.

In April of 1980 Misty and I returned to civilization and moved into Eleanor's house. I was 27 then, and while restarting my carpentry and snow-plowing businesses, I worked on transcribing the tape recordings from my winter expedition. This took another few years. In one of the summers of those years, my basketball buddy Glenn, the artists/cartoonist, went back with me to Black Mt in New Hampshire to make drawings of the camp and the kiln. Once completed, I flew to California and pitched my book to what may have been one of the first *Just Say No* organizations in this country. After reading *Staying Stoned*, they just said no.

House Calls

Mustering up my best Robin Williams impersonation, I announced, "Good Morning Merrimack Valley! Welcome to *House Calls*. This is Richard Ebner and right beside me is my cohost Joe Scaduto. For the next hour, we will ...." It was 9:00 a.m., Friday January 17th, 1992, the morning of my first live radio broadcast. Seven months later I would be at Donna and my father's wedding. The wedding I tried to stop.

My career as a once a week radio talk-show host lasted two years. Those two years overlapped the original story told here as *Saving Papa's Tales*. In addition to the radio show, I had created a newspaper column of the same name that appeared in *The Minuteman Chronicle* each week.

By September of my second year on radio I was also trying to save Papa's *tail*. When I wasn't on the phone advocating for Papa, or visiting assisted living centers, I was meeting with potential guests for the show, plaining the next show, and trying to concentrate on getting my newspaper column written by deadline.

Finding the personal space to launch a new career, maintain my struggling contracting/home inspection business during a recession, and be a supportive partner for Eleanor, while also trying to free Papa from the nursing home, was a load. Oh, and not to mention—but of course I will—my mother died during that second year of radio. I'm not complaining—just explaining. It was too much story distraction to tell during those first 33 chapters. No such problem here in sonny boy's chapter.

The idea for *House Calls* came to me while taking courses in home inspecting at Northeastern University. I had already been doing home inspections for about eight years when it occurred to me that it might be good if I learned what others in the field were doing. Seeing an ad for evening classes that were being offered by

Northeastern, I enrolled.

It was in my first class in 1988 that I met Joe Scaduto. He was a home inspector himself, had written a couple of books on the topic and was the creator of the five-course curriculum. Joe taught the introductory and overview class. Specialty subjects like plumbing and electrical inspections were taught by licensed plumbers and electricians. There was even a course on legal issues given by—you guessed it—a lawyer.

I liked Joe immediately. Much like Papa, he drew people to him with his gregarious presentation style. Less like Manny, he often showed humility or at least faked it well.

Joe introduced himself to our class as a Sicilian with a cousin named Guido whom he alluded to as a member of the mafia. When warning the class about shady things to watch out for while performing a home inspection, Joe often referred to a particularly dangerous condition he had come across as something his cousin would have done. Pennies, instead of fuses, in a fuse box were an example of a Guido job. I think this was just a shtick, but with family you can never be too sure. In Massachusetts, one Bulger brother was elected, and the other brother was convicted.

Joe and I became friends, although he never introduced me to his cousin. He was impressed with my writing skills as they pertained to the sample reports we were required to produce as homework assignments. By the end of the first semester, Joe and I formed a publishing company called ESP (Educational Specialty Publications). A workbook tailored to his two home inspection books and then used in his subsequent classes, was the first and only publication by ESP.

In my second semester, after class, Joe and I would talk shop. We'd share stories about our previous weeks' inspections; if we had any inspections that week. Joe's stories were always funnier than mine. During one such conversation I brought up the idea of doing a radio show together. My concept was modeled loosely on the *Car Talk* radio show syndicated on PBS and locally produced there in Boston. At a fundraiser for WBUR, that I had previously attended in the Good News Garage in Cambridge, I met Tom and Ray Magliozzi. In person, they seemed the same as they sounded on-air. I figured Joe and I could do something similar only about houses instead of cars.

Why not? As my mother often told me when I was little, "Teddy," she'd start, "always remember, here in America you can be whatever you want to be, even President." My mom came here from Sweden in 1920, when she was nine.

Well—maybe not President? Even though my middle name was given to me by my mother in honor of the American President she held up as her hero, not for his military heroics, but as one politician who seemed to care as much about conservation, as he did about conservatism. "Square Deal!" But I could never get myself qualified for that job anyway—too much ego needed—even more than mine. A Supreme Court justice maybe—hell—I used to like beer and I used to drink it too! But I digress, and I apologize for spearing the low hanging fruit with my sarcastic barb. I know as well as anyone, that an individual's proclivity for drinking does not concretize who they are, or all that they may have accomplished in their lives. My bad.

Anyway, Joe was intrigued with the idea of us being radio personalities, although he told me he wasn't a big fan of *Click and Clack*. I think he might have been envious and just a little jealous of the *Tappet Brothers*.

But Joe was motivated. When I got us an appointment to pitch our show idea, Joe came to the meeting with his best stuff. Apparently it wasn't good enough for NPR. About a week later

WBUR turned us down in one of those single paragraph letters I was getting used to.

We re-focused. Setting our sights a little lower, I contacted the two local AM stations in Lowell, WCAP and WLLH. After a few meetings with the station managers, WLLH accepted our proposal. Actually, Joe and I bought their counter proposal. For $150 a week, the station would give us an hour of live on-air time, minus commercials, news, weather and sports. They would also provide a producer to monitor us and screen the incoming phone calls. We agreed, and for the first year Joe and I split the cost.

The first show was awful. Our chosen topic was Radon and neither Joe or I were feeling it. The expert guest was very knowledgeable, but not the most exciting fit for a live, call-in radio show. No one called-in.

Before the next show aired, I listened to recordings of that first show. It was painful. In between the awkward moments of silence, I counted myself saying, "um" 39 times. Dead air time and repetitive stammering are the kisses of death in radio.

My producer, whom I nicknamed Jiminy Cricket as he was always in my headset, became my radio conscience. He suggested a visual to help eliminate the dreaded um. I wrote the word um on a poster board, drew a circle around it and then put an x through the whole thing. Before each show I taped my European style, road sign up on the wall behind and above where the guest expert would be sitting. It worked! Four shows later not a single um was heard throughout the Merrimack Valley.

The show started to sound better each week, but we still were not getting many callers. I began coercing friends, relatives, employees, customers and my subcontractors to be phone call plants. On-air we pretended not to know each other. I never told anyone at the station, or Joe about my behind the scenes scheming.

Near the end of year one, Joe lost interest in doing the show. "This just isn't going anywhere," he told me. "I can't afford the time—between my commute from Lynnfield and the hour doing the show—I lose three hours each week. And for this I'm also paying 75 bucks. Sorry—but I'm done at the end of our contract."

Joe had a good point. I too was suffering financially. All my attempts at finding sponsors for the show had failed. Stupid me didn't realize it was the economy—and that—no businesses in the housing industry were going to spend money advertising on a radio show with virtually no audience.

But I didn't want my dream to end just then. One of our first-year guests was a female electrician who had started her own electrical contracting business called City Lights. I convinced her to be my co-host for the second year. And I negotiated a new contract with WLLH. They still would not pay me to do the show, but I no longer had to pay them.

"Good Morning, Merrimack Valley! I'd like to introduce my new co-host Maryanne Cataldo. Good morning, Maryanne."

"Good morning, Richard—and hello to all our listeners out there."

My new radio partner was extremely smart and had already, 'reinvented' herself as Papa would call it. Having studied economics at the University of Massachusetts, she graduated *summa cum laude* and became a Phi Beta Kappa recipient. When we first met in 1992, Ms. Cataldo was already a master electrician, and in addition had just gotten her MBA from Harvard Business School that year.

But Master Electrician Maryanne told me the rigors of becoming an electrician, particularly as a woman, far exceeded anything else she had tried thus far. "I'm a card-carrying member of the International Brotherhood of Electrical Workers—Local 103—in case you want to check on me—and yet—I often get questioning looks on job sites. Men seem to wonder what I'm doing there. And some of the sleazy one's asked for services I was not interested in providing."

With Joe, I was the straight man. He and Guido were my comic relief. This approach wasn't going to work for Maryanne as she was too serious and too new to radio. Being the seasoned veteran—of a whole year—it was up to me to change my role.

During the first year of *House Calls*, most of our guests were buddies of mine or Joe's from the trades. This made introducing them easy and allowed for a friendly on-air atmosphere. Much of my job was to follow the instructions being whispered to me by Jiminy Cricket so that I could get us in and out of commercial breaks smoothly. Aside from that, I could sit back, listen, and interject only when needed. Pretty easy—really! Then, without Joe, and having already done 50 shows, I had run out of tradesmen buddies.

Maryanne advertised City Lights in a publication devoted to promoting women in the trades. This eight page directory became my expert guest list for the second-year's shows. Female plumbers, carpenters, roofers, interior designers, stained-glass artisans and faux painters were all on that list.

I didn't know any of them when I started calling their business numbers and introducing myself. A few were very suspicious at first. It seemed they thought I was trying to sell them radio advertising. Once I dropped the name of my cohost all was copacetic.

Because I wasn't familiar with any of the women's work, I felt the need to have a look at some of their past projects before having them on the show. This, combined with my father's drama, reduced the time available to find what little billable work there was to be had. As a result I was getting closer and closer to bankruptcy.

For the show I needed find a role that I could succeed in. People pleaser? Nope—already proved impossible. Good listener? Getting better every day—but something was still missing. Story teller? Oh Hallelujah!

I decided to write short fairytales as an introduction to a shows particular theme. "Once upon a time—long-long-ago and far-far-away, in a part of the world we now know as France, there lived a boy who wanted to be king …. His father sent him to the land of Faux, to….and when he saw himself in the mirror—he looked just like Elvis Presley."

Thus began the introduction to the show featuring Iris Marcus. At the time Iris was an artist that also painted houses. When I viewed her portfolio and then visited some of her work, I fell in love with her talent. She could make wood look like granite and visually turn PVC plastic into marble. Of the nearly 100 *House Calls* shows, that one with Iris remains my favorite.

For a time we became friends outside the show. Friends—with no other benefits than friendship—which was benefit enough. We saw the physical world around us from a similar perspective. Iris studied at Mass College of Art. Both of my parents exposed me to art at an early age and my mother in particular, encouraged me to be artistic. Whatever their shortcoming's as parents, I am grateful for the support and encouragement they did give to me. My artistically nurtured sole helped make a for great show that day and a wonderful, but too short, friendship between Iris and me.

Maryanne and I were also becoming friends. Aside from the weekly hour spent in the studio together, we sometimes went out for breakfast after the show. Soon Eleanor became suspicious that more than just cohosting was going on. Since the show had been moved from Friday mornings to Saturday mornings, Eleanor could listen in. She heard things that I did not.

When I told Eleanor I was thinking of inviting Maryanne to visit my father with me at Sutton Hill, Eleanor protested. She expressed her opinion that business shouldn't be mixed with family. I argued that it would be good for Papa. "Maryanne is an electrician and Manny was one a long time ago. I think both of them would enjoy comparing how it was done back-in-the-day versus how it's done today."

"I know you'd enjoy that," Eleanor responded.

Her sarcasm wasn't lost on me and I dropped my plans for introductions. I stopped having breakfasts out with Maryanne and maintained a strictly professional relationship with her to the end.

When the second year's contract was concluded in January of 1995, I terminated *House Calls*; show and column. Soon after, I filed for bankruptcy.

Homeless

I don't mean to imply I was ever "park bench" homeless, or the kind of homeless that many others are experiencing right now in tent shelters and makeshift structures all across this country of ours. Mine was the feeling of not having a personal emotional sanctuary where I could shut out the rest of the world, even if just for one night at a time.

But I always had Maslow's basics, and I was even gaining some self-actualization, although I'm not sure how I still found any space for me near the top of the triangle. I owed money to everyone, it seemed. Some of my subcontractors hadn't been fully paid for services long since rendered. Local lumber suppliers also waited as patiently as they could for me to pay up. And then there were the banks that held my numerous credit card accounts. They threatened me with collection agency letters and phone calls.

The year was 2012 and another bankruptcy was not an option. Too soon since my last one. Since leaving Eleanor's I had spent the previous year taking care of a friend's house in Chelmsford. In exchange for my property maintenance skills, I was given a sizeable break on the rent. When my friend and his wife returned from California, I needed to find a new place to live.

Without having the resources for an advance payment of the first and last month's rent, plus any security deposit, I needed to get creative. The bulk of my tools were already finding shelter in a 5x8-foot storage unit. No room left for me.

Past customers that had become friends came to my rescue once again. For the next few years I parked myself on airbeds in living rooms and spare bedrooms. Once again I used my carpentry skills to augment my financial contributions. And I also babysat dogs for a little extra income.

Harm reduction

It was the worst of times and the best of times for me during 2014-2016. My best friend, my cohost, acquaintances, and a lover died during those two years. My right knee finally said, "I'm done!" A trip to the hospital, a knee brace, and a different way to make money became necessary. I bought scratch tickets and lost more than I won. I continued to drink too much. Not too smart—even if only considering alcohol's potential gout effect on my joints.

At one of my temporary locations in Lowell, my truck was broken into for a second time and many tools were stolen. Someone else got to pawn my table saw, compressor, nail guns, etc., before I could sell them to buy more scratch tickets.

A new friend strongly suggested I get help with my gambling. Her suggestion was for me to seek therapy, and not to help finance my addiction. I called the official gambling help number—it was less than helpful.

After that, the same friend—who was not going to give up

on me even as I was giving up on myself, hooked me up with an unconventional therapist that promoted *harm reduction* as the first step in treating addiction—all types of addiction. He didn't take insurance but he also didn't insist on being paid prior to treatment. Eventually he suggested I establish a lottery budget. I could still gamble as long as I spent no more than 50 dollars a month. I agreed.

60 Columbian Street, Braintree, MA

If you live in Middlesex County, gamble, and have won more than $599 but less than 50thou in the lottery on one ticket, you've probably been to Woburn to cash in. If so, you know the drill— take a number from the deli-style number dispenser—fill out a form—sign your ticket—take a seat and wait to be called.

Once you are in front of the very friendly agent behind the glass you must provide proof of your social security number. You are then asked to take your seat again, and in a few short minutes you are called back up to receive a check for your winnings—minus the five percent you are required to share with the State. Your agent says, "Congratulations!" And you are off to the bank. But if you win more than 50thou—the process is not as simple.

On Friday, October 16, 2015, I drove to what was then Lottery Headquarters in Braintree. I filled out the form, took my seat and waited to be called. Since it was my first visit to that office, after a while I decide to get up and look around a bit. There was definitely more of the taxpayer's money being spent on that facility than at the small rented space in the strip mall in Woburn. But I already knew that when I drove up the hill to the parking lot and saw the large two-story building.

"Number 21?" I walked up to the window, presented my driver's license, a copy of my 2014 tax return with my social security number on it, my filled-out form—and—the Supreme Millions ticket number 024, with matching number eights beneath the winning numbers row and in the middle of the first row designated as—YOUR NUMBERS.

The friendly agent behind the glass collected all my documents, began to look through them, finally scanning the ticket, and said, "Oh!"

She seemed surprised but I wasn't sure why. The ticket clearly read: $1MIL. *Did the printed amount not match the barcode? Or was she new and hadn't seen one of these before?*

Then she said, "Congratulations, Richard! I'll call for a supervisor. It will just take a few moments."

Relieved, I sat back in one of the chairs and waited for the supervisor's arrival. About ten minutes later two lottery agents came down from the offices upstairs. After introductions, they whisked me away to a private room and closed the door. I was asked how I wanted my money—one lump sum of 650,000.00 dollars—or $1MIL—paid out over the course of 20 years.

I had been holding my ticket for several days before going to cash it. During that time I consulted with my accountant, who had been patiently waiting for me pay him for the previous three years of tax preparations. Being 62 and in serious debt, I decided to take the lump sum.

After signing off in front of the two agents, they began asking what my plans were for my winnings. I was reluctant to say much and gave them very evasive answers. Finally one of the agents said, "You don't seem very happy. What's up with that?"

That question triggered the response I had created in my head but never intended to verbalize. "Understand, I am grateful for wining. It will allow me to settle my debt and perhaps repair some broken friendships. But I am also troubled about the process. Gambling has been a debilitating addiction for me as it is for so many others. To simply state 'Please play responsibly', like the end of your ads tell us to do, does not excuse the State from being complicit in enabling addiction. And I've got to tell you, your helpline was no help to me."

"We are sorry you feel that way," one agent spoke for both of them. "There is only one final step before we give you your check."

It was then that I noticed the camera. And I think it was then that the agents noticed how I was dressed—dressed like the bum I was. They gave me an enlarged facsimile of my winning ticket to hold out in front of me—and then I was ready for my mug shot. Soon my face would be on the internet and on the screens of Mass. Lottery vending machines all across the state. So much for wanting to remain as anonymous as possible. I wasn't happy about that, or with myself for my own complicity in helping advertise for gambling addictions. I didn't smile for the camera.

When the awkward photo-shoot was over I got my money. Check number 40270700 for 455,000.00, as written on the check with no dollar sign. The 650,000.00-lump-sum payment had been reduced another 195,000.00 dollars for taxes on money generated by my money and other gamblers' money, which in turn had already been taxed before I bought the ticket. Later I would pay additional federal windfall profit taxes.

I will stop complaining now—and yes, I remain grateful—just not as happy as I'd like to be. Winning hasn't solved my addiction problems.

Because I was asked—Judith Helena Anderson

My mom was a working mom that never managed to save money. Despite that she had much to give, and she gave most of what she had to me—her love. Until I was about seven, my mother's love was unconditional—after that it depended on her sobriety.

Thanks to Judy I learned to cook, sew, plant and tend, a vegetable garden. She introduced me to theater and helped me rehearse my one line for, *The Emperor's New Clothes*, "But he hasn't anything on!"

That was when Judy and Teddy were members of the Sudbury Players. Later, Judy played Mrs. van Daan in the *Diary of Anne Frank*. Her little boy was in the audience on opening night and he thought his mommy's performance was fantastic!

Despite never graduating from high school, Judy taught herself the Dewey Decimal System and in 1960 she applied for a fulltime librarian's position at Digital Equipment Corporation in Maynard, one town away. After being interviewed by Ken Olsen, Judy got the job. When I asked her, "Weren't you nervous being interviewed by the man himself?"

My mother replied, "No—I just pictured him sitting on the toilet with paper in his hand about to wipe his own ass. It kind of equalized us. And, it didn't hurt being from Sweden either. Did you know his grandparents were Swedish also? We got pretty chummy in his office. A very unpretentious man for someone so brilliant and important."

At seven in my innocent world I thought my mom was amazing most of the time, but at other times I couldn't understand her nasty—hate filled expressions of anger—mostly directed at my father, but sometimes also towards her children. I didn't know about alcohol yet.

Papa and I never talked extensively about my level of alcohol intake. As my father, he didn't question my having a refrigerator filled with beer in my bedroom closet when I was just 16. In his relationship with my mother he hadn't connected her violent rages to drinking until it was too late. And yet, I don't find that strange or particularly unusual. Manny, like some people, could have one or two beers over the course of a long evening and that was always enough. It probably never occurred to him that for some of us other people, that's not always the case.

My mother was one of those people and I have been one as well. I sometimes speculate about how much of me is nature vs nurture. My propensity towards addictive behaviors could come from both camps, but it is the balance that keeps me questioning myself. Am I doomed by the DNA my mother passed on to me, so preprogrammed that it doesn't matter or even make logical sense for me to try and change? Or did the environment I grew up in have the bigger influence on me?

When I was 11, the environment started to get kicked up a notch. We had moved into 24 Ruthellen Road two years earlier, and my mom knew how unhappy I still was about leaving Sudbury.

The school I went to in Sudbury used the Montessori method of teaching. I loved school and I had a crush on my third-grade teacher and her two seat Alfaro Romero convertible. Occasionally, when I stayed late to finish a project, my teacher gave me a ride home. I missed the neighborhood, the corn field, the pond, the two Costa Rican brothers across the street, and the tree fort down the block, where our three mutual girlfriends innocently played house with us and we all pretended to be a family.

In Chelmsford, I had difficulty adjusting to the old-school way of teaching, and I found it hard to make friends in the all-white, mostly Catholic suburban development. Other than being white skinned, I didn't fit in.

To help ease the pain of missing life in Sudbury, my mother got me a six-month-old Standard Poodle puppy, (the tallest of the Full-Doodle-Poodles). Remember, this was before they started breeding labradoodles and golden doodles and such. Judy loved animals and me, so she knew a dog was just what I needed. Over time I trained

Jacque do tricks like; rollover to the left and right, crawl through a tunnel and walk up and down a three-step, stepladder.

My mother encouraged me to have a show. We made tickets together and she sold them at work. Many of her friends and coworkers came. I started to feel some happiness again thanks to my mom and the superstar dog she had gotten for me.

One day Jacque asked to go out, ostensible to pee. It was fairly early in the morning and I wasn't dressed yet. I opened the front door for him and then started getting my clothes on. While I was dressing, my circus dog attempted his last death defying trick—he slid under the real wheels of a garbage truck. Sad, I know, but I can't make this stuff up—or I suppose I could, but I didn't. The reason I've put this awful childhood experience back in the book is so that you can have context and some empathy for my mother's next decision.

I was miserable for the rest of that day as you might imagine. By evening I still cried. After Judy had finished her second glass of wine and was well into her third, she asked me to come sit with her. Then she poured me my own glass. My introduction to alcohol had begun and I started to learn that, happy or sad, booze was there to get you through.

During the next year my mother started to work longer days. To hear Judy tell the story, she'd become the right-hand woman for Ken Olsen. She presented me with a job proposal instead of an allowance—cook supper for the family five-days a week—she would help me plan the menu and we'd shop together. For this she offered to pay me $5 per meal. *Are you kidding me? $25 a week and I'm only 12!* I took the job.

In school I read even slower than I now write. Timed tests for reading comprehension were a killer for me, as I typically only finished reading about a third of the required material. Ask me anything about that 33% and my recall was spot-on, but that still left me near the bottom of my class.

Before the Children with Specific Learning Disabilities Act was passed in 1969, which federally mandated support services for students with dyslexia and other learning impairments, my mother went to my school and gave the principal her own mandate— "Turn the clock off when you're testing my son!" The school complied and it worked. Suddenly I was up in the 90th percentile for reading comprehension.

Saturdays were mother and son days. In the summer when I was taking a break from boring public school, Judy enrolled me and paid for Saturday classes held at the deCordova Museum in Lincoln, MA. I took play writing, acting and watercolor painting.

On the way there, mother and I talked nonstop. She waited in the car for me to finish my three hours of artistic schooling, and then we went off to Walden Pond or the Drumlin Farm Wildlife Sanctuary together. My mother, like the atomic bomb, was awesome!

When I turned 16 all I wanted was a car so that I could escape the warzone that had become my parents' marriage. With the money I had saved from cooking our family meals, I purchased a 1964 Ford Galaxy 500 convertible with black bucket seats, a V8 engine and miles of flashy chrome. A lot of car for me at 16.

Later that year I bought a 1940s—overbuilt—under-engineered, perfectly functioning refrigerator. After cleaning it, I painted a peace sign on the front and stocked it with 96 bottles of Carling's Black Label. Judy provided the id—I provided the cash. We became drinking buddies my mother and I, although she preferred 1/2 gallon jugs of inexpensive wine over beer.

The word got out and Judy's friends started questioning her about this style of parenting. She defended herself by telling them, "Teenagers are experimenters and they will discover alcohol whether you forbid it or not. At least my son isn't out drinking and driving." Nice try, but in reality having access to beer at home only meant there were no bottles or cans in the car after my friends and I got hammered in my room before going out on the road.

As I got close to 18, the age when it was required that males register for the draft, Judy took the training to become a draft counselor. She helped me prepare my conscientious-objector application. In order to be accepted as a CO you needed to prove to the Draft Board that you were sincere about not wanting to kill—and that you were not just trying to avoid being killed yourself. If you were a Jehovah's Witness or among the Amish you were a shoo-in—atheists not so much.

I wrote a ten-page dissertation about how killing has never solved anything for very long and that I refused to kill any humans, unless in self-defense. Judy helped edit my thesis paper, but she knew it would not be enough by itself. As a fully trained draft counselor she had learned that references from non-family, preferably members of the military, were essential in order to convince the Board of sincerity.

One night, my father came home from work, stepped over the threshold, and with door still open, he was greeted with, "Hypocrite!"

"Excuse me my dear?" he responded.

"You! You preach peace while you profit from war. Hypocrite."

"My job puts this roof over your head," was the best my dear-old-dad could come up with. The practical pragmatist, never acknowledged Judy's emotions back then.

Sylvania, which was one of many defense contractors operating during the Vietnam War, was our families only connection to all things military. Part of my father's self-created position with the company as their Value Engineer, made him responsible for interfacing with top military brass. It was his job to convince them that Sylvania wasn't wasting the government's money.

"I don't give a shit about this roof! Do you realize they are trying to kill our son?"

"What do you want from me?"

"We need a reference from a high ranking military officer to keep your war machine from killing him. He's your son too!"

A few days later I met with an Air Force Colonel that my father had invited to our house. He read my application, talked with me, and tried to convince me I was wrong. And yet I liked him because he didn't patronize. I almost wanted to tell him about killing my dog when I was only 15 and how sick that made me feel about myself. I couldn't even imagine what I'd feel like if I had to kill a human Sargent—or any person—military or civilian, but I thought it best not to mention my having killed anything.

Within a week I received his written letter of reference for me. In it, the Colonel disagreed with all my conclusions for why I felt killing was wrong, and he restated his opinion why killing is a necessary evil to protect this country, but he also totally supported my right to disagree, and more importantly expressed his impression that I was sincere in my beliefs. I got my CO status.

Although I never made the trip to Woodstock, I considered myself as a member of the peace movement. But when some of our membership started spitting on, and trying to guilt trip returning vets about atrocities based on our relatively safe societal norms, my mother and I left the movement altogether. To this day I always say, "Thank you for your service," whenever I see a vet wearing their well-earned cap. It's not much I know.

Before my brother Carl was about to be drafted, our mom encouraged him to join the Coast Guard. Carl was the only one in our immediate family that served this country. During his tour of duty, he saved sailors from their burning boat off the coast of Scituate, MA, was on patrol aboard the Coast Guard cutter Casco in the North Atlantic, and towed targets for the Navy to shoot at in Guantanamo. Peter avoided service with a student deferment—and good for him.

When Carl died in 2005, the Coast Guard sent a two-person detail with a nicely folded American flag to present to his widow. Nice gesture; however, I would have preferred that our government took better care of him near the end of his life when he spent over a month at the Jamaica Plain VA Medical Center. But that's another story.

As my parents faced divorce, my father borrowed money from his future bride and settled Judy's half-ownership in our family home. My mother used those funds to; study transactional analysis, rent a studio/storefront in Chelmsford Center where she offered workshops on TA, and to produce a board game called *EEGO*. The Lowell Sun wrote an article about her invention in 1976. If you clicked on her invention you will find my perception to be in conflict with the official newspaper version. In the article I am credited with inventing EEGO as a birthday gift—that much is true—but Judy hired the professionals to make it a purchasable product. Five games remain from the 1,000 she paid to have produced. All are in their original shrink-wrapped sealed boxes, in case anyone is interested. Make me an offer.

A few years later my mother was broke and her downward spiral was in full rotation. As she drank more, and more often, I was continually engaged trying to rescue her from various unhealthy living situations and conditions. Eleanor told me I was just being an enabler. She suggested a family intervention and introduced me to the concept of, "tough love."

After I brought Judy for detoxification at Lowell General Hospital, my mom agreed to attend a month long, in house, aftercare program in Maine. Sundays were family participation days and I drove up for all of them. When released, she began going to Alcoholics Anonymous meetings, but that didn't last long as god got in the way—the word '*god*' that is.

Eleanor suggested I cut off all contact with my mother unless she returned to AA. I cut off contact. My mother got drunk, ran her car off I-495, and spent a month in Emerson Hospital. I didn't visit. When she had healed enough to be released, she had nowhere to go, and because no family stepped-up she became a ward of the state.

On November 20th, 1994, I took Papa to Walden Pond where Judy's family and friends gathered at a memorial service for her. Eleanor was there—along with those women that were still around from Judy's old consciousness raising group. The venue was chosen by me with help from Henry David. Thoreau's *Walden* was one of my mother's favorite reads.

For once I had no words, so I hired a humanist from Harvard University to say a few. But I did still have a flare for the spectacular. I made a cardboard Viking ship, filled the hull with Judy's ashes, set the boat on fire, and pushed it into Walden Pond. If the authorities question me—I'll say I made this up.

My brothers and I had agreed, that because our mother used our father's affair with Donna as her final reason for divorcing him, it would be inappropriate for Donna to attend. But we also all felt Judy would have wanted our father there when she set sail. As a result, Papa became confused about who had died. I had to continually reassure him that his current wife was still alive, while also telling him over and over again that it was his ex whom had died. Each time he reacted with relief about Donna—followed by disbelief and tear-streaked cheeks at the loss of Judy.

When the service was over, the accolades came pouring in as the guests left. "You did such a beautiful job with the service, Richard. Your mother would be so proud of you." That one quote pretty much sums it up. But no one knew that all the fanfare was my cover-up of a more complete story.

On the day that my mother actually died, I ignored her requests for me to come to her. While performing a home inspection for one of my plumbers, I got a call from Newton Wellesley Hospital that my mom didn't have long to live, and that she was asking for me. I chose to finish the inspection.

In my opinion, tough love was a ridiculous concept in the way I thought I'd been told to practice it. I wish I knew about the loving kindness of *harm reduction* back then. It was perfectly fair for me to set boundaries; like refusing to spend time with my mother while she was intoxicated. Drinking with her was definitely disabling for both of us. But not visiting Judy, my mother, on her deathbed, that was just plain cruel of me!

Settling up—and—moving on

I thought I had already forgiven myself for shunning my mother at the end of her life. After just writing about it, I realize this is still in process—something I must settle-up with just me if I am to truly move on.

A much easier settlement came after winning the lottery. I paid, in person, all subcontractors and suppliers that I owed money to, and with whom I also had a human connection. All of them treated me with dignity and surprised me by waiving any penalties or interest charges. The credit card companies that were willing to settle, I dealt with over the phone or on my newly purchased Apple MacBook Pro.

With the money I had left I took care of my friends and gave a little over 10% of the remainder to various charities that I could now afford to support. After that I only had two targets for the rest of my funds—buy a modest house near the ocean in Maine—a home that no one could ask me to leave—and publish my two books.

Naturally I had to finish writing this one first before I could publish it and I needed art for the cover. I thought of Glenn. We talked on the phone about the project and kicked around the idea of a "Marmadukeish" cartoon to represent Baby. Now I could afford to pay him for the new book's cover and for those sketches inside *Staying Stoned* that he had already drawn for me some 33 years earlier. We made loose plans to meet in a few months when Glenn was next scheduled to be up from Maryland.

Glenn

On a pleasant, early October afternoon, I jumped my borrowed motorcycle up over the curb at the front of the South Row Elementary School in Chelmsford; the school I attended in the fourth grade when my parents moved us from Sudbury to Chelmsford over my objections—my nine-year-old's irrelevant objections.

Once firmly on the sidewalk, I popped a less than impressive wheelie, and road up to one of the two, black asphalt basketball courts. A pickup game was in process on the first court. I parked the bike 15 feet, or so, away from the second court, shut the engine off, removed my helmet placing it on my lap, and sat for a while watching my potential competitors and/or possible teammates.

The Power Wagon was in the shop with a blown engine—too much overly aggressive plowing during the past winter without enough attention to oil fill levels. My little Honda had been stolen several years earlier. So that I would have some means of transportation while the truck got a new engine, my brother Peter was generous enough to loan me one of his motorcycles. I didn't want to risk cracking it up so I stayed close to home. Eleanor's house was only a mile and a half from *South Row*, as us locals called it.

It was 1981 and a little over a year had passed since returning from my drug-free zone in the mountains. More importantly to most New Englanders, the Boston Celtics won the NBA title that year. The new season would be starting at the end of the month and there were basketballs being dribbled between legs and shot into the air at most all of the school playgrounds. I was looking for new friends—non-using friends. Basketball courts seemed like a good place to find them.

When the game I was watching ended one of the players walked over to me. He reached out his hand, and from beneath an unkempt beard he revealed the most genuinely disarming and completely welcoming smile I had ever seen in my relatively short life by then, and has not yet been surpassed since. "Hi—Glenn Foden," he introduced himself.

I responded in kind, but with a much less intoxicating smile, "Richie," I called myself. That was strange as I had never used that as a nickname for myself and I'd never been called that by others. The name stuck. With my soon to be new basketball buddies I'd be Richie forevermore.

At 6 foot 3 and 235 pounds Glenn was a big lad—3 inches taller and 50 pounds heavier than I. From having watched him rebound the ball I could tell his weight was mostly comprised of muscle and bone. His handshake confirmed this; however, it wasn't overly forceful as some first handshakes tend to be with men. Glenn had nothing to prove.

Very quickly Glenn and I became friends, but unlike other

rapid-fire friendships of mine, ours lasted a lifetime. Politically we were polar opposite—me, the conscientious objector—die-hard-hippie, and Glenn with a republican's conservative disposition. After basketball games we often sat for hours in his vehicle or mine and discussed our differing world views. We expressed ourselves passionately but always with civility and never in a personally judgmental manner. Glenn became my role model for how to be a man, how to treat women and how to just be a good human being. A role model I have not thus far lived up to. Right now I wish there were more men like Glenn in this country to help keep our civil and political discourse positive.

As Glenn was practicing his cartooning craft and looking for full-time work in his field, I remember him glibly telling me, "Richie, I read the obituaries first thing every day to see if any prominent cartoonists have died—and then I read the rest of the news to figure out what I want to satirize that day. You never know—my ticket to success might just be one death away."

For me Glenn was already successful. He was a success in how he treated others, particularly strangers, and in how he valued friendships. In 1986, he'd find further success at a newspaper in Maryland, and after meeting Teresa at that same paper, as a faithful husband and a devoted father of twins.

In the interim, I hired Glenn, part-time. His work ethic was great and what he lacked in carpentry skills, which was mostly everything, he made up for by his sunny disposition and uplifting spirit on construction sites. Being damn strong didn't hurt either.

Glenn had some great guiding principles for life. One of those principals was his willingness to do anything for a friend with no payback expected, as long as it didn't pertain to his marketable artistic skills. If you needed his help to move furniture or rake leaves—you could count on him. Need art and you'd have to pay. When I told him about *Staying Stoned* and asked him if he'd go back to the campground with me to make some sketches, he replied yes with enthusiasm. He also made an exception to his rule by not charging me on completion of his pen and ink drawings. He told me he was willing to wait until the book was published. Poor Glenn is still waiting.

Outside of work and basketball, Glenn and I orchestrated summertime trips for us and our mutual basketball friends. Camping at Baxter State Park in Maine was our most common destination. From there we would go whitewater rafting by day and play cards in the portable screen house at night. We played for peanuts; literally.

Most nights, after staying up until morning, Glenn and I were the last to crawl back into our separate tents. Sometimes moose would wander through our campsite and delay our getting to sleep even longer. Once, upon encountering two of those impressive animals, a cow and calf, Glenn whispered, "Richie aren't they amazing and we get to be with them for free." My friend always had an appreciation for simple, inexpensive, and natural pleasures.

On a few rare occasions we played our own version of picture charades. If Glenn was on your team you were likely to win. His abilities as a cartoonist allowed him to express most anything in as little as three lines. I remember some of my early paintings of the mill buildings in Lowell. Every individual brick was drawn. It was Glenn who taught me that the viewers' imagination completes the image. "Draw three bricks in detail, then just elude to more, and if done well, the hundreds of other bricks will appear to be there also," he told me.

After Glenn and Teresa's daughters were born our excursions to the backwoods of Maine and the mountains of New Hampshire were replaced by summer visits on Eleanor's back porch. Those

Foden family trips up north to keep in touch with relatives almost always included one day spent with Eleanor and me.

Other than that, Glenn and I stayed in touch by phone, not weekly or even monthly, sometimes only yearly. But always on Groundhog Day—Glenn's birthday—an easy date to remember— no Facebook reminders required. And whenever we did speak, other than catching up about the events in our lives, it always felt like time had stood still for us. Our relationship remained solid, and as if we had just been together the day before.

So when I needed him to draw the cover for this book—he was willing and able. On Friday, March 18, 2016, at 6:22 a.m. EST, I received the following text from him: "Hey Richie! Sitting in the airport waiting to head north… I'll give you a shout for coffee and maybe a donut or two…c u soon." This was Glenn's way of setting up a business meeting.

A day passed without my hearing a "shout" from him. When I called his cell phone there was no response. The weekend passed. On Monday I decided to call his dad's house in Chelmsford where I knew he was staying. "Hi, Donald—it's Richie. I understand your *Sunny* boy is up visiting with you."

"Glenn is gone, Richie," he offered no more than that at first.

I questioned him further, "Is everything all right in Maryland? Did he have to go back early?"

"No, Richie—Glenn died last night," Donald told me, and then started sobbing before hanging up.

It was the worst of times for me and anyone who knew Glenn. Even those that only met him once or twice were saddened. He had that rare impact on people. I am grateful for the hours I had alone with Glenn and I am pleased we maintained our closeness for 35 years despite miles of separation for many of those years. At 60 a prominent cartoonist died; that cartoonist was Glenn Foden. No satire today.

A message from Beyond

For two years after Glenn's passing this book writing process slowed down once again. The artist I wanted to create the cover for me was gone, and I was forced to bone up on my drawing skills. Cartooning was not within my abilities, so *Marmaduke* was out of the question. I got my brushes out and began working on a watercolor painting. While I practiced painting Baby, I started receiving invitations from Beyond.

"Dear Richard,

I am an associate producer with HGTV's My Lottery Dream Home, produced by Beyond.

Congratulations on your Lottery win! We are currently casting for Season 2 of our hit series, featuring real lottery winners who've recently bought their dream home. It doesn't matter if this is an extravagant home or a simple investment, it's all about how the lottery has helped you achieve this amazing goal. If you are interested in being part of our uplifting and inspirational TV program featuring host David Bromstad, call or email us, hope to hear from you soon and all the best!"

They didn't hear from me soon, as I didn't respond by phone or email. I was still very uncomfortable about doing further advertising for my shared addiction. All I wanted was to be left alone to finish this book.

When Beyond started casting for Season 3, I received a phone call while cooking supper at one of my temporary residences in

Lowell. This time the associate producer's boss, the producer, tried to convince me to do the show. We went back and forth for a while, with me asking many questions and the producer doing his best to answer me—not knowing how distracted and disinterested I was. When he told me the show had an audience of 2 million viewers, I put dinner on hold and started to listen more attentively.

Since I already knew I was going to self-publish, marketing would be up to me. I remember thinking, *two million viewers are a lot of potential readers.* I asked, "Will I be able to talk about my writing on the show?" The answer was a conditional yes. I could talk about being an author, but I wouldn't be allowed to mention the name of my books. *Close enough.* I agreed to do the show.

The Maine Attraction

Traveling north on I-95 just past the Portsmouth Circle in New Hampshire, as the highway veers left and begins to elevate, a magnificent arched bridge, that seems to rise instantly, place itself over the Piscataqua River, and magically appear in front of the windshield, reveals the final approach to Maine.

After crossing over a large sign proclaims, "Welcome to Maine" and a slogan underneath used to read, "the way life should be." I know Papa would have taken issue with that tagline. *Too judgmental and presumptuous for him.* He might have rephrased it to say, "the way life can be." For me—Maine is the way life is—and—where I want to be welcomed home.

Halfway through the summer of 2017, I was in Rockland, Maine, to be filmed for, *the Maine Attraction: Episode 12— Season 3, of HGTV's my Lottery Dream Home.* I had cleared all the preproduction hurtles and been approved for TV. And I must admit I was reasonably excited.

The weather cooperated nicely for the four-day shoot. In Maine there was sunshine every day. On one afternoon the wind off the ocean did prohibit flying the camera carrying drone. The next morning though, aside from some wardrobe consistency issues, all was peaceful again and the breathtaking, aerial images of Rockland's famous Breakwater were captured. If you haven't walked the rocks of the Breakwater to the lighthouse, which is almost a mile out, you should try it sometime. I recommend: sensible shoes, a hat, sunscreen, and no alcohol. Miss a step out there and it might be more than your breath, being taken away. And never, never go out when lightning is predicted—others have and they are no longer with us.

Better than the weather, was my surprise at how pleasant the TV shooting experience wound up feeling for the previously reluctant me. That reluctance was assuaged by the director, who had an easy going and reassuring way about her. The whole crew was wonderful to be around and all of them helped keep me calm.

When lunch times came around, the two cameramen, sound guy, gofer, director, host and the host's personal assistant, ate with me at local restaurants—all paid for by Beyond. In some respects, those were the best moments, as everyone, except the gofer perhaps, could relax and be more real—whatever that means, considering all of them were thousands of miles away from their homes and love one's in order to help me make my TV debut.

The first day we lunched at Claws, a lobster shack overlooking the harbor. From outdoor speakers, I bathed in music from the '60s. There were happy reminders of The Beach Boys, the early Beatles, The Supremes, and Lesley Gore—it's my party and I'll laugh if I want too. Every few minutes the music would be interrupted for a couple of seconds. "Number 14—your order is ready." It was very Americana and quite nostalgic for me, as Eleanor and I used to love stopping at diners with old-fashioned jukeboxes whenever we traveled. The food at Claws was delicious as well.

Day two found our group at the Home Kitchen Café'. As the name implies, everything was homemade—even the warm bread and sticky buns. I am a reasonably good cook but my omelets cannot compare to theirs. Warmer still was the staff at that busy eatery across the road from the bay. Now, when in Rockland, I make breakfast in my new house six days a week and try to go out at least one morning to Home ....

And then there was the host—David Bromstad, who did not have a calming effect on me. His enthusiasm was completely contagious and I quickly developed the on-camera bug. At the same time, David steadfastly kept to our agreement. He not only allowed me to mention that my reason for wanting a home in Maine was to write—and going beyond my expectations—he kept mentioning it for me, at all three houses we looked at together.

However, I must confess I exaggerated about how many kitchens I had already renovated. On camera I said, "I've probably done 40 kitchens in my 40-year career." The camera didn't lie, but I had. The real number is less than half that. I cringed as soon as I heard myself, but I said nothing to revise the inaccuracy and didn't ask for a retake. The only hope for correcting my faux pas was for it to be edited out.

Show business, like feng shui—is powerful stuff—if you've already watched Our episode than you probably get my little joke. I call it "Our" episode because my partner doesn't want her name in print—so—if you are curious as to who this mystery woman is—buy the show. I tried to find a way to hyperlink it for you, but that process failed, and creative intellectual property is to be respected. Only $1.99—less than a low-end lottery ticket. And no—I don't get a cut!

In the late afternoon of the last day in Maine we filmed at

Archer's on the Pier. The restaurant was open to the public while the team was filming. It was a little difficult for me to concentrate. Between the sailboats coming and going in the glistening sunlit water, happy customers, tantalizing aromas, mountains and the shoreline as a backdrop, there were lots of distractions. This was the segment where David Bromstad asked which house I liked best. Naturally I liked the one I bought.

I had to wait until January, of 2018 to see how I fared on the screen and to discover what the editors had made of me. At that time I didn't own a television in Maine or anywhere else—watching television I felt would just slow my writing process even more. I watched at a friend's house. It was decidedly weird to see myself on the tube. *Perhaps I hammed-it-up a touch too much?* None the less, I was happy that the edited version of the filming still emphasized my desire to be a published author. *And now I am!* Unfortunately, the 40-kitchen gaffe was not left up in the digital cutting room cloud.

When I returned to Rockland about a week later, weirder things began happening, as strangers that recognized me from the show wanted to talk. I was first accosted in the checkout line of the supermarket. "Excuse me, but didn't I see you on TV the other night?"

"I cannot tell a lie—it was I," was my first response. Then I added, "Well, I have told some lies—but my having been on television is true."

These impromptu interactions continued to occur every few days at the gas station, in shops and at restaurants. Mostly the fascination with me had to do with my winning the lottery. Which in fairness is only human nature. *But did you miss the fact that I'm a writer?* You know if David said it's so, it's so-to-speak—so.

I am working towards the goal of making Rockland, Maine

my permanent home. But for now, my 1998 Ford Explorer is registered in Massachusetts where my full-time residence is officially recognized, and so I still have a MA license plate. The locals' have a somewhat tongue-in-cheek way of referring to us self-absorbed Bay Staters as, "Massholes."

Being that Maine is a fairly large state, generalizing about what Maine is, is tricky. In the past I saw it as *vacation land* like so many of us out-of-staters do. But here, women ride motorcycles, drive pickup trucks and pretty much do anything men can do. And the men, although being mostly rugged individualists, always hold the door open for me even when I am still 15 paces away, and they always thank me when I do the same for them—kind of a refreshing return to civility. Maine is so much more to me now than a place to visit, and aside from the obvious beauty, it is the people here that truly make me feel welcome. Thanks to my winnings I was able to choose the house I wanted, but that didn't allow me to select who'd be living next-door. I love my neighbors.

Addiction

While in Lowell being treated for my gambling addiction I was invited to participate in informal get-togethers with some of my therapist's other clients. Although attending was not required, I thought *why not?* Meetings were regularly scheduled on Saturdays and usually at least eight to ten people showed up. A wide range of issues were discussed and a myriad of addictive behaviors expressed through shared anecdotes.

I was alone with gambling as my personally recognized addiction—or as I described it to the group in a typically defiant gambler's terms, "Gambling is not my problem—losing is." As I listened to others talk about their struggles with—addictions to—sex, alcohol, cocaine, pornography, internet gaming, crystal meth, and opioids—I was struck with how most of their issues were my mine as well. Well—with the exception of internet gaming, pornography and opioids. The first two I found boring—and the last one too terrifying!

When my mother was coerced by me and Eleanor to attend AA meetings she had trouble dealing with why God should have anything to do with her journey—if such an entity did exist, why focus on her? But on reflection I think she had more trouble standing up and saying, "My name is Judy and I am an alcoholic."

It took me years to convince my brother Carl to go with me to a support retreat for people with multiple sclerosis. He didn't want to associate with the diseased. When he finally agreed, he introduced himself as Carl Ebner. No one expected him to say, "My name is Carl and I am multiple sclerosis." No guilt trip when your illness isn't something you can't just say no to. You are not your disease!

Don't get me wrong, I understand that AA works for many people, and the Lord knows, we need many approaches to the problems of alcohol addiction. Those raised with the concepts of original sin and such, before their brains were even capable of abstract thinking, probably do pretty well giving up their autonomy to a god. For some of us this makes no sense. When I think of collecting poker chips to represent my days staying sober—all that comes to mind is placing them at 0-00 on the roulette wheel, just to cut into the house advantage.

Heroin was always a scary drug for me and something I knew I'd never do—and not for any fear of needles—I've donated blood many times and it was no big deal—milk and cookies after. However, it wasn't until I met some of those who had taken the opioid ride, that I better understood my fears. I was told, "My first high on heroin was like nothing I had ever experienced. It was like I understood everything in the universe—felt totally loved—

and couldn't imagine feeling any better." And then I heard how an endless search began to repeat that experience. Too often only ending in death.

I have no statistical data for how the concept of *harm reduction* helps with recidivism rates for heroin usage as compared to how very structured no tolerance drug programs work—but some of those I've met seem to truly appreciated Suboxone and a joint or two to push the edge of desire back just a nudge. Whatever works!

For some of us who continue to struggle with addiction despite having been through traditional types of treatment programs, we need professionals that are capable of thinking more creatively about alternative methods to help us. Just like diapers—one size does not fit all.

During one of our Saturday group sessions I shared my having written a story about my personal attempt to free myself from drug use. All of my fellow addicts seemed curious, but it was the therapist who was most interested. He asked to read it. I dusted off my only copy of *Staying Stoned* and gave it to him. His reaction after reading it was very gratifying for me. So after I finish this book, I'll be back at work cleaning up my first one.

Simultaneously, parents and other relatives of heroin users associated with our group started a non-profit called, Recover a Life. Because I had some knowledge of Robert's Rules from my experience on the board of a Jewish temple, I was asked to join Recover a Life's board.

Yes, you read that right—me, a non-Jew, agnostic, sat on the board of a Jewish congregation—for five years in fact—just stepped down in April of 2019. Those Reformists are as inclusive as the Unitarians. I think there is room for all religious beliefs as long as they include tolerance of others and don't promote hate. Maybe we should just Coexist?

At Recover a Life I was installed as vice president. The position was really just a convenient placeholder, as all the other officer positions had already been filled. Then in a fluke, when the president needed to resign her position, I became president. Judy was right.

Like many well-purposed non-profits, we lacked sufficient funds to achieve our goals. Our mandate being to help support entire families and friends of those affected by the opioid crisis, we needed to raise a significant amount of money. Many other groups were competing for a limited number of grants. After I won the lottery, I donated ten-thousand dollars to our cause in general. It was not enough and Recover a Life—died.

Before I was even aware of *harm reduction*, I instituted several of my own techniques to try and limit, both the quantity, and the frequency of my drinking alcohol. Addressing the quantity issue, I started purchasing nips of vodka, and only the number of nips I planned to drink that day—usually no more than four—twice the recommended daily dose I know. For frequency I went with established norms—starting with happy hours at 5pm on Friday's and stopping sometime late Saturday night, into Sunday morning.

As long as I didn't drink alone and not during the week I felt I was normal. Everyone gets high on the weekend—right? But they don't let you bring your own booze to bars, so sometimes after consuming my nips, I exceeded my self-imposed limit when out for the night.

Although I was always able to walk back to my vehicle, and once driving it I never ran off the road killing myself so far, obviously, or others—that might just be dumb luck—kind of like scratching a winning lottery ticket. More change was required.

The process of completing this book is just the motivation I need. Despite the fact that many writers recognized as brilliant at their craft—also may have had a few too many, too often—I have never felt alcohol enhanced my writing skills.

However, when in group therapy sessions, I tended to assume the role of assistant counselor—thus avoiding my own issues. I wasn't facing the fact that I don't like who I become when I drink. Most of the time I am pretty happy with the sober me, so why do I think I am not enough without alcohol? Writing about my addictions leaves me no escape from dealing with them. I'll keep you posted about how successful I am at reducing my own *personal harm*. Regardless of my success—I want you to triumph over your own demons—whatever they might be.

Optimism

Tell me something reader— "… are you happy in this modern world, or do you need more?" I thank, Bradley Cooper and Lady Gaga for asking—even if the question in their song is different—from mine in posing it. Having been raised by atheists, I met many of that consortium—they seem to flock together. Most of the atheists I've known want less *God* and they want it now. They tend to blame all the world's problems on religion and hold out little hope for change.

While Manny was indeed an atheist, he was not a pessimistic one. My father believed that as science and technology evolved, religion would become irrelevant. He envisioned a day when there would be no borders—no walls between countries—no countries at all actually—only one world with everyone speaking the same language. The one language part seems a tad boring to me—but I fully agree with the spiritual aspects of the concept.

If Papa were alive today he would embrace social media. He'd have his own blog and he'd be all over Twitter, Instagram and Facebook. I can imagine him advocating for us to stop playing the "blame game." Oil companies are not evil—he'd tweet. They provide a need. Did you drive a gasoline powered car today—or ride in an airplane?

There are serious problems that need to be solved, so maybe we should stop arguing whether humans are the one's responsible for rising temperatures, or if it is just a cyclic event of nature. Call it global warming or climate change if you prefer, but if there is reasonable evidence that the water is rising—let's put humans to work building walls to keep the sea out.

I too am searching for something more and I am no defeatist—perhaps for different reasons as well as some overlapping one's as my Papa. I heard a radio interview recently that made me say to myself, "Duh? —how simple!" A young person was asked whether they identified as a boy or a girl. They responded by saying, "Sometimes I feel like a girl and sometimes I feel like a boy." But my *duh moment* came when the interviewee turned the question around by asking, "What does it matter?"

A few years ago I brought a male friend of mine to the Manchester, NH airport. Three weeks later I picked her up at the same airport. He had gone to Pennsylvania for sexual reassignment surgery. I can't imagine—and I have a robust imagination—how it must be for someone to feel trapped in the wrong body. For people who are transgender, it is more than just pronouns.

I need unpolluted air to breath—clean water to drink—truly nutritious food to eat—and shelter. As does every other human being on this planet—no matter their religious beliefs—none beliefs—education level—political affiliation—income level—ethnicity—race—or gender identity. And I need acceptance—the essence of *Love* as I feel it is—so I am willing to be the first to give love and acceptance in any situation. I have no better answers for myself.

For me technology is a tool, like a table saw is a tool, only much more complicated and confusing to the carpenter in me. Fortunately those younger than I, the vast majority, have grown up with the internet, so knowing which tools they need is more like my choosing the right screwdriver from my toolbox. Hopefully as a nation, and later as world, technology will help us find the right tools to provide at least the basic needs for all people. I read recently that more people have access to a cell phone than they do to clean water. And yet, I am confident that our country will lead by example as we have done before.

Listening to many millennials and younger in the process of writing this last chapter, I am pleasantly surprised by what I heard. Despite the mess my generation and those few older than me have left them, most said they remain hopefully optimistic about their future.

Many of those who expressed their concerns, are also facing thousands of dollars in college-related debt, even before entering their careers. It is my understanding that only taxes and student loans are not eligible for relief through bankruptcy proceedings. Having gone bankrupt twice myself, I'm just glad I never went to college. But seriously—I wish I had done a better job managing my own finances. Sometimes the only *trump* card you have to play is to pass your losses on to someone else. The rich, in the business of staying rich, know this, but somehow college graduates are exempt.

Not every twenty-something has given up and given in to drugs. But too many have and that is a tragedy for them, their loved ones, and a huge loss for our country in general. Let's fix that!

The end—almost

I started this chapter by asking—So what is the story and how does it end? My father already told you, "It is what you say it is."

Groucho Marx might have said, "Everyone from New York City thinks they can write a book—and unfortunately they do." Did I tell you I was born in the Big Apple? Lol—only about 20 references. Right?

Manny could have considered it as an introduction to Alfred Korzybski, critical thinking and general semantics—where—the word is not the thing.

Baby would be content to just hangout on the cover and only respond when her name is mentioned—no other words needed.

Regarding my misunderstandings of the importance of family, and more particularly—honesty, loyalty and commitment in relationships—I was recently visited by Eleanor in a dream. "It's about time," is all she said.

If Papa was wrong and there is some form of existence after death, then I hope Judy knows how much she is still loved by both of us.

Students of Musar know the story is also about *space* and *place*—with many questions raised—but no true answers given for this continuum of life—other than the need for ethical behavior between all fellow humans.

Those who have—or know someone who has substance abuse issues—might relate to my own personal struggles with such things.

Since *Saving Papa's Tales* is technically a memoir—it is certainly about how fleeting and unreliable memories are.

It could also qualify as a book about writing a book—or how not to write a book—unless you have 24 years to spend.

If you are a critic who prefers commas, to em—dashes, I could easily imagine you thinking, *This last chapter sucked even more than the first 33 did.* And I am fully aware that I often violate the two-em dash maximum per sentence—as one's eyes get older those em dashes are easier to recognize than commas. But being a wordsmith yourself—I know you will post your constructive criticism more politely in writing than you may be thinking.

For me, *Saving Papa's Tales*, is my confession, as well as a coming-of-age story that goes all the way to becoming aged—with pitfalls to watch out for along the way. Rich or poor, if I live long enough, at some point I won't be able to care for myself on my own—so as I suggested to Papa, "I'll try to remember to be kind to my caregivers."

You may have noticed that concepts—as well as specific lyrics—in popular music from many periods—have had a big influence on me and thus in my writing. So here I go once again. There is a recent popular song being played occasionally on Kiss-FM here in Rockland, Maine. The repeated refrain advises me to, "Always be humble and kind."

I totally get the *kind* thing. Trying to be a good human being has been a continuing battle for me, and gets more complicated when I overthink it. Many times I've gotten caught up in arguments just to prove I'm better at arguing—usually the best according to me.

Then I consider how good it feels if I let others' win—even when I think I know they are wrong. Humility is more *powerful stuff* and I realize I need more of it—but here's my dilemma—how do I remain humble without losing my curiously outgoing precocious nature? I've decided that doing all things with love and caring kindness, is my ticket to happiness. Definitely not there yet—but working it every day. As the Moody Blues pointed out, it's all, *A Question of Balance*.

A contest

Dear Reader,

Tell me not to do something and I'll find 10 ways to do it. Did you see what I did just there? I was inconsistent. I used the numeral 10 instead of spelling out ten. My editor Teresa has told me at least a million times not to exaggerate, and to, "Find your style for writing, but once you do—be consistent. If your style is to leave participles dangling, just keep them dangling. Deliberately misspell a word, make sure it is misspelled everywhere. Preferably don't do any of those things, but if you do, consistency is most important!"

But if you are a rebel like me with only one cause, you like to break the rules whenever you can, as long as no one gets hurt. It ain't the Chicago Style—it's the Richie Style.

So here's the thing, this was a deliberate act of defiance on my part and the basis for this contest. The first reader who finds another, stand-alone numeral 10 not spelled as ten will get $50 dollars from me personally, or fifty-dollars if you prefer.

This contest only applies to the word *ten* when standing alone in the first 33 chapters. All Chapter 34 inconsistencies are exempt. It does not include the transcribed numbers taken from nurses' notes, or ten when representing figures used in measurements and dimensions. All other inconsistences are also excluded.

Naturally, I will need proof of purchase for *Saving Papa's Tales*. Printed versions only. Electronic books do not qualify. However, electronic readers have already gotten the extra benefit—or the unnecessary distractions depending on your perspective—of additional hyperlink information about various topics, tunes, and names within the text of this last chapter.

So—if you have read *Saving Papa's Tales* in paperback form, enter the contest absolutely, but also consider re-reading this book electronically. Remember what Papa said, "… I always re-read books many times to see what other meanings I can squeeze out."

Shameless self-promoting, I know. Isn't America Great! Or is America going to be Great Again? Our choice.

Only one payout for all books sold. Sorry, but I am not really a millionaire—I just played one on TV. If you enjoyed your read please recommend it—but don't be too kind by giving your copy away—let your friends buy their own. I have a mortgage too.

Thanks for reading,
Richie